D1564108

DATE DUE

Selling the CIA

Selling the CIA

Public Relations and the Culture of Secrecy

David Shamus McCarthy

 University Press of Kansas

Published by the University Press of Kansas (Lawrence, Kansas 66045),
which was organized by the Kansas Board of Regents and is operated and
funded by Emporia State University, Fort Hays State University, Kansas State
University, Pittsburg State University, the University of Kansas, and Wichita
State University.

Library of Congress Cataloging-in-Publication Data
Names: McCarthy, David Shamus, author.
Title: Selling the CIA : public relations and the culture of secrecy / David
    Shamus McCarthy.
Description: Lawrence : University Press of Kansas, 2018. | Includes
    bibliographical references and index.
Identifiers: LCCN 2018010428
    ISBN 9780700626427 (hardback)
    ISBN 9780700626434 (ebook)
Subjects: LCSH: United States. Central Intelligence Agency—History. |
    Intelligence service—United States—History. | Public relations—United
    States—History. | BISAC: HISTORY / United States / 20th Century. |
    POLITICAL SCIENCE / Political Freedom & Security / Intelligence.
Classification: LCC JK468.I6 M422 2018 | DDC 327.1273—dc23.
LC record available at https://lccn.loc.gov/2018010428.

British Library Cataloguing-in-Publication Data is available.

Printed in the United States of America

10 9 8 7 6 5 4 3 2 1

The paper used in this publication is recycled and contains 30 percent
postconsumer waste. It is acid free and meets the minimum requirements
of the American National Standard for Permanence of Paper for Printed
Library Materials Z39.48-1992.

For my mom and dad

Contents

Preface: The "Family Jewels"

When Gerald Ford ascended the presidency on August 9, 1974, he famously declared, "our long national nightmare is over."[1] President Ford, of course, was referring to the Watergate scandal, which had dramatically unfolded over the previous two years, culminating with the resignation of his predecessor, Richard Nixon. Ford was never elected vice president, and he sought to reassure the American people that he could be trusted to lead the country, reminding them: "Our Constitution works; our great Republic is a government of laws and not of men. Here the people rule."[2] Ford was hoping for a honeymoon, but shortly before Christmas, he was confronted with a shocking scandal. For officials at the Central Intelligence Agency (CIA), the scandal quickly became a nightmare.

The crisis began on Sunday, December 22, 1974, with a front-page scoop in the *New York Times*. In what remains the most sensational news story ever printed about the CIA, reporter Seymour Hersh revealed that the agency had "conducted a massive, illegal domestic intelligence operation during the Nixon administration against the antiwar movement and other dissident groups in the United States."[3] Hersh had been pursuing the story for approximately two years.[4] Established in 1947 under the National Security Act, the CIA was prohibited from engaging in domestic operations. In 1967, however, Richard Helms, then the director of central intelligence (DCI), approved Operation MHCHAOS, a secret program that targeted American citizens opposed to the Vietnam War.[5] James R. Schlesinger, who replaced Helms in 1973, served as DCI for exactly five months, and he made a decision in May 1973 that unintentionally helped Hersh's investigation. Concerned about allegations of CIA involvement in Watergate, Schlesinger signed a memo that was distributed to all agency employees, informing them, "I have ordered all the senior operating officials of this Agency to report to me immediately on any activities now going on, or that have gone on in the past, which might be construed to be outside the legislative charter of this Agency."[6] The memo instructed "every person presently employed by CIA to report to me on any such activities of which he has knowledge. I invite all ex-employees to do the same. Anyone who has such information should call my secretary . . . and say that he wishes to talk to me about 'activities outside CIA's charter.'"[7]

Schlesinger's memo produced a 702-page collection of internal CIA documents that outlined activities and operations since March 1959 that were considered violations of the National Security Act. Behind closed doors, agency officials humorously titled the secret compendium "the Family Jewels."[8] John Prados has persuasively argued that "the Family Jewels is probably the most sensitive secret document ever produced by the Central Intelligence Agency."[9] Given Hersh's ability to cultivate sources deep within the intelligence establishment, it was only a matter of time before he would be in a position to expose "the Family Jewels." The article about Operation MHCHAOS that appeared on December 22 would have profound consequences for the CIA. Hersh's reporting directly contributed to three major investigations: the Rockefeller Commission in the executive branch, the Church Committee in the Senate, and the Pike Committee in the House of Representatives. In fact, 1975 became known as the "Year of Intelligence."[10]

President Ford initially hoped to head off a congressional investigation by appointing Vice President Nelson Rockefeller to launch an inquiry into the allegations of domestic wrongdoing. The Rockefeller Commission issued a report, hereafter the Rockefeller Commission Report, in the summer of 1975 that confirmed the existence of Operation MHCHAOS. According to the report, "the Operation compiled some 13,000 different files, including files on 7,200 American citizens. The documents in these files and related materials included the names of more than 300,000 persons and organizations, which were entered into a computerized index" that was housed inside a secure vault in the basement of CIA headquarters in Langley, Virginia.[11]

Two congressional investigations followed the Rockefeller Commission. Senator Frank Church (D-ID) chaired "the Senate Select Committee to Study Governmental Operations with Respect to Intelligence Activities," while Congressman Otis Pike (D-NY) led "the House Select Committee to Study Government Operations with Respect to Intelligence Activities."[12] Both committees held hearings in 1975 that received extensive media coverage. The House of Representatives voted not to release the Pike Report, but the document was leaked to the *Village Voice* in February 1976.[13] After completing its sixteen-month investigation, the Church Committee published six detailed reports in April 1976.[14]

The "Year of Intelligence" was a watershed moment in the history of the intelligence establishment. The investigations—and the barrage of shocking headlines—directly challenged the culture of secrecy at the CIA, and there was fear within the agency that covert operations might be abolished. To protect covert operations and the culture of secrecy, CIA officials turned to public relations. The book that follows is the story of how this happened.

Selling the CIA

Introduction

"A Fundamental Public Relations Problem"

What is it with you people? You think not getting caught in a lie is the same thing as telling the truth.
—Joe Turner, *Three Days of the Condor* (1975)

On March 4, 1976, George H. W. Bush delivered a speech to CIA employees in which he acknowledged that the agency had developed "a fundamental public relations problem" that was unprecedented.[1] Bush had been DCI for less than two months, and he was already frustrated with recent opinion polls. In the summer of 1973, only 19 percent of Americans questioned in a Gallup poll had a negative view of the agency. Two years later the number of negative responses would rise to 39 percent,[2] and by January 1976, a separate polling service found that almost 50 percent of those surveyed disapproved of the CIA's performance.[3] "We're going through a time in our country's history where the American people seem to take delight in tearing down our institutions," Bush observed. He went on to say, "there were some mistakes made here . . . but I'll not be troubled by these numbers because I'm not sure that the CIA, in terms of basic support from the American people, is suffering more than other institutions."[4] Although he attempted to downplay the polling data, Bush was worried; Americans no longer trusted the CIA, and something needed to done.

Scholars have struggled to precisely explain the historical context of the crisis that Bush faced in 1976. Most agree that the CIA reached the height of its power during the 1950s, but that the political climate shifted in the following decade. Simon Willmetts contends that the turning point was the CIA's failure to overthrow Fidel Castro in April 1961. The CIA had trained Cuban exiles for the operation, but within three days of their landing at the Bay of Pigs on the southern coast of Cuba,

Castro's army defeated them: 114 were killed, 1,189 were captured. The debacle at the Bay of Pigs was described as "a perfect failure."[5] In the aftermath of the operation, observes Willmetts, "the CIA became a lightning rod for the public's wider anxieties regarding US government secrecy."[6] The event "began the process of questioning US foreign policy—of pointing out the gap between reality and the official story, and of penetrating the mythologies that had hitherto gilded American foreign policy, and in particular, the activities of the CIA."[7]

Tity de Vries, on the other hand, minimizes the significance of the Bay of Pigs, arguing that the defeat was "mostly covered over by the blanket of Cold War consensus."[8] She emphasizes the important role of *Ramparts* during the 1960s. Based on the West Coast, the left-wing magazine was closely connected to opposition to the Vietnam War. In 1966, *Ramparts* exposed the secret relationship between Michigan State University and the CIA. The following year *Ramparts* published an article that accused the CIA of covertly funding the National Student Association. The agency had funneled at least $200,000 to the organization through private foundations since the 1950s, but only a handful of the students were informed of the relationship.[9] The scandal prompted a brief investigation of the CIA.[10] According to de Vries, what happened in 1967 "can be seen as the prelude to the Watergate affair and the subsequent exposure of a series of other secret CIA operations in the 1970s."[11]

From another perspective, the Watergate scandal, which unfolded between 1972 and 1974, was the most important event prior to the "Year of Intelligence." Americans learned that several of President Richard Nixon's "plumbers" had ties to the CIA. It later became clear that the break-in had been authorized by the White House, not the CIA, but revelations about the agency's initial willingness to cooperate with E. Howard Hunt, the CIA retiree who directed the operation, exacerbated the public's disillusionment with intelligence agencies. In the opinion of Thomas Powers, "Watergate did what the Bay of Pigs had not: it undermined the consensus of trust in Washington which was a truer source of the Agency's strength than its legal charter, and it gave outsiders their first good look at CIA files and tables of organization. . . . Watergate, in short, made the CIA fair game."[12]

So, was it the Bay of Pigs, the 1967 scandal, or the fallout from Watergate that undermined America's trust in the CIA? The obvious answer is that all three were critically important in setting the stage for the "Year of Intelligence." During the early years of the Cold War, the culture of secrecy at the CIA was never significantly challenged. Agency officials carefully protected this culture; in effect, they constructed a metaphorical floodwall. For the first time in CIA history, water came crashing over the floodwall after the Bay of Pigs. Lyman Kirkpatrick, the CIA inspector general who investigated what went wrong, heavily criticized the agency's involvement in the tragedy; rather than accepting his recommendations, however, a decision was made to cover up his report. The document remained classified for nearly four decades.[13]

Kirkpatrick was a loyal servant of the CIA. Like so many founding members of the agency, Kirkpatrick began his espionage career with the Office of Strategic Services during World War II. After contracting polio while on assignment for the CIA, he was confined to a wheelchair for the rest of his life. He never understood why his superiors largely ignored his findings. "Rather than receiving [the report] in the light in which it had been produced, which was to insure that the same mistakes would not be repeated in the future," he lamented, "those that participated in the operation resented it and attacked it bitterly."[14] Most copies of the Kirkpatrick Report were destroyed, while the rest "were locked away in the director's office."[15]

In retrospect, the CIA should have listened to Kirkpatrick; they should have also recognized that it was time to accept greater congressional oversight. Instead, they focused on rebuilding the damage to the metaphorical floodwall. When the scandal involving Michigan State University broke in 1967, the CIA was ready; the agency had been illegally investigating *Ramparts* magazine for at least a year. President Lyndon Johnson subsequently ordered the agency to clandestinely monitor opponents of the Vietnam War, which became known as Operation MHCHAOS.[16] Much to the delight of the intelligence establishment, one of the three men assigned to investigate the CIA in 1967 was DCI Richard Helms.[17] What eventually destroyed the metaphorical floodwall surrounding the CIA in the mid-1970s was not the *Ramparts* exposés or even Watergate; it was the illegal surveillance of *Ramparts* employees and antiwar activists, which Hersh revealed in December 1974. The damage was entirely self-inflicted.

In the months leading up to Hersh's article, the floodwaters were rising quickly. From the perspective of CIA leaders, Victor Marchetti was making the situation worse. Marchetti had once been a rising star at the CIA; in 1966, eleven years after joining the CIA as an analyst, he became the assistant to the deputy director, and he worked for the next three years on the elite seventh floor of headquarters in Langley, Virginia. He resigned from the agency in 1969 disillusioned with the Vietnam War, the agency's old-boy bureaucracy, and the excessive use of covert action in the Third World. Marchetti soon joined forces with John D. Marks, a former State Department official, to write *The CIA and the Cult of Intelligence,* which they published in June 1974. They left spaces in the text to show readers where the agency had censored material.[18]

In the book, Marks and Marchetti disclosed aspects of CIA covert intervention in Chile before Salvador Allende's inauguration as the president of that South American country in 1970. The discussion of Chile, which appeared at the beginning of the second chapter, had been heavily censored during the CIA's review process. For instance, the authors were forbidden to include Henry Kissinger's now infamous comment at a meeting a few months before the Chilean election: "I don't see why we need to stand by and watch a country go communist due to the irresponsibility of its own people."[19] The CIA also prevented Marks and Marchetti from sharing information on what the agency had done after Allende was democratically elected in September 1970. "Attempts were made to undercut Allende through continued propaganda, by encouraging a military coup d'état, and by trying to enlist the support of private U.S. firms, namely ITT, in a scheme to sabotage Chile's economy," they explained.[20] Although this passage was withheld from the first edition of the book, Hersh began to put the pieces of the puzzle together, and in early September 1974, he wrote a front-page story for the *New York Times* that detailed the CIA's destabilization operation against Allende.[21] A few weeks after Hersh's story, a photograph of then DCI William Colby appeared on the cover of *Time* with a provocative question emblazoned over his horn-rimmed glasses: "The CIA: Has It Gone Too Far?"[22] The revelations about the intervention in Chile served as the prologue to the headline on December 22 of the *New York Times*: "Huge C.I.A. Operation Reported in U.S. against Antiwar Forces, Other Dissidents in Nixon Years."[23]

Scholars have written extensively about what happened in the immediate aftermath of Hersh's article.[24] In essence, there are three basic interpretations of the "Year of Intelligence."

The Straitjacket Interpretation

The investigations forever changed the CIA, and the changes were bad. This argument became incredibly popular among conservatives after the attacks of September 11, 2001. During an ABC interview on the afternoon of the attack, James Baker, who served in the cabinet of both President Ronald Reagan and President George H. W. Bush, blamed the tragedy on the Church Committee. Baker alleged that the investigation in 1975 "unilaterally disarm[ed] . . . our intelligence capabilities."[25] From this perspective, the intelligence establishment became risk averse as a result of the Church Committee, and turned away from human intelligence and covert operations. James Jesus Angleton, the longtime director of counterintelligence at the agency who was fired just days before the publication of Hersh's article, pioneered this thesis in 1976. Claiming that the Church Committee had undermined the CIA, Angleton railed against "the straitjacket Senator Church and the Committee's staff have brazenly tailored for it."[26]

Defenders of the CIA often attempt to connect the failure to infiltrate terrorist groups in the 1990s with events from the mid-1970s, and they would likely agree with Stephen F. Knott's *Secret and Sanctioned: Covert Operations and the American Presidency*. Although the book primarily focuses on the history of covert operations before the Cold War, Knott devotes his final chapter to an extended rant against the Church Committee. He claims the "majority report can thus be regarded as a disturbing mixture of historical ignorance and moral fastidiousness."[27] Presidents George Washington, Thomas Jefferson, and James Madison all believed in covert operations; therefore, Knott argues, the American people should stop worrying about the CIA. In fact, Knott recommends the abolition of the oversight committees in Congress "and the restoration of the system that existed from 1947 to 1974."[28] Knott covers the early history of the CIA in just four pages.[29] Although he contends that the Church Committee hamstrung the CIA, the agency embarked on a massive covert operation in Afghanistan after the Soviet invasion in December 1979.[30] He conveniently omits any mention of this operation. In the final analysis, Knott's interpretation of the "Year of Intelligence" is undermined by the facts. It is also important to point out that the bipartisan 9/11 Commission determined that congressional oversight had been too weak. "Of all our recommendations," the 9/11 Commission concluded, "strengthening congressional oversight may be among the most difficult and important."[31]

The Johnsonian Interpretation

The investigations forever changed the CIA, and the changes were positive. Moreover, Congress demonstrated that American democracy works. The scholar most closely connected to this interpretation is Loch K. Johnson, who served as the special assistant to Senator Frank Church during the investigation. In 1979, Johnson joined the faculty at the University of Georgia, and he quickly became the leading figure in the burgeoning field of intelligence studies, publishing more than one hundred articles and several books. In *A Season of Inquiry: The Senate Intelligence Investigation,* Johnson contends, "the intelligence investigation of 1975 succeeded. Though flawed, the inquiry satisfied the primary standard by which a legislature must be judged in a democracy: it enhanced the freedom and well-being of the citizens."[32] As Johnson explains, permanent intelligence oversight committees were established in both the House and the Senate, and President Ford issued an executive order banning assassinations. It was truly "a new and promising era of intelligence oversight."[33]

The Olmstedian Interpretation

Reform was badly needed, but in the end, the investigations did *not* significantly change the CIA. Kathryn S. Olmsted disagrees with Johnson's conclusions, arguing in *Challenging the Secret Government* that the CIA and other intelligence agencies "clearly emerged the winners of their long battle with the investigators."[34] Rhodri Jeffreys-Jones shares Olmsted's overall skepticism: "Attacks of the 'rogue elephant' type [from Senator Church] were painful for a while but, in the process of being debunked, they actually helped the Agency. The CIA emerged from its trial with a refurbished reputation."[35]

It may appear at first glance that it is impossible to reconcile the second and third interpretations. Johnson has been critical of Olmsted's analysis; in his assessment, he wrote, "she too easily discounts the improvements that have come about as a result of the investigations in

1975."[36] Johnson correctly points out that congressional oversight was transformed as a result of the inquiry: "The creation of the two intelligence oversight committees has led to a much closer check on America's secret government than existed earlier."[37] More recently, however, Johnson has embraced a slightly more moderate position, acknowledging in 2008 "that the level of rigor displayed by intelligence overseers in Congress has fallen below the expectations of the [Church] Committee's reformers in 1975."[38] In other words, the Church Committee successfully reformed congressional oversight, but the new system can only succeed if members of the intelligence committees are vigilant.[39]

This study illustrates that there is a middle ground between the interpretations of Johnson and Olmsted. At the same time, however, it disagrees with Jeffreys-Jones's argument that the investigations "refurbished" the agency's standing. In reality, the events that unfolded in the mid-1970s badly damaged the CIA's mystique, which had been assiduously cultivated since the agency's inception in 1947. In *The CIA and the Cult of Intelligence*, Marks and Marchetti specifically warned that "secrecy and deception in intelligence operations are as much to keep the Congress and the public from learning what their government is doing as to shield these activities from the opposition."[40] As the agency withheld information from Congress and the American public, they observed, it simultaneously promoted a clandestine mystique "designed to have us admire it as some sort of mysterious, often magical profession capable of accomplishing terribly difficult, if not miraculous, deeds."[41] Marks and Marchetti recognized that public relations and government secrecy were simply two sides of the same coin, but unfortunately, they failed to elaborate on this crucial insight.

With the passage of time, as Jeffreys-Jones suggests, the CIA's image did improve, but this development should be attributed, at least in part, to the public relations strategy of the CIA. In 1989, Marchetti delivered a conference paper that revisited several of the themes that he had raised fifteen years earlier. Rather than focusing on the inner workings of the CIA, he chose to examine the ways in which the agency aggressively guarded its own history. These public relations schemes presented a unique challenge to scholars interested in studying the agency, as Marchetti notes:

> By suppressing historical fact, and by manufacturing historical fiction, the CIA, with its obsessive secrecy and its vast resources, has posed a particular

threat to the right of Americans to be informed for the present and future by an objective knowledge of the past. As long as the CIA continues to manipulate history, historians of its activities must be Revisionist if we are to know the truth about the agency's activities, past and present.[42]

This study, which confirms Marchetti's accusations, provides the first systematic history of CIA public relations and it simultaneously analyzes *both* CIA secrecy and CIA public relations, since they have been inseparable from each other.

The analysis of CIA public relations presented here serves as an important corrective to existing scholarship. Drawing extensively on documents that the CIA first released in response to one of my own Freedom of Information Act (FOIA) requests, Tricia Jenkins offers an excellent assessment of the CIA's determination to influence American popular culture in *The CIA in Hollywood: How the Agency Shapes Film and Television*.[43] Although many of Jenkins's conclusions are correct, the central weakness of *The CIA in Hollywood* is its failure to provide the broader historical context of CIA public relations.[44] While Jenkins focuses narrowly on the CIA's activities in Hollywood, Mordecai Lee takes a more expansive view of government public relations in *Congress vs. the Bureaucracy*. Published in 2011, this landmark book examines the history of congressional attempts to restrict the use of public relations at federal agencies. Lee concludes that "when Congress has tried to exert its statutory and financial powers to threaten bureaucratic autonomy by limiting agency public relations, the bureaucracy has almost always succeeded in negating Congress's will and protecting its ability to communicate externally."[45] This is undoubtedly true, but Lee also concludes that the bureaucracy's success in outmaneuvering Congress contributes to "the overall balance and viability of the federal system of governance in the modern era."[46] In reality, the opposite is true: the CIA has implemented a public relations strategy that directly threatens American democracy.

The five chapters that follow outline how the CIA has used public relations to fight back against its critics since the mid-1970s. Both William Colby, DCI between 1973 and 1976, and George H. W. Bush, his successor, recognized that the agency was confronting a major public relations crisis. Colby and Bush responded cautiously, and former CIA officials such as David A. Phillips helped develop the initial public relations strategy. In 1977, Admiral Stansfield Turner, the CIA director under President Jimmy Carter, established a modern Office of Public

Affairs at Langley. There has been tremendous continuity in CIA public relations since then. First, and most importantly, the public relations staff has attempted to project an image of openness and accountability. Second, they have perpetuated the CIA's mystique, portraying the agency as the heroic guardian of national security. "Our failures are known, our successes are not" has been the mantra of this initiative. Third, public relations officials have done their best to put a positive spin on secrecy. Admiral Turner's director of public affairs went so far as to suggest that there was "more openness with greater secrecy."[47]

In March 1977, the CIA embarked on a far-reaching public relations campaign. The history of public relations at the CIA may appear fairly innocuous at first glance, but this history must be considered in conjunction with the agency's successful efforts to withhold documents from historians and the media. While Turner described the CIA as the most open intelligence agency in the world, he was trying to undercut FOIA and the ability of former employees to publish memoirs. Turner's successor, William Casey, continued the fight against FOIA and secured passage of the CIA Information Act in 1984. He also employed public relations in a clandestine domestic campaign to win public support for covert action in Central America. In the years following the end of the Cold War, the actions of CIA directors have repeatedly contradicted their public rhetoric. In February 1992, then DCI Robert M. Gates boldly promised a new era of openness, but he failed to deliver. While claiming in 1998 that the agency did not have enough funds in the budget to continue the voluntary declassification program, George Tenet, the CIA chief from 1997 to 2004, had no trouble acquiring the money to sponsor a covert program to "reclassify" CIA documents at the National Archives.

The poisonous relationship between public relations and secrecy is not unique to the CIA. In *The Presidency and Individual Liberties*, published in 1961, Richard Longaker recognized the widespread abuse of the classification system: "Exploiting the legitimate claims of secrecy, the executive branch habitually overclassifies documents, absurdly segments scientific research, and maintains convenient shields to protect administrators from the curiosity of the public and the press."[48] Unless something was done to challenge the excessive secrecy, he warned, "the public will be forced to subsist on the sugar-water of the public relations man, and important aspects of public policy as well as administrative errors will go unobserved by Congress, the press, and the electorate."[49]

Over half a century after Longaker wrote these words, the twin dangers of public relations and secrecy have assumed more importance than ever before. This book will use the CIA as a case study to illustrate how the complex interplay between secrecy and public relations undermines historical research. Similar to any institution within a democracy, the CIA must be held accountable for its actions—past and present. But by withholding documents from scholars, agency officials have effectively manipulated the historical record to create a mystique that has been repeatedly used to thwart calls for greater oversight.

1 | "Telling the Intelligence Story"
William Colby, ARIO, and the
CIA Counteroffensive, 1973–1976

Until we create some sort of "watchdog committee" . . . we will have nothing but continued anxiety about the Central Intelligence Agency and its widespread activities.
—Senator Mike Mansfield (March 1954)

In the same speech where he admitted "a fundamental public relations problem," DCI George H. W. Bush explained to CIA employees that he "made the mistake" during the holiday season of going to see the film *Three Days of the Condor* with his daughter, "who is madly and passionately in love with Robert Redford."[1] He described the movie as "a fairly good shoot-em-up and, if I were totally untutored in this business, I might have got a yak out of it"; despite this complimentary remark, however, he warned that "it was a very vicious and sinister piece because what it did was to lay at the CIA's doorstep all kinds of outrageous things that the CIA by its severest critics has never been accused of."[2]

It is easy to understand why Bush was so concerned about the film. *Three Days of the Condor* was released in September 1975, and it opens with Joe Turner (played by Robert Redford) arriving late for work one December morning at the American Literary Historical Society, which is a CIA research office in New York City. Turner, whose codename is Condor, gets paid to read and analyze books to provide the CIA with new ideas as well as information about potential intelligence leaks. Turner leaves the building for lunch using a basement exit, and when he returns, he discovers that all six people in the office have been gunned down. Turner ultimately becomes convinced about the strong possibility that "there's another CIA, inside the CIA."[3] According to Vincent Canby, "Turner . . . comes close to wreaking more havoc on the C.I.A. in three days than any number of House and Senate investigating committees have done in years."[4]

The film culminates with a meeting between Turner and Higgins (played by Cliff Robertson), the deputy DCI, outside the *New York Times* building. Turner has concluded by this point that there was a rogue plan to invade the Middle East. When he confronts Higgins about these suspicions, Higgins replies, "We have games. That's all. We play games. 'What if,' 'How many men,' 'What would it take,' 'Is there a cheaper way to destabilize a regime?' That's what we're paid to do."[5] Higgins admits that a colleague at the agency had embarked on "a renegade operation," but he proudly observes that "there was nothing wrong with the plan. No, the plan was all right. The plan would have worked."[6] This response leads to a famous exchange that is worth quoting at length:

> TURNER: Boy—What is it with you people? You think not getting caught in a lie is the same thing as telling the truth.
> HIGGINS: No, it's simple economics. Today it's oil, right? In ten or fifteen years, food, plutonium. Maybe even sooner. Now what do you think the people are going to want us to do then?
> TURNER: Ask them!
> HIGGINS: Not now, then. Ask them when they're running out. Ask them when there's no heat in their homes and they're cold. Ask them when their engines stop. Ask them when people who've never known hunger start going hungry. You want to know something: they won't want us to ask 'em. They'll just want us to get it for 'em.
> TURNER: Boy, have you found a home.[7]

While nearby Christmas carolers sing "God Rest Ye Merry Gentlemen," Turner explains that he has revealed the operation to the *New York Times*. Yet Higgins insinuates that the CIA might have the power to kill the story when he asks: "How do you know they'll print it?"[8] The movie ends with a dramatic freeze-frame of Turner looking at Higgins over his shoulder, which reinforces the ambiguity of the ending. Turner's facial expression suggests defiance, but it also appears he understands that he is "about to be a very lonely man."[9]

Defenders of the CIA did not enjoy *Three Days of the Condor*. In his assessment of the film's ending, William F. Buckley Jr., conservative icon and former CIA officer, observed with a hint of sarcasm that "the director failed only to emblazon under [the *New York Times* building], 'Daniel Ellsberg slept here.'"[10] Buckley criticized promotional material for the movie, which said that the filmmakers wanted to describe "the climate of America." "They really mean," he complained, "the climate of America as seen by I. F. Stone, Seymour Hersh, Susan Sontag and Shirley MacLaine."[11] *Three Days of the Condor* also upset Benjamin Stein, and in an article in the *Wall Street Journal* titled "Let's Tar and Feather the CIA," Stein called the movie "complicated and simple-minded at the same time."[12] Stein criticized the filmmaker and other critics of the intelligence establishment for failing to consider "the possibility that the CIA might serve some valuable function for the nation and that the Soviets may not be the friends they seem to be. Fashion must be served."[13] From the perspective of DCI George H. W. Bush, moreover, the accusation that the CIA could manipulate the press seemed irresponsible and downright foolish: "Well, if we control it [the *New York Times*], we're doing a hell of a job with the editorial content they're coming out with! This is tough propaganda."[14]

Although Bush characterized the film as Hollywood paranoia, the agency had been closely linked to the media since its establishment in 1947. Carl Bernstein, the reporter who became famous for his coverage of the Watergate scandal, left the *Washington Post* in 1977, embarking on a six-month investigation of the CIA's relationship with newspapers and television networks. In October 1977, Bernstein published what remains the definitive account of that relationship in *Rolling Stone*. He alleged that "more than 400 American journalists . . . in the past twenty-five years have secretly carried out assignments for the Central Intelligence Agency, according to documents on file at CIA headquarters."[15] Bernstein's number was significantly higher than previous estimates. As Loch K. Johnson has noted, DCI William Colby admitted in 1973 that the CIA employed "some three dozen" American reporters, while the Church Committee believed that there were fifty.[16]

Hugh Wilford, David P. Hadley, and other historians have meticulously researched the CIA's clandestine use of journalists during the Cold War. Wilford explains "that the CIA constructed an array of front organizations that Frank Wisner, the agency's first chief of political warfare, liked to compare to a 'Mighty Wurlitzer' organ, capable of playing any propaganda tune he desired."[17] CIA officials used the media to advance their evolving propaganda strategies.[18] Hadley correctly points out that it is inaccurate to portray the agency as completely immune from criticism prior to the Bay of Pigs.[19] However, it is abundantly clear that the CIA wielded tremendous power in this pivotal era. "During the 1950s," Hadley observes, "the press/CIA relationships were largely congenial and mutually beneficial. The CIA was for the most part able to present itself as an effective, useful, and trustworthy tool for the United States in the struggle against communism."[20] It is important to emphasize that, in most cases, the agency did not use heavy-handed tactics to achieve compliance from the press. In fact, many journalists never hesitated when the CIA called on them. Perhaps Bernstein's most revealing interview was with Joseph Alsop, one of the country's prominent columnists during the early Cold War. Alsop admitted to Bernstein that both he and his brother, a fellow columnist, had done work for the agency: "The Founding Fathers [of the CIA] were close personal friends of ours. Dick Bissell [former CIA deputy director] was my oldest friend, from childhood. It was a social thing, my dear fellow. I never received a dollar, I never signed a secrecy agreement. I didn't have to. . . . I've done things for them when I thought they were the right thing to do. I call it doing my duty as a citizen."[21] Alsop strenuously dismissed the idea that his actions had been unethical. "The notion that a newspaperman doesn't have a duty to his country is perfect balls," he declared.[22]

Although the Alsop brothers certainly helped the CIA, agency officials devoted far more attention to CBS and the *New York Times*. "The Agency's relationship with the [*New York*] *Times* was by far its most valuable among newspapers, according to CIA officials. From 1950 to 1966," says Bernstein, "about ten CIA employees were provided [*New York*] *Times* cover under arrangements approved by the newspaper's late publisher, Arthur Hays Sulzberger."[23] Wilford explains that not only was Sulzberger a close friend of Allen Dulles, DCI between 1953 and 1961, he also "signed a secrecy agreement with the agency, although he delegated liaison duties to subordinates so as to give himself plausible deniability."[24] Upon the request of Dulles in June 1954, Sulzberger directly intervened to prevent Sydney Gruson, a correspondent with the *New York Times*, from leaving Mexico City to investigate allegations about CIA activity in Guatemala. The agency had spied on Gruson for at least two years. This surveillance was finally revealed in 1997, and it provided further confirmation of Bernstein's earlier description of Sulzberger's willingness to do the bidding of the CIA. When interviewed about the revelations, Gruson was not surprised: "I had a reputation with the C.I.A. I got in their hair. I knew that they kept very detailed files on me and for years they thought I was a Red."[25]

When Allen Dulles became DCI in 1953, he led the agency into what is commonly known as the "golden age of operations."[26] Dulles, more than any other person, cultivated the mystique of the CIA that would be directly threatened during the "Year of Intelligence." At a meeting in the summer of 1954, Dulles provided an excellent summation of his commitment to public relations. "I know perfectly well this 'shop' is run by the case officers, but by God I'm going to run the public relations," he proclaimed.[27] Reflecting on the contributions of "the Great White Case Officer," one of his protégés perceptively observed that "Dulles loved [the mystique], helped create it, and in many ways embodied it."[28] Dulles controlled the covert dimension of American foreign policy under President Dwight Eisenhower, while his brother, John Foster Dulles, ran the State Department.

Despite the Cold War consensus that emerged in the 1950s, Dulles's clandestine power did not go unchallenged. In July 1953, just five months after President Eisenhower selected Dulles to be the country's top spymaster, Senator Mike Mansfield (D-MD) made a proposal that stunned the intelligence establishment. Mansfield, a former history professor who had been elected to the Senate the previous fall, offered a resolution that would establish a congressional oversight committee on intelligence with ten members drawn from both the House and the Senate.[29] Dulles's supporters on Capitol Hill easily quashed the resolution, but in March 1954, Mansfield tried again. This time he delivered a stirring speech on the floor of the Senate, declaring, "secrecy now beclouds everything about CIA—its cost, its efficiency, its successes, and its failures."[30] Mansfield even included a prophetic warning in his address: "until we create some sort of 'watchdog committee' . . . we will have nothing but continued anxiety about the Central Intelligence Agency and its widespread activities."[31]

The evidence now available indicates that Dulles was reluctant to challenge Mansfield publicly.[32] Dulles fought back against the senator indirectly using a masterful display of public relations, the crowning achievement of which appeared in the form of a three-part series in the *Saturday Evening Post*. The articles, written by Richard and Gladys Harkness, would have been impossible without insider assistance at the agency. Peter Grose, Dulles's biographer, claims that Dulles did not leak stories to the reporting team, but he does concede that the DCI granted them full access and later proofread their articles over dinner, "making a few corrections or suggestions here and there."[33]

Judging from the content of the series, however, Dulles most likely had far more control over the articles than Grose suggests. In fact, "The Mysterious Doings of the CIA" nicely illustrates what historian Jonathan Nashel has called "the incestuous and corrosive mix between the government and the media that developed during the Cold War years."[34] The first article, which appeared on October 30, 1954, revealed to readers that the CIA had been covertly involved in Guatemala. The reporters claimed that this intervention was justified since Dulles had "proof that the communist-dominated government of Guatemala was part and parcel of a Red conspiracy, hatched in Moscow, to give Russia a military toehold in Latin America hard by the Panama Canal."[35] President Jacobo Arbenz of Guatemala had been a "communist puppet," and his supporters were Soviet hardliners posing as reformers.[36] Thankfully, from the perspective of the authors, Dulles and his CIA operatives "met the Reds early enough to hand Russia its defeat in Guatemala."[37] As a consequence, the United States had averted the possibility of a large-scale military intervention "to save Latin America."[38] It is evident, however, that Dulles and his subordinates withheld crucial information during interviews for the story. In the aftermath of President Arbenz's downfall, the CIA conducted Operation PBHISTORY, an examination of thousands of captured documents. This secret study firmly indicated that Arbenz had not been Moscow's puppet.[39]

The second article in the series told readers that the CIA had achieved a similar success in 1953 when "the strategic little nation of Iran was rescued from the closing clutch of Moscow."[40] Like Arbenz, Muhammad Mossadegh was in cahoots with the Communists, according to the authors, and they obviously took pleasure in boasting that the Iranian prime minister "was captured as he lay weeping in his bed, clad in striped silk pajamas."[41]

If the coverage of Iran was propaganda masquerading as journalism, the final article on November 13 was even worse. The Harkness duo described Dulles as "a tough-minded, hardheaded, steel spring of a man with an aptitude and zest for matching wits with an unseen foe."[42] On the final page, they editorialized about the necessity and cost effectiveness of the agency: "A helping hand in the rescue of one country such as Guatemala or Iran from communism is worth CIA's annual budget many times over."[43] In the event that readers had somehow missed the implicit rebuke of oversight proposals, they were reminded that "qualified observers in Washington believe that CIA deserves the trust and confidence of Congress and the people."[44]

The public relations campaign ended in success for the CIA when the most recent Mansfield oversight proposal was defeated 59–27 in April 1956.[45] Dulles remained committed to CIA public relations in the ensuing years. As Nashel reveals, the DCI became so interested in the Hollywood adaptation of Graham Greene's *The Quiet American* that he was willing to help the production team shoot the movie on location.[46] Unlike Greene's original story, the movie version celebrated America's involvement in Vietnam. Edward Lansdale, the CIA's point man in Southeast Asia, helped director Joseph Mankiewicz modify the script to transform "Pyle [the American character] into a hero and Fowler [the British character] into a communist stooge."[47]

Although Dulles successfully developed the agency's mystique, public relations was never institutionalized at the CIA in the way it was at J. Edgar Hoover's FBI.[48] In fact, the CIA did not establish the Office of Public Affairs until March 1977. The internal history of CIA public relations, which was declassified in 2005, is only four-pages long. Between 1947 and 1951, the agency lacked an official spokesperson. In May 1951, however, DCI Walter B. Smith, Dulles's predecessor, "appointed Colonel Chester B. Hansen—a former public relations aide to General Omar Bradley—as the agency's first 'spokesman.'"[49] Reporters often joked that Hansen and his successors were actually "nonspokesmen" or "no comment" men.[50] Shortly after Hansen joined the CIA, Eugene B. Rodney, a producer, expressed interest in developing a television series about spying with assistance from the agency. Smith declined to participate; "the C.I.A. deliberately cherish[es] anonymity," he explained.[51]

Hansen probably authored the "Public Relations Policy for CIA" before leaving the agency in 1952. This document recommended a more comprehensive public relations strategy for the CIA: "The sooner we acknowledge that the overt activities of intelligence are normal everyday functions that a government must exercise if it is to exist, the sooner people will accept intelligence as a routine part of the policymaking processes of government."[52] Colonel Sheffield Edwards, the longtime director of the Office of Security, carefully reviewed the recommendations. Edwards was arguably one of the most powerful officials at the CIA during the "golden age of operations," and he later became an instrumental figure in the agency's attempt to recruit the mafia to kill Fidel Castro. In a thoughtful and polite memorandum, Edwards offered his assessment of the public relations recommendations—"the question of a 'silent service' [versus] a 'not-so-silent service.'"[53] Even though he agreed with the proposals, he strongly defended the prevailing culture of secrecy. From his perspective, "too much publicity will do more to wreck our reputation than all the preventive work done so far or which could be done by public relations."[54] Edwards wanted to follow the example of the intelligence agencies in France and England. "Neither has permitted any publicity about its activities," he observed.[55] He was fearful that public relations had the potential to open a Pandora's box. "Public Relations must constantly feed the press additional bits and pieces of intelligence. Newspapermen will not accept old stuff nor a rehash of trite material," he warned. "These bits and pieces eventually result in an accurate picture of what the Agency does or, more important, hasn't been able to do."[56]

Prior to the late 1970s, top officials at the agency, like Edwards, were adamantly opposed to public relations. Dulles's embrace of public relations should be considered the exception rather than the norm.[57] The seven CIA spokesmen between 1951 and 1977 were essentially practitioners of crisis public relations. When they discovered a reporter was working on a story about the agency, they worked aggressively to prevent publication. Although this was relatively easy in the 1950s, it became increasingly difficult after 1961. "The CIA had known significant failures before the Bay of Pigs," says David P. Hadley, "but the agency was not prepared for the magnitude of its failure and the very public drubbing it received."[58]

Because Dulles had such a close relationship with the media, he did not need an entire office devoted to public relations. Colonel Stanley J. Grogan, the CIA spokesman between 1952 and 1963, helped implement Dulles's public relations strategy (see table 1).[59] Grogan corresponded frequently with newspapers and television networks; according to CBS records, for instance, the news division provided extensive assistance to the agency during this era. Sig Mickelson, then the president of CBS news, was fully aware of the clandestine relationship. In September 1957, Mickelson was informed that "Grogan phoned to say that [J. B. Love] Reeves [a CIA official] is going to New York to be in charge of the CIA contact office there and will call to see you. . . . Grogan says normal activities will continue to channel through the Washington office of CBS News."[60] At least one CBS reporter was a CIA employee, according to Bernstein. "Once a year during the 1950s and early 1960s," says Bernstein, "CBS correspondents joined the CIA hierarchy for private dinners and briefings."[61]

Table 1.1 CIA spokesmen, 1951–1977

Name	Years Served
Colonel Chester B. Hansen	1951–1952
Colonel Stanley J. Grogan	1952–1963
Paul M. Chretien	1963–1965
Commander George F. Moran	1965–1966
Joseph A. Goodwin	1966–1971
Angus M. Thuermer	1971–1976
Andrew T. Falkiewicz	1976–1977

Source: "History of CIA Public Affairs," Central Intelligence Agency, Office of Public Affairs (CREST).

The CIA's ties to the media continued after the debacle at the Bay of Pigs, but in the words of author Don DeLillo, "nothing was the same."[62] Forced out in November 1961, Dulles continued his public relations activities in retirement. He enlisted E. Howard Hunt, the CIA officer who later became infamous for his role in Watergate, and agency veteran Howard Roman to ghostwrite his memoir, *The Craft of Intelligence*.[63] Before the book was published, Dulles shared a copy with the CIA. Simon Willmetts explains that Grogan compiled a detailed summary of the manuscript, which contained "a series of acerbic annotations."[64] Grogan was not pleased with his former boss. In his memo to the DCI, he observed that the book "does go into intelligence methods and sources, does contain anecdotes, and takes the reader well inside the CIA."[65] He also noted that "the Soviet propaganda machine will find much to quote from the book."[66] If the CIA allowed Dulles to publish the memoir, Grogan warned, a dangerous precedent would be established. He worried the book "will open up the flood gates to *all* CIA employees to write or speak of their experiences to the same degree and in the same manner as does Mr. Dulles, some with their eye on a Hollywood series on espionage, which will bring them a pot of gold."[67] While Grogan could not prevent the book's publication, it does appear that Dulles agreed to make changes.

Dulles had helped perfect the "Mighty Wurlitzer," but in the early 1960s, the system was beginning to malfunction. CIA officials responded poorly to this turn of events, often utilizing heavy-handed tactics that made the situation worse. For instance, when the CIA discovered that journalists David Wise and Thomas B. Ross had written an exposé of the intelligence establishment, DCI John A. McCone invited them to lunch at CIA headquarters. When Wise and Ross refused to comply with McCone's request for deletions, McCone turned to Random House, offering to purchase all copies of the book. As Wise and Ross later recalled, the publisher "responded that he would be happy to sell the first printing to the CIA—but that he would then order another printing for the public, and another, and another."[68] Published in 1964, *The Invisible Government* quickly became a best seller. CIA officials should have moved on, but they were determined to sabotage the authors. "All [CIA] stations were deluged with dispatches giving instructions [on] how to handle the matter," according to Joseph B. Smith.[69] Stationed in Argentina at the time, Smith learned that the agency's Propaganda Guidance Section had prepared critical reviews of the book that were planted in foreign newspapers.[70]

Victor Marchetti and John D. Marks, a former State Department official, encountered similar tactics when they teamed up to write the manuscript that became *The CIA and the Cult of Intelligence*. After submitting a draft to the CIA in August 1973, they discovered that agency officials defined "classified" rather broadly. According to Marks's account, the CIA "said that the book could only be published if we deleted 339 items, [an estimated] 15 to 20 percent of the book."[71] Marks, Marchetti, and the American Civil Liberties Union (ACLU) protested the number of deletions, and within five months, the CIA had reduced the list of deleted items to 168.[72] The authors were now allowed to reinsert information that had obviously never presented a threat to national security; they could, for instance, tell readers that DCI Richard Helms had incorrectly pronounced the name of an African country during a meeting, and they also received permission to include budget information that had been published in the *Congressional Record*.[73] They decided to sue the CIA over the deletions that remained in effect, and in early 1974, Judge Albert V. Bryan Jr. granted them the right to print all but 27 of the items.[74] When the CIA appealed the case, however, Marks and Marchetti published their book in June, excluding the 168 contended items in order to avoid further delays. They left spaces in the text to show the extent of the censorship.[75]

In 1972, just months after Marks and Marchetti's legal battle began, the CIA once again attempted to interfere with a book critical of the agency when they convinced Harper & Row to send them a copy of Alfred W. McCoy's *The Politics of Heroin in Southeast Asia* prior to its publication. Concerned with the accusations leveled by McCoy about the CIA's knowledge of illegal drug trafficking, agency executives lobbied Harper & Row to reconsider sections of the manuscript, but the editors refused.[76] Since McCoy, then a PhD candidate at Yale University, had never worked for the CIA, the agency could not legally censor his writings. Ironically, he believed that the CIA's actions "actually improved his book—he insisted the CIA fully document every change it wanted. He [then] used that material to extend his analysis."[77]

The CIA's forays into public relations in the early 1970s were comically disastrous. DCI Helms allowed the director of the movie *Scorpio* to film the exterior of agency headquarters in Langley, Virginia. But unfortunately for Helms, he was apparently unaware that the screenplay called for the protagonist in the movie to gun down a high-ranking CIA official.[78] A few years later Helms accepted an invitation to visit the movie set for *Three Days of the Condor.* He was then serving as ambassador to Iran, and according to the film's director, Sydney Pollack, Helms appeared to be "having a great time" and was even "giggling." The actor who played Higgins, Cliff Robertson, recalls that at the moment Joe Turner confronted him about CIA involvement in assassinations, he glanced over and noticed that the former DCI was grinning. "As his grin wrapped around his mouth, the hairs on the back of my neck stood upright at attention," says Robertson.[79]

By the time *Three Days of the Condor* was released in 1975, however, CIA officials were not laughing. Colby, who headed the CIA during this contentious era, decided that it was necessary to reveal some of the agency's darkest secrets in order to ensure its survival. As John Prados has explained in *Lost Crusader,* Colby became "the man in the middle."[80] Not only was he caught between congressional investigators and the White House, he also found himself in the middle of two opposing factions within the CIA. The first believed that it was acceptable for him to share information with Congress and the public, while the second lobbied aggressively for him to stonewall Congress.[81] Even though Colby infuriated the old school Cold Warriors for cooperating with the investigations, it is now clear, as Prados concludes, that the embattled DCI was "far less open to inquiry than his critics claimed."[82] In the end, Colby managed to protect what he referred to as the "good secrets."[83] Colby explained in his memoir, *Honorable Men,* that "the CIA must build, not assume, public support, and it can do this only by informing the public of the nature of its activities and accepting the public's control over them."[84] Rather than weakening the CIA, Colby concluded, creating the perception of greater openness would reinvigorate it: "A public informed of the CIA's accomplishments and capabilities will support it. A public aware of its true mission and the limits of its authority will accept it. . . . A public convinced of the CIA's value will help protect its true secrets."[85]

On October 30, 1975, an ad hoc task group chaired by Lieutenant General Samuel V. Wilson sent Colby a memo entitled "Telling the Intelligence Story." Not surprisingly, Wilson and his colleagues noted that "publicity on the CIA in the last year has not resulted in a rounded story. Much attention has been focused on specific sensational bits and pieces of information."[86] The authors of the memo proposed a strategy for overcoming the negative publicity. "Altering this situation will require patience and a gradual approach. It will also require a more open and forthcoming attitude in the Agency's dealings with the media, which provide our only significant access to the American public," they advised.[87] The group outlined four recommendations for improving the CIA's relationship with the media. They began with the suggestion that the agency "collaborate with the media when asked to do so in developing features articles, articles for publication on selected topics, or television features," and in an attachment, they listed several topics that might interest journalists.[88] Second, the committee thought that "the present program for providing substantive background briefings [for columnists] should be expanded as opportunities arise."[89] They also believed that high-ranking CIA officials should consider making more "public appearances and speeches," while their final recommendation sought to highlight "CIA contributions to the advancement of technology and keeping the peace."[90]

In addition to their proposals for dealing with the press, the ad hoc group hoped that other people might be encouraged "to help tell the true story of intelligence."[91] The CIA should ask "senior statesmen" to get involved, and perhaps more importantly, they pushed for a stronger relationship with ex-officers: "We can provide judicious assistance to selected former Agency employees and retirees who want to defend the CIA in books, articles, or public appearances. 'Judicious' and 'selected' are the operative words."[92] Although the memo did not explain how "judicious" and "selected" would be defined in practice, it is obvious that the authors were only interested in dealing with individuals willing to support their former employer.

Since Colby had already embraced similar ideas before receiving "Telling the Intelligence Story," the memo should be viewed as a synopsis of pre-existing polices that offered a blueprint for modifications in the future. President Gerald Ford fired Colby only a few days after the document was prepared, and although he stayed on for a few more months, he did not have much time to implement changes. Yet there is no question that Colby desperately wanted to change public perceptions of the agency. As he explained in his memoirs, the CIA adopted a "gradual strategy" for public relations during his tenure at Langley,[93] an approach intended "to get our story out to the American people."[94] In order to maintain ties with ex-officers, for instance, he established an event called "alumni day." This reunion was viewed as more than an opportunity for intelligence veterans to reminisce about old adventures, since Colby intended "to arm them with the answers they needed to defend the institution to which they had given their loyalty."[95] There was undoubtedly a recruitment dimension to Colby's efforts. Groups of high school students on trips to Washington, DC, visited CIA headquarters every Tuesday night during the spring, and the agency also opened its doors to several college delegations.[96]

Colby's efforts were not always successful. Seeking to improve relations with the media, he initiated a briefing program for reporters that proved disastrous. The first session with journalists, which Colby thought would focus on world events, led to a confrontation over the CIA's relationship with American businessmen. Finding himself cornered, he accidentally blurted out the approximate number of agency contacts in the business community. Colby learned from the embarrassing incident; in the future, such briefings were done on a smaller scale that enabled the CIA to retain more control over the topics discussed.[97]

Unlike many of his colleagues in the clandestine service, David A. Phillips, a twenty-five-year veteran, supported Colby's strategy. At the same time, however, he worried that the backlash against previous wrongdoing might lead to the CIA's destruction. The media, which Dulles had manipulated with such ease in the 1950s, had turned on Phillip's beloved agency. He described the "Year of Intelligence" as "the storm which changed my life," a crisis that he believed could be solved using public relations.[98]

Phillips drew inspiration from the plight of Ray S. Cline and Harry Rositzke. Cline had been deputy director for intelligence (DDI) at the

CIA before leaving in 1969 to run the State Department's intelligence division (INR), and Rositzke was previously a high-ranking officer in the Directorate of Plans (renamed the Directorate of Operations in 1973).[99] In October 1974, Rositzke reviewed the history of the relationship between the CIA and the executive branch in a *New York Times* editorial, noting that the agency did not operate independently of the president. "Political-action operations—secret support of foreign leaders, political parties and labor unions, and the preparation of coups and countercoups—have been carried out under the aegis of every postwar President," he observed.[100] While Rositzke advised that paramilitary operations like the Bay of Pigs should be moved to the Pentagon, he believed that "more post-mortems" were unnecessary.[101] Cline argued in the *New York Times* the following month that covert action was vital to national security: "We should not be obsessed with piety but instead should think earnestly of every way possible short of total war to insure that our society and political structures and alliances with like-minded peoples will continue to flourish."[102] As the "Year of Intelligence" unfolded, Cline and Rositzke also appeared on television to defend the intelligence community.[103] Phillips admired their efforts, but it was obvious to him that they were badly outnumbered.

If he had learned one thing during his years of service in the CIA, however, he realized that low manpower was not an insurmountable handicap. His understanding of propaganda convinced him that even though Colby should be forthcoming at the congressional hearings, the agency had to simultaneously push back against critics. Phillips approached Colby with his concerns, hoping to convince his boss to launch a more aggressive public relations campaign aimed at restoring the public's confidence in the CIA. Though he agreed with Phillips in principle, Colby considered the approach too risky. He reminded Phillips about *The Selling of the Pentagon,* a documentary that CBS had first broadcast in February 1971.[104] Narrated by Roger Mudd, the exposé outlined the Pentagon's massive efforts to win the support of the American public, from displays in shopping malls to promotional films that showed how the military was winning in Vietnam. It revealed that the annual public relations budget at the Defense Department had risen from $2.8 million in 1959 to $30 million in 1971. According to the Twentieth Century Fund, the budget in 1971 was actually closer to $190 million.[105] Colby understood that the CIA could not allow a similar controversy to happen to them. After Hersh's story, critics might characterize any public relations venture as nothing more than sinister propaganda. "We're just going to have to take the heat," Colby declared.[106]

Phillips accepted Colby's decision, but he could no longer tolerate watching events from the sidelines. He retired from the CIA in the spring of 1975 to form the Association of Retired Intelligence Officers (ARIO). When Phillips began planning ARIO, he hoped that Cline might be interested in serving as president. Cline, an executive director at Georgetown University's Center for Strategic and International Studies at the time, declined the offer. "You know that I have been trying to build up a reputation as a scholarly commentator on intelligence as distinct from a 'committed' defender of CIA," Cline explained in a letter to Phillips. "While I am not sure my tactics have been entirely successful, I do want to stay in the public view as an independent rather than a partisan 'CIAnik.'"[107] Although it is unclear whether he sought out anyone else about the position, Phillips ultimately became the first president of ARIO.

Taking addresses from the mailing list that his family used for Christmas cards, he had sent out a letter to fellow intelligence officers in March announcing his objective "to explain why our country needs an intelligence service and to help clear up some of the erroneous impressions and sensationalism surrounding us by explaining what CIA is and, more important probably, what it is not."[108] Membership was open to anyone who had previously worked within the American intelligence community, and annual dues of $10 included a subscription to *Periscope*, ARIO's newsletter. More than anything else, the organization provided a network for ex–intelligence officers. Starting in 1975, for instance, ARIO held conventions every year.[109] Over 1,000 people had joined by the fall of 1976.

Phillips hoped to address what he referred to as "a tough credibility problem" for American intelligence.[110] ARIO established a speaker's bureau for anyone in the organization who wanted to publicly defend the intelligence establishment against its detractors. Phillips, arguably the most prolific speaker in ARIO, made multiple appearances across the country after leaving the CIA. He spoke about his adventures with the agency, and he assured audiences that the policies of reform were working effectively. Not everyone accepted what Phillips had to say. In fact, when he appeared in Madison, Wisconsin, to deliver a speech in 1976, approximately four hundred people protested.[111] But for the most part, demonstrations of this magnitude were uncommon.

In addition to their speeches in front of local groups, Phillips and select colleagues from ARIO spoke to journalists and went on television to provide a counterpoint to opponents of the CIA. Kathryn S. Olmsted correctly observes, "he guaranteed reporters that pithy, pro-CIA quotes were just a phone call away."[112] On an ABC morning show, Phillips squared off against John D. Marks and Philip Agee, the former CIA officer who revealed the names of agency operatives in *Inside the Company*, and on another show he sparred with Victor Marchetti.[113] Unlike Agee, who Phillips called "the first CIA defector,"[114] Marchetti had not ousted any CIA employees. Marchetti contends that Phillips put pressure on him to renounce any connection to *Counter-Spy*, the radical magazine in Washington, DC, that was exposing the identities of agency officers. "Marchetti respected the CIA's power and took the warning to heart," says Angus Mackenzie. "He withdrew from the magazine and talked others into leaving with him."[115] Phillips briefly mentioned in his memoir that Marchetti left *Counter-Spy*, but he omitted any reference to his conversation with the noted CIA critic.[116]

The omission was not especially surprising, since ARIO members typically wrote their memoirs with the intention of shaping public opinion. Having seen how effectively former officers such as Marchetti, Agee, Frank Snepp, and Patrick McGarvey had used their books to criticize the agency, they believed that the genre offered a terrific opportunity to counterattack. Less than three weeks after leaving the CIA, Phillips complained in the *New York Times* that the media was treating the agency unfairly. Phillips placed stories about the CIA into three categories: "factual," "sensationalist," and "fact-and-fallacy."[117] The first type "we can endure stoically," he explained, while the second "we can also endure because the ridiculous is patently short-lived."[118] What most frustrated Phillips and his colleagues was "the hybrid (fact-and-fallacy) story" because it "refuses to die or be straightened out, and sinks into the public subconscious as durable myth."[119]

Ironically, despite Phillips's concerns about so-called hybrid news stories, he and fellow CIA defenders did not respond with "factual" accounts of the agency; on the contrary, they used their memoirs to create their own "durable myths." Phillips published *The Night Watch* in 1977, a skillfully written account of the various positions he held at the CIA between 1950 and 1975. After his initial recruitment in Chile, he gained extensive experience with the agency throughout Latin America—in Guatemala, Cuba, Mexico, the Dominican Republic, Brazil, and Venezuela—before finishing his career as the head of the Western Hemisphere Division in the Directorate of Operations. In reflecting on his quarter century of service, Phillips admitted the CIA had made mistakes. He condemned the MKULTRA experiments that the agency secretly conducted in the 1950s and 1960s. "Without question," Phillips acknowledged, "conducting the drug research on unwitting persons or in a manner that could lead to suicide, as in the instance of one man [Dr. Frank Olson], was unjustifiable."[120] He also criticized the CIA's actions leading up to the Bay of Pigs invasion of April 1961. Phillips, who had participated in these events, concluded, "at some time we [the CIA] should have cried 'enough.' When told the plan was to be changed from a classic guerilla landing at Trinidad to a military operation we should have protested individually to the point of refusing to go along."[121]

Phillips's primary objective, however, was not to apologize. Throughout *The Night Watch*, he attempted to refute negative allegations that had been leveled against the agency. For instance, to counter the accusation that the CIA lacked diversity, he casually mentioned, "one of my friends became the first black Chief of Station,"[122] and later described how he "appointed the first female Chief of Station in CIA's history."[123] Interestingly, when Janine Brookner successfully sued the CIA in 1994 for gender discrimination, evidence came to light that contradicted Phillips's assertion that he had named the first woman station chief. Brookner, who joined the agency in the late 1960s, had served as acting deputy chief of station in Venezuela, and she later became chief of station in Jamaica in 1989. Brookner's lawyer described her as the first female director of a CIA station in Latin America.[124] If this information is indeed accurate, Phillips appears to have misstated the facts in his book.

There are also significant flaws with the information he provided on covert actions. In 1954, four years after the CIA first recruited him in Chile, he helped overthrow President Arbenz in Operation PBSUCCESS. Phillips's version of Operation PBSUCCESS evoked memories of the *Saturday Evening Post* series "The Mysterious Doings of the CIA." He referred to Arbenz as "a Soviet sycophant" who "would have undoubtedly succumbed to the political flattery and pressures of his [communist] advisers."[125] Phillips proudly told readers how the radio broadcasts he initiated on May 1, 1954, were designed to convince Arbenz that the opposition forces of Castillo Armas were too powerful for his government to stop. "Arbenz would not have resigned had he not been manipulated into what he conceived as an impossible situation by the rebel radio," Phillips observed, "especially in creating a climate in which he would not allow his pilots to fly or permit the colonel from St. Cyr to commit his troops."[126] He relaxed in Guatemala City after Armas prevailed, playing golf at a local course; in a somewhat bizarre twist, he learned afterwards that the spikes he wore during the outing actually belonged to Arbenz.[127] Not only did Phillips perpetuate the well-worn myth that Arbenz was a Soviet pawn, he also appears to have exaggerated the effectiveness of his propaganda campaign, Operation SHERWOOD.[128]

Since Phillips portrayed covert action as a method of spreading democracy and containing communism, he went to great lengths to explain away the CIA's intervention in Chile. After Salvador Allende was democratically elected in September 1970, President Richard Nixon ordered the CIA to prevent the Chilean leader from taking office. The agency established the secret Chile Task Force to execute this mission and appointed Phillips to direct it. Phillips said in his memoirs that he was aware he would be working to undermine democracy, which made him reluctant to take the job: "Track II [Nixon's covert policy for Chile] was the only episode in my CIA career which disturbed me to the point that I even considered resigning in protest."[129] Instead of resigning, however, Phillips accepted the position to run the task force. Starting in the middle of September, he spent over forty days plotting against President Allende, and by his own estimation, he typically "worked twenty hours a day" during the operation.[130] Declassified CIA records indicate that Phillips and his task force sought to establish "a coup climate [in Chile] by propaganda, disinformation and terrorist activities."[131] Phillips and the head of the Western Hemisphere Division sent a cable to the CIA station in Santiago on September 28 that bluntly outlined their objectives: "We conclude that it is our task to create such a climate climaxing with a solid pretext that will force the military and the president to take some action in the desired direction."[132]

Phillips attempted to disassociate the CIA from the assassination of General Rene Schneider, the official designated to protect Chilean democracy, but he neglected to mention that the agency provided $35,000 to the conspirators after the murder.[133] He also kept secret the praise that he had lavished upon CIA officials in Santiago after hearing about the attack on General Schneider. "The Station has done [an] excellent job of guiding Chileans to point today where a military solution is at least an option for them," he said in an October 23 cable.[134]

Even though he later claimed that he had been reluctant at first to participate in Track II, the sentiment expressed in this cable reveals that Phillips took great pride in his work once he committed himself to the covert project.

Phillips blamed Track II on President Nixon and National Security Advisor Henry Kissinger, calling the covert policy of the White House "inexcusable."[135] The condemnation of a plan that he implemented with such determination seems rather self-serving to say the least. Some might be inclined to sympathize with Phillips's situation in the fall of 1970: after all, he received orders from his superiors, and he loyally followed them despite significant reservations. Yet the evidence demonstrates that Phillips was a willing participant in events rather than a hapless victim. After Schneider was gunned down on October 22, Phillips claimed in his memoir that the CIA aborted Track II.[136] He argued that the CIA was not responsible for the military coup that toppled Allende on September 11, 1973. Rather than destabilizing the Chilean government, Phillips maintained, the objective of the CIA after 1970 "was just the opposite—to stabilize [Chile] by keeping alive democratic institutions until the election . . . scheduled for 1976."[137] Cord Meyer, a retired CIA officer who published his memoir three years after Phillips, essentially made the same argument about Allende. Track II was an "unhappy incident" and a "secret Nixonian aberration" in Meyer's assessment, but "the Agency was specifically enjoined from any action that might be construed as supporting coup plotting" once the program ended in October 1970.[138] Like Phillips, Meyer said that the purpose of CIA involvement in Chile after Track II "was to ensure the survival of a democratic coalition that would have a reasonable chance of winning back the Chilean presidency in the election scheduled for 1976."[139]

Denying CIA complicity in Allende's downfall was central to the defense of covert action, since agency supporters recognized that the American public would not tolerate an institution that undermined democracy and promoted dictatorships. Recently declassified CIA files show that the assertions of Phillips and Meyer were significant distortions of the historical record. Meyer served as the assistant deputy director of the Directorate of Plans between 1967 and 1973, and in June 1973, Phillips took over as chief of the Western Hemisphere Division. Given their high-ranking positions within the clandestine service, both men would have known that the covert operations against Allende continued in the three years preceding the September 1973 coup. Thomas

Karamessines, who ran the Directorate of Operations during this era, later admitted "Track II never really ended."[140] Although the CIA avoided any involvement in the logistical aspects of the coup, an agency report concluded in 2000 that Langley "provided assistance to militant right-wing groups to undermine the president [Allende] and create a tense environment."[141]

Phillips and Meyer developed a clever disinformation campaign to hide what the CIA had done in Chile. Phillips believed that the truck strikes in the months prior to the military takeover directly contributed to the success of Chilean dictator Augusto Pinochet, but he denied that the CIA had financed the truckers.[142] This denial was literally true; at the same time, however, it was completely misleading. Instead of directly funding the labor unrest, the agency offered money to other groups—"cutouts"—who, in turn, "supported . . . key sectors fomenting economic and social upheaval, notably the truck owners and strikers that paralyzed Chile in 1973."[143] The CIA also supported the newspaper *El Mercurio*, which, rather than stabilizing Chilean democracy, sought to destroy it using propaganda to force the resignation of Carlos Prats in August 1973. Peter Kornbluh has eloquently summarized the tragic implications of Prats's resignation: "Like his predecessor, General Schneider, Prats had upheld the constitutional role of the Chilean military, blocking younger officers who wanted to intervene in Chile's political process."[144]

Phillips, a true believer in the power of propaganda, who once owned a newspaper in Santiago, took over the Western Hemisphere Division at the same time that events began to escalate in Chile. Was this simply a coincidence? Perhaps. But it is certain that Phillips knew about ongoing efforts to undermine Allende, participated in them, and then worked assiduously to cover up the CIA's ties to the Chilean right-wing. "The argument that these [CIA] operations were intended to preserve Chile's democratic institutions was a public relations ploy, contradicted by the weight of the historical record," Kornbluh notes in *The Pinochet File*.[145] Phillips and his ARIO friends were key architects of this "public relations ploy," and they unleashed their propaganda techniques on Americans to mislead them about what really happened in Chile during the early 1970s.

Phillips and Meyer downplayed the domestic operations of the agency using similar tactics of obfuscation. In his famous exposé of the CIA in December 1974, journalist Seymour Hersh revealed that the agency had "conducted a massive, illegal domestic intelligence operation during the Nixon administration against the antiwar movement and other dissident groups in the United States."[146] Defenders of the CIA took issue with Hersh's decision to use the words "massive" and "illegal" in the opening sentence of the article, which appeared on the front page of the *New York Times*. "Based on the extensive evidence that is now available," argued Meyer, "my own view is that the domestic surveillance activity involving antiwar activists conducted by the Agency was neither massive in scope nor clearly illegal at the time that it was undertaken."[147] Operation MHCHAOS led to the infiltration of antiwar groups, but he rationalized the activity by claiming that the informants were simply attempting to establish whether the protestors were the puppets of Moscow. While he acknowledged that the CIA team implementing Operation MHCHAOS had "clearly exceeded its instructions" on three occasions,[148] Meyer concluded that "[Richard] Helms was correct in his judgment that the foreign dimension of domestic dissent was clearly within the Agency's jurisdiction and that there was no choice but to trace down every lead."[149]

Not surprisingly, Meyer blatantly distorted Helms's assessment of Operation MHCHAOS. In February 1969, Helms had sent a letter to National Security Advisor Henry Kissinger, informing him that "this is an area not within the charter of this agency, so I need not emphasize how extremely sensitive this makes the paper [on the antiwar movement]. Should anyone learn of its existence, it would prove most embarrassing for all concerned."[150] Both Meyer and Phillips cited the Rockefeller Commission Report to support their claims. Phillips first developed this strategy in 1977: "these violations were not 'massive'; the undisputed findings of the Rockefeller Commission established less than a dozen cases which could be described as clearly illegal."[151] Phillips embraced a puzzling definition of the word "massive." In reality, the Rockefeller Commission disclosed that the CIA had created files on approximately 7,200 Americans while simultaneously maintaining a secret computer database in the basement of Langley with "the names of more than 300,000 persons and organizations."[152] In outlining their defense of the CIA, these agency veterans also chose to sidestep one minor detail: the National Security Act of 1947, which established the CIA, specifically prohibits it from engaging in domestic operations.

Skeptical observers in the 1970s charged that there was an active relationship between Langley and ARIO. The organization's decision to move into an office building that was a short drive from CIA headquarters did nothing to diminish this perception. While Colby approved of the project and became a member after his retirement, he told Phillips that "he [Phillips] could have no special help from or relationship with CIA or we would be pilloried for attempting to run a covert operation on the American public."[153] Phillips vehemently denied any connection. "I wish to make it absolutely clear that the C.I.A. management has not had, and will not have, a hand officially, unofficially or otherwise in this organization and its efforts," he said to the media in 1975.[154]

At first glance it appears that ARIO, which was renamed the Association of Former Intelligence Officers (AFIO) in 1977, had a fairly innocuous relationship with CIA headquarters. Evidence suggests that they made referrals to each other if they considered it appropriate. For instance, when a staffer on the Senate Select Committee on Intelligence contacted the agency's Office of Legislative Counsel in January 1976 to see if Phillips could make a speech in Texas, the counsel's office extended a cautious response. "I told [the staffer] we are at arms length with Mr. Phillips but provided him the phone number where Mr. Phillips can be reached," wrote the official.[155] Referrals also worked in the other direction, since members like Cline kept contact numbers for the CIA's public affairs office on hand. One member, an assistant professor at Canisius College in Buffalo, New York, sent the CIA a letter to arrange for students visiting Washington to meet with agency officials. The professor described the proposed meeting as "an opportunity for the Agency to contact a group of highly motivated, intelligent, and patriotic young men and women."[156]

The editor of *Counter-Spy* magazine leveled one of the most sensational charges against agency veterans connected to AFIO, alleging in 1979 that Cline and thirteen other Georgetown University employees were still working for the CIA. Cline lashed out at the accusation in the campus newspaper while claiming that the magazine was "set up by Cuban intelligence, run by the KGB [Soviet secret police]. . . . Where do you think they get their funds from?"[157] He further defended himself in a memo on the episode, saying he had "received no compensation of any kind from CIA since [resigning in 1969] except for three or four lectures given to training classes at CIA. My total income from fees for such lectures is only a few hundred dollars spread over several years."[158] In truth, Cline had remained in contact with the CIA even though he was not on the payroll. Shortly after Admiral Stansfield Turner succeeded George H. W. Bush as DCI, Cline offered to assist him. "If there is anything at all that I can say or do to help you," Cline wrote in March 1977, "please let me know."[159] He sent a more detailed letter about four months later:

> I wish I had an opportunity to counsel with you and your staff with a view to supporting from outside of government the legitimate goals of coordinated central intelligence. I have consulted your staff several times in the past month to see if you ever have any time for sympathetic old hands, so far with no response. . . . If you can think of any way in which I can be helpful to the intelligence community, please let me know.[160]

It appears that Admiral Turner never followed up on Cline's overtures.[161] Yet there is also no question that other AFIO members received assistance from inside Langley. Trevor McCrisken revealed that a founding member of ARIO visited CIA headquarters in March 1978 and met with DCI Turner, discussing the possibility of a television show about the agency. In pitching the idea, the producers promised to "fight back in defense of the CIA and other U.S. intelligence organizations."[162] Nick Cullather has found similar evidence of collaboration. While working for the CIA's history staff in the early 1990s, he discovered that Phillips's chapter on the Guatemala coup in *The Night Watch* had been "copied almost verbatim from a debriefing report that is still classified."[163] Assuming that Phillips did not possess a photographic memory or steal documents from headquarters before he retired, Cullather's remarkable finding suggests that the president of ARIO was actually receiving assistance from friends still working at Langley in the mid-1970s. This directly contradicts the official proclamations of both Colby and Phillips, in which they denied a relationship between Langley and ARIO. CIA officials apparently had no problem leaking classified information as long as Phillips could spin it to make them look good. Ironically, when two authors filed a FOIA request for documents on the Guatemala operation, the agency turned them down and ultimately prevailed in the legal battle that ensued.[164] CIA lawyers failed to disclose that at least one of the documents requested had been published already in *The Night Watch*. If this information had not been withheld from the court, it would have been far more difficult for the agency to win the case.

What most united the former intelligence officers was their belief that the intelligence community needed to operate in secrecy.[165] After terrorists murdered Richard Welch, the CIA station chief in Athens, the White House used the tragedy to turn public opinion against the investigations of Senator Frank Church (D-ID) and Representative Otis Pike (D-NY). Frederick A. O. Schwarz Jr., the chief counsel of the Church Committee, has described it as a Machiavellian public relations campaign: "They danced on the grave of Welch. They egregiously and unfairly took advantage of the situation. In a short-term, tactical way, they rejoiced in his death."[166] It is important to remember that the Ford administration received assistance in this effort from ARIO and Colby, who did everything in their power to portray Welch as a fallen hero.

To commemorate the arrival of Welch's remains at Andrews Air Force Base on the morning of December 30, 1975, Phillips, Colby, and about twenty-eight others formed a receiving line and watched as an air force honor guard escorted the casket from the C-141 transport plane to a nearby hearse. Television crews filmed the brief ceremony, and thousands of Americans saw the footage on the news. Perhaps the most iconic image of the event was of Colby standing next to Welch's ex-wife and crying daughter, all three with hand over heart.[167] The CIA organized a memorial ceremony for Welch inside the auditorium at Langley, also known as the Bubble, and although the press was not allowed to attend, the agency released detailed information about the service. It began with the national anthem and closed with "America the Beautiful." In between the songs, Colby delivered a eulogy for Welch.[168] President Ford granted a special waiver to authorize Welch's burial at Arlington Cemetery on January 6. The funeral, with an estimated five hundred people in attendance, garnered national media attention.[169] "Although the Welch family requested that reporters be barred from the chapel where the funeral service was performed," observed Laurence Stern of the *Washington Post*, "provision was made for news coverage of what the Ford administration clearly conceived of as an important event."[170] As Senator Church recognized, the White House carefully "stage-managed" the entire event.[171]

Phillips nicely complemented the Ford administration's public relations efforts. He spoke out against the editors of *Counter-Spy* for disclosing the names of American operatives, and just three days after Welch's killing, the *Washington Post* ran a front-page story drawn almost exclusively from information he provided. Dan Morgan, the *Washington Post* reporter who wrote the story, focused on Phillip's claim that Welch had foreseen the possibility of terrorists murdering CIA officers. He quoted

Phillips several times in the article, which allowed the ARIO president to shape the story's content. The reporter's sources portrayed Welch as a CIA martyr, "an 'erudite' man with a mastery of classical and modern Greek, Spanish and French," and a person who "reportedly would enliven government meetings on current topics by citing anecdotes and precedents from ancient Greek and Roman history."[172] Phillips described Welch, who worked for him in the Western Hemisphere Division, as someone "who had the potential for aiming at any position in the agency, given time and experience."[173] Phillips later dedicated *The Night Watch* to Welch, and he even based the title on a comment that Welch made to a CIA recruit at Camp Peary's bar: "[that intoxicated instructor is] trying to tell you that the night watch can be lonely, but that it must be stood."[174] Phillips and his organization would keep alive the memory of Welch, lobbying forcefully in the years ahead for a federal law to guard against the disclosure of intelligence officers. This effort directly contributed to the passage of the Intelligence Identities Protection Act in 1982.

In order to turn Welch into a martyr, however, important evidence was withheld from the American public. Kathryn S. Olmsted points out that the CIA had unsuccessfully encouraged Welch to use a home in Athens that was less conspicuous,[175] and John Prados found in his research that Welch's house "was regularly pointed out on sightseeing tours of the Greek capital."[176] Yet in the immediate aftermath of Welch's death, agency officials kept secret the warnings that they had sent. Supporters of the CIA placed blame for the assassination on *Counter-Spy*, and a *Washington Post* article even claimed that *Athens News* contacted the magazine's editors before deciding to print Welch's name on November 25. Although a CIA investigation concluded the *Washington Post* story was "untrue," the agency only released this information after a FOIA request forced its disclosure.[177]

On January 8, 1976, two days after the Welch funeral, *New York Times* columnist Anthony Lewis perceptively observed that the events were "being manipulated in order to arouse a public backlash against legitimate criticism [of the intelligence community]."[178] He expressed concern about the "careless legitimizing of secrecy," predicting that President Ford and Langley would exploit the situation "to prevent any thoroughgoing reform of the C.I.A."[179] Lewis was arguably the first person to recognize that the forces of secrecy were turning the tide against the congressional investigations. These inquiries, which initially threatened the future of the CIA, ended within four months of Lewis's editorial. It is true that both the House and the Senate established intelligence oversight committees, but at the same time politicians refused to take more radical action.

In describing how Americans viewed the agency prior to the congressional investigations, Jonathan Nashel offers an interesting observation: "The fact that the American public simultaneously respected, feared, and approved of the CIA's actions until the 1970s was the result of one of the most successful promotions undertaken by the U.S. officialdom."[180] Allen Dulles, of course, was the mastermind behind the "promotions." But if Dulles built up the agency with public relations wizardry in the 1950s, it is equally fair to say that William Colby and David A. Phillips helped save the institution two decades later using the same techniques. These men correctly perceived that the American public had not completely lost their fascination with the agency despite all the ugly revelations that emerged in the mid-1970s. It was not accidental that Phillips evoked the CIA mystique by emphasizing the anonymous heroism of intelligence officers on the final page of *The Night Watch*. "They have been in dark alleys working hard—with some mistakes and some success—to protect those [American] values," he observed, and then hopefully predicted: "American intelligence will survive."[181]

In retrospect, public relations deserves at least part of the credit for making this prediction come true.

2 | Admiral Stansfield Turner, Herbert Hetu, and the Legend of CIA Openness, 1977–1980

Write the music and play him [the reporter] like a violin.
—Pickett Lumpkin

In March 1992, William Colby provided a succinct and convincing description of his objectives during the "Year of Intelligence": "I was fighting for (a) survival of the agency, [and] (b) survival of the covert action mission. We won both."[1] Public relations helped Colby achieve this victory, and it would also assist his successors in their efforts to repair the CIA's tarnished image. When Admiral Stansfield Turner became DCI in 1977, he immediately revamped how the agency interacted with the public. Two years earlier Colby had shied away from using the Department of Defense as the model for his public relations campaign; citing the fallout from *The Selling of the Pentagon,* a documentary that aired on CBS, he worried the agency might be accused of violating the National Security Act's prohibition on domestic activity. Given Admiral Turner's naval background, he was much more willing than Colby to institutionalize public relations at the CIA. He recruited an outside public relations expert to establish a modern Office of Public Affairs, and between 1977 and 1981, this office developed media strategies for the agency that are still in use. Turner and his advisors sought to create the impression that the CIA had learned its lessons from the previous intelligence scandals; that agency officials accepted and welcomed the newly established oversight committees; and that the reforms were working effectively. By projecting an image of openness to both Congress and the American public, Turner and his advisors hoped to avoid further investigation of the intelligence community. The public relations hype served simultaneously to obscure what was happening at the CIA in the late 1970s and early 1980s. Ironically, at the same time that agency executives talked publicly about their acceptance of greater openness, they worked forcefully to undermine FOIA and the ability of former intelligence officers to criticize the CIA.

Agency employees distrusted Admiral Turner and the outsiders he brought to Langley, but it immediately became clear to them that the new policies on public relations were not open for debate. In April 1977, E. Henry Knoche, Turner's deputy, sent his boss a packet of material titled "Suggestions for CIA Outreach to the Public"—two pages of which remain classified—that contained proposals for addressing public relations. For each recommendation, the report's authors provided a short description, estimated the related costs, and assessed the idea's advantages and disadvantages. Not only did Turner read the packet thoroughly, he also made notations at the bottom of several pages. He approved most of the recommendations, even offering detailed suggestions for improvement in certain cases. One of the proposals was to provide tours of the agency's headquarters for groups from congressional offices that would offer politicians "the chance to look good in front of the constituents."[2] In response to the idea that these visitors could watch "old Agency P.R. films," Turner enthusiastically wrote: "Let's get a new one."[3] He also advised that there should be an exhibit in the passageway between the main building and the Bubble.[4]

The packet contained a proposal to bring regional experts from universities to CIA headquarters for a visit, a recommendation that had obvious benefits for recruitment. Turner was warned that "many of the target academics have been hostile or critical of the Agency in the past, and at least a few might well choose to make an issue of such an effort."[5] Yet despite the potential challenges, such visits represented a tremendous opportunity: "The target academics are among the most prestigious and influential regional experts in the United States, and in each instance where we succeed in improving their understanding and appreciation of the intelligence process there would be an extensive multiplier effect among both faculty and students."[6] Similar proposals were made for think tank directors; meetings with these officials could "identify areas in which the research of private centers complements our own with an eye toward possible contractual relationships in areas where they are especially well qualified."[7] In addition to embracing the above suggestions, Turner approved a plan to participate more extensively in career fairs at high schools and colleges.[8]

The packet on public outreach included ideas that would have delighted David A. Phillips. The Office of Public Affairs wanted to recruit a "group of well-qualified public speakers to represent the Agency at local level speaking engagements . . . throughout the country. Retired employees could be used for this purpose along with public personalities."[9] The proposal did not make reference to the speaker's bureau that ARIO had already established, but it is clear that the intention was to institute a similar program under agency auspices. The CIA apparently no longer worried that the project might be characterized as a domestic operation. Turner wanted to pursue an ambitious public relations campaign, and few ideas were off limits. His staff even proposed holding an "open house" at Langley that would be "advertised in advance to which the public at large would be invited."[10] Turner, however, ultimately decided against the plan, most likely because of concerns about "a staged incident" and the possibility that the event could be condemned "as a 'Disneyland' approach to selling the Agency's image, i.e., 'huckstering.'"[11] Agency officials wanted to sell their image, but they planned on closely guarding their tactics.

The person responsible for "selling the Agency's image" was Herbert Hetu, a jovial public relations man with over two decades of experience in the navy, who Turner would later praise for implementing "a far-reaching but carefully controlled plan."[12] Since public affairs at the agency had been conducted internally in the past, Hetu's arrival proved somewhat controversial at first, especially since he reported directly to Turner and received the title assistant to the director. Hetu recalled in a 1984 interview that he joked privately about looking underneath his car for explosive devices before driving to Langley in the morning: "Going in there perceived as the guy who was going to let the press in, open the windows. . . . Oh boy, [there was] a lot of hostility."[13]

During a series of interviews in 1996, Hetu explained that his introduction to public relations began while serving on the USS *Salem*. The Ionian Islands in the Mediterranean sustained extensive damage in August 1953 after several earthquakes, and the *Salem* provided emergency assistance to the disaster victims. Hetu, the assistant public affairs officer on the cruiser, submitted reports on the situation that were used in newspaper accounts of the tragedy. *Time* magazine even printed a quote from one of Hetu's dispatches.[14] After completing his tour on the ship, the navy selected him to run the magazine and book division of the Office of Information where he soon became a protégé of Pickett Lumpkin. Hetu described Lumpkin as a member of the "40 Thieves," the moniker given to the founding fathers of the navy's public relations apparatus in the early Cold War years.[15] Hetu fondly remembered the advice that Lumpkin bestowed on junior officers before sending them to meet with a reporter: "Write the music and play him [the reporter] like a violin."[16] Lumpkin made it perfectly clear that the objective of public relations officers in the navy was to emphasize the positive and downplay the negative. This might sound like government propaganda, but Hetu perceived it differently: "We were always trying to think about telling the good side of the Navy. I suppose that's, in the classic [sense] of the definition, propaganda in a way, but [it was] not propaganda in that we didn't manipulate the message to be untrue or to say something that wasn't honorable or truthful."[17]

Yet the evidence indicates that the navy did "manipulate the message" on several occasions. In fact, Hetu was directly connected to the two most important books published about Vietnam during the 1950s. While running the magazine and book division, he arranged for Admiral Arleigh A. Burke, then chief of naval operations, to write the foreword for Tom Dooley's *Deliver Us from Evil.* He also helped organize a national tour to promote the book. Seth Jacobs, author of *America's Miracle Man in Vietnam,* observes that "*Deliver Us from Evil* was a brilliant work of cold war propaganda in which the communist enemy was irredeemably evil and the Americans and their South Vietnamese allies were virtue incarnate."[18] Dooley, a navy doctor in Vietnam, ultimately became a public relations liability when, in Hetu's words, "they found out that he and his sailors were running more than a dispensary."[19] After discovering Dooley's homosexuality, Hetu admitted, the navy forced him to resign.

Hetu left the navy's magazine and book division in 1956 and spent the next three years with the Pacific Fleet in Hawaii. He briefly shared an office there with William Lederer, who was in the process of coauthoring *The Ugly American* with Eugene Burdick. The novel, which was published in 1958, inspired countless Americans to more aggressively confront communism in the Third World, most notably in Southeast Asia. "Few books have had greater influence on American popular and elite opinion," argues Jacobs.[20] Since Lederer asked Hetu for feedback on drafts, the young public affairs officer had the opportunity to "read the book as it came out of the typewriter."[21] During his tour of duty in Hawaii, Hetu received another interesting job when asked to be the location scout and technical advisor for the 1958 movie *South Pacific.*[22] He subsequently served a year in Hollywood using his public relations skills to convince producers to portray the navy "in a good light."[23] Hetu and his public relations colleagues actually collaborated with writers to achieve this objective, even developing the entire plotline for an episode of the television show *The Real McCoys*. He believed that their efforts improved perceptions of the navy: "Some people would think it was a waste of time, but the McCoys then had a . . . big audience. . . . They were one of the top shows. We said something about the Navy to those people and that's what we were trying to do."[24]

With guidance from Lumpkin, Hetu learned how to persuade reporters and producers to focus on the navy's best attributes. During the 1960s, however, he also became a pioneer in the field of crisis public relations. In April 1963, the USS *Thresher* sank off the coast of Massachusetts, and CBS soon informed the navy that they had plans for an hour-long program on the loss of the nuclear submarine. Navy officials initially wanted nothing to do with the documentary, but the public relations experts convinced their superiors that it was possible to "at least get a positive spin on the story" if they provided assistance to CBS producers.[25] By getting involved with the project, Hetu discovered, "we were able to turn the thing around."[26]

Hetu pursued his interest in crisis public relations at Boston University by writing a master's thesis on peacetime naval disasters. He stressed the importance of disaster plans in the thesis: "The single most important conclusion of this study is that the success or failure of public relations in a naval disaster is the result of detailed preparation and planning, or the lack of it."[27] Hetu outlined strategies for dealing with the media in the aftermath of a tragedy, including a comprehensive "do" and "don't" list. "Be alert to positive stories which may develop, such as the heroic work of relief workers, [and the] number of doctors and nurses working to treat survivors," he advised.[28] In June 1969, after the USS *Frank E. Evans* was sliced into two pieces by an Australian aircraft carrier during a naval exercise, Hetu applied his theories to handling the crisis. He coached the survivors on the most effective way to deal with the media:

> If you do want to tell stories, from what I've heard just talking to some of you guys, there's some real heroics that went on, people helping people out [in] the dark, out in the middle of the night. People helping other people off the ship and in the water. . . . And those stories, you can't tell enough of those.[29]

He obviously hoped that these instructions would shift news coverage away from the mistakes that caused the tragedy and toward the heroism of navy survivors.

Given Hetu's expertise on crisis public relations, he was a perfect match for the CIA in 1977. He had warned in his thesis about the dangers of cutting ties to the media when confronted with a tragedy. Hetu understood that this was an understandable psychological response to a traumatic situation, but nevertheless, he concluded that isolation only made matters worse.[30] He argued that the media was an indispensable ally in repairing the image of an institution under attack. Colby had previously attempted to regain the trust of reporters, but his understanding of public relations was limited. Hetu, on the other hand, knew how to handle tough questions without giving the appearance of stonewalling. "I had a standing order in my office," he explained. "We never said, 'No Comment.' I thought it was important, even if we couldn't comment, to tell the reporter why."[31] While Hetu was in charge of CIA public affairs, journalists frequently contacted him to discuss stories that they were preparing. He listened to their information, provided assistance if possible, and made sure that the names of covert operatives were not revealed accidentally.[32] If the media needed a favor, Hetu was more than willing to help. For example, when *Time* magazine asked the CIA to participate in an event that it was hosting for European businessmen, he helped set up a meeting for them with Turner in October 1977.[33]

Hetu also moved quickly to combat unexpected public relations problems. In November 1977, Paul M. Chretien, the CIA spokesman between 1963 and 1965, visited a high school, and in addressing concerns about the MKULTRA experiments, he criticized the program but defended its underlying objective, observing that "if you could control the mind of [Soviet Premier Leonid] Brehznev it could be useful."[34] Displeased with the incident, Hetu sent a memo to the deputy director for administration in which he complained that Chretien was "meeting with the public on a regular basis with little or no guidance from, or contact with this office. . . . I am really concerned that Paul [Chretien] may get himself or the Agency inadvertently into some serious difficulties by trying to field questions such as the ones described in this article."[35] He emphasized the necessity of coordinating all public appearances through his office to prevent public relations gaffes.

Rather than obsessing about minor mishaps, however, Hetu focused on larger objectives. He developed plans for CBS to film a "Who's Who" segment inside Langley shortly after joining the CIA, and not surprisingly, he had to overcome the skepticism of some agency employees. One official worried that Dan Rather might "air his own [Rather's] personal views about CIA and the Intelligence Community" during the show,[36] while Robert Gambino, the CIA's director of security, expressed concern that permitting "CBS to film this program would be setting a precedent which has unknown future complications."[37] Gambino requested that CBS producers allow the agency to view the footage before the show aired to ensure that employees in classified positions did not appear on screen.

Even though he acknowledged the risks involved, Hetu advised Turner that CIA officials could "positively impress [Dan] Rather and realize an overall good show."[38] The CBS visit represented an excellent opportunity for the agency to receive positive media publicity, and it would be, in effect, a preemptive strike against those who continued to criticize the culture of secrecy at Langley. "If we don't open our doors under our own terms, we could be forced to do so by external pressures (Congress, White House, media, public opinion, etc.)," wrote Hetu. "I think it better to move in the direction of openness voluntarily and in an orderly fashion. We may as well get credit for opening our own doors and enjoy the credibility that goes with such a decision."[39] Breaking with long-standing agency fears about outsiders, Turner signed off on the project.

Hetu's "openness" initiative was an image-making operation and nothing more; when he spoke about "opening our own doors," he was not signaling the end of Langley's obsession with secrecy. He wanted to protect the agency's mystique, but he also hoped to draw the public's attention away from the scandals that had occupied headlines just a few years earlier. In the summer of 1977, Hetu began collaborating with ABC's *Good Morning America* on a program devoted to the thirtieth anniversary of the CIA. The two-hour show, which aired on September 19, 1977, contained short segments on the agency that had been formulated in consultation with Hetu and his public relations staff. In addition to "a live interview with the DCI at the ABC studio in Washington," there were proposals to feature the following aspects of the CIA:

    the automated cartography program
    the headquarters library facilities
    the recruitment process employed in hiring employees for several
        diverse positions

the preparation of analytical material on such issues as Soviet economy, PRC [People's Republic of China] oil, weather, and ecology
the Operations Center
the support activities of the [Directorate of Administration]
various aspects of security—burn baskets, safes, and vaults.[40]

"We will have no control over the narrative or story content," Hetu acknowledged to Turner, "but I am confident that, as in the case of [the
CBS show], the product will sell itself."[41]

Part of Hetu's confidence stemmed from the fact that his cooperation with ABC made it unlikely that *Good Morning America* would deviate
from the script at the last minute. In fact, the only uncertainty was the
questions directed at Turner during the broadcast. After receiving the
authorization to move forward with the project, Hetu made arrangements for ABC to shoot four segments at Langley on a Saturday. He knew
in advance which topics the producers had selected from the list created
in early August, informing the acting deputy DCI that the camera crew
would be filming "a walking tour of the building" as well as features on
security procedures, cartography, and employee recruitment.[42] Then,
on the morning of September 19, *Good Morning America* conducted a
live interview with Turner at 2430 E Street, the landmark building that
housed the Office of Strategic Services during World War II and the CIA
between 1947 and the early 1960s. Although it is unclear who made the
decision to use 2430 E Street instead of the studio at ABC, the new location was a vivid reminder of the mystique that developed around the
CIA in the early years of the Cold War. William Donovan, the legendary
chief of the Office of Strategic Services, and several DCIs had used the
office where the interview took place.[43]

Since the CIA continues to withhold records on Hetu's tenure at
the CIA, it is difficult to evaluate the effectiveness of his overall strategy. However, the statistics for 1979 are revealing. That year the public
affairs office scheduled about thirty speaking engagements for agency
officials; provided tours of Langley for over forty groups; and conducted
139 press briefings.[44] In October 1980, Acting DCI Frank Carlucci nom-
inated Hetu and his office for a congressional public service award,
praising them for developing programs that "resulted in an overwhelmingly favorable reaction from a greatly enlightened and supportive segment of the American public."[45] Carlucci explained that the Office of
Public Affairs had helped implement "a new policy dedicated to the

belief that a well-informed and supportive public is essential to the ful-fillment of the Agency's mission, and that the public has a right to know as much as possible about the role of intelligence and the responsibili-ties of CIA."[46] He emphasized, however, that the public's "right to know" did not extend to CIA secrets. From his perspective, "the new policy [of openness] had a vital counterpoint: secrets essential to an effective intelligence organization must be protected at all costs."[47] Informing Americans of the need for secrecy was "a major objective" of Hetu's of-fice.[48] In other words, CIA officials believed that public relations could be exploited to tutor the public about the positive aspects of secrecy. In the briefing book that Hetu assembled to prepare Turner for the *Good Morning America* interview in 1977, for instance, he advised his boss to argue that there was "more openness with greater secrecy."[49]

Despite Hetu's concerted effort to spin the American public, there was a fundamental incompatibility between openness and secrecy. The rhetoric of openness diverted attention from the real strategy of the CIA during the late 1970s. Rather than working to reform the culture of secrecy at Langley, agency officials were actually attempting to reinvig-orate it. The former CIA officers who published memoirs critical of the intelligence establishment were directly threatening this entrenched culture. Patrick McGarvey, Victor Marchetti, and Philip Agee differed significantly in their motives and methods, but they all accused the CIA of using secrecy to hide evidence of incompetence and malfeasance. In responding to these unprecedented exposés, CIA officials viewed the Publications Review Board (PRB) as a convenient tool to reassert control over disgruntled intelligence officers. George H. W. Bush had created the PRB in June 1976 "to review nonofficial writings of current employ-ees," but as Turner took over at the CIA in early 1977, the board re-ceived a much broader mandate.[50] In addition to examining the writings of individuals still on the agency payroll, the PRB now had the power to inspect anything written by former personnel. Given the board's respon-sibility for protecting classified information, one might expect that the person chosen to supervise it would have been an agency veteran, some-one with the years of operational experience necessary to determine what information could conceivably threaten intelligence sources and methods. But the man selected as the chairperson of the PRB was none other than Herbert Hetu, the head of public affairs at Langley.

During the years that Hetu chaired the PRB, the board received a wide range of submissions, from articles and books to speeches and editorials. The annual number of PRB reviews increased from 42 in 1977 to 148 three years later.[51] Hetu informed a congressional subcommittee in 1980 that the members of the PRB, Hetu included, should "consider [themselves] negotiators. We often sit down with authors and work out the differences. In other words, it is not an arbitrary, cold-blooded process."[52] Hetu said that the board objectively evaluated each item submitted without taking into consideration the author's opinions of the agency, asserting that defenders of the CIA and its critics received equal treatment. Observers of the PRB, however, have accused the board of more readily approving the submissions of agency loyalists. "While it gave the appearance of an orderly, even-handed approach," charges Angus Mackenzie, "its purpose was to increase the CIA's ability to censor the writings and speeches of CIA officers."[53] Congressman Les Aspin (D-WI) offered a similar analysis of the PRB in 1980, calling it "a very arbitrary and capricious system."[54]

In an internal assessment of the Office of Public Affairs written in 1981, the CIA's inspector general found only two recorded complaints against the board. One person had appealed a PRB ruling to the deputy DCI, while another had filed a lawsuit.[55] The report did not disclose the percentage of submissions modified by the PRB during the review process; however, it did reveal that members of the board attempted "not only to delete specific classified items but to recast entire passages and segments of manuscripts that the DO [Directorate of Operations] considers damaging."[56] Although the inspector general never explained how the agency defined "damaging," one suspects that there was an overarching concern about potentially embarrassing information.

When Kermit Roosevelt informed the CIA that he planned to write a book about Operation TPAJAX, he initially received the agency's blessing. He met personally with DCI Bush on June 3, 1976, and he apparently agreed to submit his manuscript for prepublication review. In the summer of 1953, Roosevelt implemented Operation TPAJAX, which led to the overthrow of Iran's prime minister, Muhammad Mossadegh. As Roosevelt recounted the event years later, "Mossadegh was out. The Shah was in."[57] The Shah allegedly told Roosevelt: "I owe my throne to God, my people, my army—and to you!"[58] Since CIA officials then viewed the operation as one of their greatest victories in the Cold War, it makes sense that Bush wanted to publicize the event as Allen Dulles had done over two decades earlier.[59] As the book neared completion in 1978, however, the situation had changed. The Iranian Revolution was unfolding, and in early 1979, the Shah would be forced into exile. CIA officials traveled to Nantucket Island on August 2, 1978, to meet with Roosevelt. Much to Roosevelt's surprise, the deputy director for operations would not allow the publication of the book. "The book has cost me two years of my life. Why wasn't I told earlier?" he exclaimed.[60] In reply, PRB officials told him that "the Agency [has] different management today and different ground rules concerning publication of manuscripts."[61] In the negotiations that followed this meeting, the PRB demanded 156 changes when it became clear that Roosevelt was determined to publish the book. According to the Directorate of Operations, the manuscript was gutted; it was now "essentially a work of fiction."[62]

In November 1977, less than a year after Hetu became the PRB's chairperson, the CIA discovered a critical flaw in the review system when Frank Snepp published *Decent Interval*. Snepp, a CIA officer who had witnessed the fall of Saigon in 1975, violated the agency's secrecy agreement by publishing his book without submitting it to the board for review.[63] While Philip Agee had hoped to stop covert operations, Snepp had entirely different objectives. He accused the CIA of betraying agents in South Vietnam, leaving hundreds of them behind and failing to destroy classified documents that revealed the identities of several informants. Snepp vehemently condemned the Saigon withdrawal: "It is not too much to say that in terms of squandered lives, blown secrets and the betrayal of agents, friends and collaborators, our handling of the evacuation was an institutional disgrace. Not since the abortive Bay of Pigs invasion of 1961 had the agency put so much on the line, and lost it through stupidity and mismanagement."[64]

The following February the CIA initiated a landmark lawsuit against Snepp.[65] Rather than claiming that the former CIA officer had disclosed classified material, agency lawyers focused instead on Snepp's violation of his secrecy agreement. Judge "Roarin'" Oren Lewis ruled against Snepp in a bench trial that was far from impartial. Fred Barbash of the *Washington Post* observed that the outcome was hardly a surprise, since "throughout the one and one-half–day-long non-jury trial, [Judge] Lewis had made little effort to conceal his personal view of what Snepp, whom he generally referred to as 'Shepp,' had done, lecturing him angrily when he took the stand and saying at one point that 'it won't make any difference' what the evidence is."[66] Lewis ordered Snepp to turn over all profits from *Decent Interval* to the federal government. Although an appeals court concluded in March 1979 that Snepp had indeed violated the secrecy contract, they overturned most of Lewis's decision.[67] But in February 1980, the Supreme Court upheld the original verdict without bothering to hear oral arguments.[68] Some attributed the 6–3 decision, one of the most reckless ever issued, to an exposé of the court that Bob Woodward and Scott Armstrong had recently published. Not only did the court rule in favor of the agency, they described the CIA as "essential to the security of the United States and—in a sense—the Free World."[69]

As a result of the Supreme Court's judgment, Snepp would ultimately forfeit over $140,000. The decision was an undeniable victory for the "culture of secrecy" and a massive defeat for the advocates of openness. After the PRB received the high court's sanction, Turner wasted little time in pursuing John Stockwell, who had refused to submit his scathing account of the agency's covert operation in Angola to the board. This operation had occurred at the height of the congressional investigations.[70] Turner, however, did not target all former CIA officials in violation of the secrecy agreement. Even though the agency discovered that the French edition of William Colby's *Honorable Men* was not submitted to the PRB before its publication, the former DCI received no punishment and was allowed to the keep the money he earned from his memoir. Colby, unlike Snepp, had even revealed classified information.[71] Nothing happened either to Cord Meyer, who had started a second career as a syndicated columnist. Hetu attempted to convince Meyer to allow the PRB to review his columns, but according to the findings of the inspector general, Meyer refused, "insisting that as a journalist he [Meyer] writes only his opinions of current developments in foreign affairs without discussing operations or other activities which he knows about as a former Agency officer."[72] The inspector general discovered "some believe that Meyer has maintained close ties with still active former colleagues and periodically visits Agency Headquarters."[73] Despite the evidence that Meyer was possibly receiving insider information, the CIA did not take him to court. "We have less concern that Mr. Meyer would deliberately reveal a secret or would deliberately do harm," agency lawyer Ernest Mayerfeld explained in congressional testimony.[74]

Mayerfeld came close to admitting that there were two sets of guidelines. Agency supporters like Colby and Meyer would be forgiven for clear violations of the secrecy agreement, while Snepp, Stockwell, and other CIA critics received no such mercy. In the aftermath of the Snepp ruling, the PRB wielded its authority even more subjectively than before. Wilbur Eveland, a former National Security Council employee who had assisted CIA covert operations in the Middle East during the 1950s, had recently finished writing a manuscript about these activities when he learned of the Snepp verdict. Eveland had been secretly assigned to Allen Dulles in 1955 and participated in a covert CIA mission to undermine the government of Syria. After contacting the CIA to determine if he had signed a secrecy agreement, a CIA lawyer informed him in March 1980 that since the agreement was "contained in a document which is currently properly classified, I am not at liberty at this time to forward it to you."[75] Eveland knew that he had not signed any secrecy agreement prior to September 1957, so he balked at the CIA's demand to review the entire manuscript. "I'm sure as hell not going to let you get into anything before I signed the agreement [in 1957]," he declared.[76]

The CIA's tactics were on display again a few months later when the PRB analyzed a novel that Snepp had written. In it, Snepp included the identities of actual CIA operatives in the book, and the board instructed him to remove one of these names in early July. The PRB, however, apparently forgot that they had permitted David A. Phillips to identify the same person in *The Night Watch*. "That gives you an idea of how good the clearance process is," Snepp wryly observed. "They'd allowed one of their 'good old boys' to release a name and now they were trying to get me to help squeeze the toothpaste back in the tube."[77] He would ultimately remove the name from the book, but not before chastising the PRB for the inconsistencies of its reviews: "I have gone to great lengths to avoid exposing a secret, a name or an intelligence source whose confidentiality is crucial to the effective functioning of our intelligence services. Although your own review staff has shown itself to be somewhat less diligent, I will not violate my own moral responsibility."[78]

The PRB reacted with even greater hostility to a manuscript Ralph McGehee submitted one week after the Supreme Court ruled against Snepp, demanding that he delete 397 items. When McGehee protested these deletions, agency officials were less than gracious. "It's too bad you didn't work for the Israeli intelligence service," he was told. "They know how to deal with people like you. They'd take you out and shoot you."[79] The CIA reviewers took issue with McGehee's discussion of Langley's liaison arrangements with Thailand even though he could demonstrate the "relationship was so well known that books had been written about it, academic studies discussed it, pictures of CIA station chiefs appeared in the Thai press, and high-level Thai officials openly bragged in the media about CIA support for their organizations."[80]

Another PRB deletion pertained to McGehee's criticism of "the Agency's long-term operations against mainland China."[81] McGehee quickly pointed out that they previously cleared Peer de Silva's *Sub Rosa*. De Silva, an Agency supporter who had once headed the CIA station in Hong Kong, had criticized the operations as well.[82] The board initially reversed their decision on that item, but then the China division of the Directorate of Operations developed an entirely different justification for blocking the undesired commentary on their past failures, alleging that the manuscript divulged a technique associated with CIA methods. "That technique, recruiting persons from the other side, was just slightly newer and less well known than prostitution," argued McGehee.[83] The PRB backed down when McGehee demonstrated that agency defenders such as Phillips revealed extensive information about recruitment techniques in their writings.[84] Based on his experiences with Hetu's board, McGehee believed that the double standard was self-evident:

> The PRB, taking its responsibilities seriously, labels just about everything secret until an author who is critical of the Agency can prove this not to be the case. But the situation for ex-employees who are advocates of the CIA is the opposite. They are given almost *carte blanche* to discuss operations and techniques, and in some instances they are assisted in the research and writing of their works.[85]

Moreover, he contended that the board wanted to protect the CIA's image even in cases where there was no legitimate reason for withholding material. "Agency officials show no hesitation in trying to censor embarrassing, critical, or merely annoying information," he warned.[86]

While the PRB made it increasingly difficult for current and former employees to criticize the agency, there was a simultaneous effort to combat FOIA. The CIA and other members of the intelligence community had been largely exempt from FOIA, which President Lyndon Johnson had grudgingly signed in 1966, until Congress passed an amendment to the law that took effect in early 1975.[87] This amendment, inspired in part by the Watergate scandal, made it possible for requesters to gain access to agency records, but the CIA could still withhold documents for a long list of reasons. When speaking publicly, CIA officials went so far as to cite the FOIA amendment as evidence of the new era of openness and accountability at Langley. In 1977 Acting DCI John F. Blake, who also chaired the CIA committee in charge of complying with the new law, told a subcommittee of the Senate Judiciary Committee that the legal changes "constituted a somewhat traumatic experience" for the agency.[88] At the same time, however, Blake proudly reported: "My colleagues have worked very hard during these past 30 months to make the act work according to the letter and spirit. We have been able to make the necessary adjustments. I am pleased to report that, in fact, I think the Agency is better off for it [the 1974 FOIA amendment]."[89]

Blake's optimistic testimony did not accurately reflect what was happening behind closed doors at Langley. In reality, as an ACLU lawyer explained in 1984, the agency hierarchy "developed a siege mentality toward the public and the FOIA" in the 1970s.[90] About fifteen months after he gave the impression that the CIA had benefited from the increasing number of FOIA requests, Blake, then deputy director for administration, forwarded a report on FOIA and the Privacy Act to Deputy DCI Carlucci. The study indicated that there was a backlog of 2,700 FOIA requests, that around 70 full-time CIA employees were needed to respond to those inquiries, and that the agency spent nearly $2.4 million in 1977 on FOIA processing.[91] Rather than outlining the benefits of FOIA to researchers, it referred to "the burden imposed on the CIA."[92] Thus, the author of the report informed his superiors that "a good case could be made for total exemption from the Act, or, if that is impossible, partial relief."[93] While he warned that there would be opposition to such an exemption, the official argued, "all of our old 'dirty linen' has by now been thoroughly exposed to public scrutiny. The public's interest in preventing future abuses or illegalities by U.S. intelligence organizations will be adequately served by the elaborate oversight mechanisms that have been established in the Agency, the Intelligence Community, the White House, and the Congress."[94] In referring to the increased oversight of the intelligence establishment, the report came close to describing FOIA as a wasteful redundancy. "There is no compelling need . . . for the Freedom of Information Act to be a means of monitoring Agency activities," it concluded.[95]

Although there is no question that CIA officials wanted to press for exemptions to FOIA, they recognized that lingering memories of the "Year of Intelligence" would make politicians reluctant to assist them. In fact, as the author of the 1978 FOIA study acknowledged, "the prospects for obtaining relief through amendments to the Freedom of Information Act are not bright."[96] Instead of abiding by the law and opening their files in response to FOIA requests, the CIA adopted unethical tactics to thwart these inquiries. Stockwell, the CIA officer who served in Angola, disclosed in his memoir the existence of "blind" memos, documents which were not even allowed into the filing system, and as a result, "the inner-most records of the war [in Angola] would forever be immune to any Freedom of Information Act disclosures, or congressional investigation. Technically they did not exist: legally they could be destroyed at any time."[97] Stockwell asserted that the tactics used by the Africa division were directly connected to concerns about FOIA: "Since the Freedom of Information Act, the agency increasingly uses a system of 'soft,' 'unofficial,' or 'convenience' files for sensitive subjects, especially any involving surveillance of Americans. Such files are not registered in the agency's official records system, and hence can never be disclosed under the FOIA."[98] Interestingly, Blake revealed that the CIA did indeed use "soft files" in his 1977 testimony.[99]

At the same time Admiral Turner publicly talked about the CIA's greater openness, his deputy was quietly attempting to undercut the new FOIA statute. Carlucci began to lobby Congress for broad relief from FOIA in April 1979. In order to downplay concerns about civil liberties, the CIA said that it did not want to eliminate individuals' abilities to file first-person requests to determine if they had been subjected to agency surveillance or experimentation. The agency would also allow people to submit FOIA requests for completed intelligence reports prepared by the Directorate of Intelligence. In essence, Carlucci argued that all of the so-called operational files should be placed off-limits to FOIA. After Carlucci shared his concerns with Congress, Representative Robert McClory (R-IL) drafted H.R. 5129, a bill that used "language which [was] all but identical to [the CIA's]."[100]

Carlucci, unsuccessful in 1979, appeared in front of a subcommittee of the House Committee on Government Operations the following February to continue his support for the proposed exemptions, offering a variety of reasons why Congress should allow the CIA to more easily reject FOIA requests. He told members of the subcommittee about the backlog of 2,700 cases, and he claimed that requests for operational material inevitably forced agency personnel to search through mountains of documents that they ultimately could not release.[101] Such processing wasted time and money, argued Carlucci, and the backlog could be substantially reduced if the CIA was allowed to simply deny any request for operational files at the outset. Even though the CIA's own study of FOIA had acknowledged that the risk of accidentally releasing classified information in response to a request was minimal, Carlucci warned about the dangers of human error. If the FOIA processors made a minor mistake, an enemy of the United States might be given the final clue needed to damage national security—a concern known as the mosaic theory.[102] The deputy DCI even suggested: "There still exists the very real possibility that an orchestrated effort by persons hostile to the Agency could literally swamp the Agency with FOIA requests."[103] By covertly inundating the agency with FOIA requests, in other words, the communists could potentially cripple the intelligence establishment. In reality, the CIA report forwarded to Carlucci for his review had concluded that there was no evidence that the Soviet Union or China had filed any FOIA requests.[104]

Carlucci focused extensively on the alleged difficulty of convincing potential intelligence assets and foreign governments that they could share secrets with the agency. He claimed there had been situations "where agents have cited the FOIA as the reason for [their] unwillingness to either cooperate initially, [to] continue to cooperate, or [to] cooperate as fully as in the past."[105] Carlucci admitted that the agency had the complete power to protect secrets under the existing laws, but he believed that foreigners "have an entirely different perception."[106] Although he recognized that there were reasons other than FOIA that might explain why agents were reluctant to turn over information to the CIA, he described the act as an important "symbol" of the problem.[107] He was essentially asking Congress to grant the CIA an exemption to correct a problem that did not exist. Perhaps even more troubling, Carlucci denied that FOIA should contribute to the oversight of the agency. The internal safeguards within the intelligence community and the designated committees in Congress were responsible for holding the CIA accountable, "not . . . 23,000 foreign and American FOIA requesters."[108]

Several representatives on the subcommittee responded skeptically to Carlucci's testimony. Congressman John Erlenborn (R-IL) wondered why the agency "wanted relief from a misperception."[109] When Congressman Peter Kostmayer (D-PA) further pressed Carlucci on this point, Carlucci offered an *Alice in Wonderland* reply: "I think that we have to base this decision on the reality in which we live, and the world of perceptions in the intelligence business is the world of reality."[110] Later in the hearing, Congressman Kostmayer expressed concern that changing the current FOIA law might make it easier for the CIA to withhold information on illegal operations, observing, "the record of the

Central Intelligence Agency leaves a great deal to be desired in terms of upholding the law."[111] This comment led to a testy exchange:

> CARLUCCI: Mr. Kostmayer, you are posing hypothetical upon hypothetical based on an assumption that nobody in the CIA is an honorable person, and I frankly cannot accept that.
>
> KOSTMAYER: I am not suggesting that, and you are basing part of your testimony on assertions which you acknowledge are not valid, so I do not think you are in a position to criticize my hypothesis.[112]

Carlucci also faced tough questioning from other members of the subcommittee. Father Robert Drinan, a Democratic congressman from Massachusetts, drew attention to the fact that the agency had a perfect record in FOIA litigation, and Congressman Ted Weiss (D-NY) was apprehensive about the lack of judicial review.[113] Congressman Weiss recognized that if the CIA received an operational files exemption, a judge would be obligated to reject all appeals from FOIA requesters any time the CIA claimed that the relevant documents were considered operational in nature. Like Kostmayer, Weiss forcefully reminded Carlucci that Congress had every reason to be suspicious of the promises made by CIA officials. "The gentlemen who preceded you . . . were thought to be every bit as high minded, and noble, and patriotic American citizens as you are, and yet all kinds of terrible things happened during their directorships," he declared. "And I think the reason for our concerns—the reason for FOIA—is that . . . terrible things can happen, and that is why we need the protections of the law."[114]

When the hearings on the proposed exemptions resumed three months later, the ACLU, historians, and other groups stepped forward to block the legislation. The Center for National Security Studies, a division of the ACLU, submitted a detailed report that provided a point-by-point refutation of Carlucci's testimony. The study reiterated: "As of March 1980, not one sentence has been released to the public under a court order in circumstances where the CIA has argued that release would injure the national security."[115] Moreover, the Center for National Security Studies highlighted the dangers associated with reducing the intelligence community's accountability to the public: "The CIA says it is willing to give all information to the Congress for purposes of oversight and that this is further reason for granting the exemption. Yet disclosures under the FOIA have shown that the CIA did not turn over all information about past operations to the Congress."[116]

Lloyd Gardner, a history professor representing the Organization of American Historians, joined the ACLU in denouncing the CIA's campaign to restrict FOIA. "This will be a tragedy if it is allowed to go unchallenged," he argued.[117] Gardner told Congress that the exemptions would seriously undermine historical scholarship on American foreign relations. He lamented that "the post-Vietnam backlash against declassification and against FOIA can only remind the historian of days when kings banished prophets who displeased them and sent messengers bearing bad news to oblivion. Surely, we are not prepared to go that route."[118] William Corson, the author of *The Armies of Ignorance*, elaborated on Gardner's protest, bluntly advising, "Congress should be encouraged by the CIA's attempt to gain further exemptions from the FOIA. That, to me, is the best evidence that the FOIA is working, albeit not completely as some might prefer, but nevertheless still working."[119] He called the proposed legislation "a bureaucratic Trojan horse," since it would enable the agency to withhold any document from FOIA requesters by simply labeling it an operational file.[120]

The forces aligned against the CIA in 1980 confirmed what agency officials had anticipated two years earlier: the political climate, still shaped by the legacy of the Church and Pike Committees, was not conducive to rolling back FOIA. Since Congress refused to grant the CIA's request for exemptions to FOIA, many requesters were able to obtain fascinating information from the agency between 1975 and the early 1980s. John D. Marks, for instance, gained access to sixteen thousand pages of records on MKULTRA, which enabled him to write *The Search for the "Manchurian Candidate": The CIA and Mind Control*. "Without these documents," he admitted, "the best investigative reporting in the world could not have produced a book, and the secrets of CIA mind-control work would have remained buried forever, as the men who knew them had always intended."[121] The legal battle with the agency had taken three years, but Marks remained optimistic about FOIA, observing in October 1978, "the system has worked extremely well."[122] Journalists also used FOIA successfully at this time. Students at the College of William & Mary learned in April 1980 that the CIA had conducted surveillance of "radicals" on their campus during the Vietnam War.[123] The Office of Security at Langley ran the operation as part of Project Resistance, a program of domestic espionage that targeted faculty and students at several colleges. The college newspaper at William & Mary, the *Flat Hat*, had acquired the sensational information through a FOIA request, which had been filed two years earlier.[124]

The victories of FOIA requesters in the 1970s gave credence to the image of openness that Hetu worked so hard to create. The tragedy of CIA history during these years is that agency officials wanted nothing to do with openness. They complied with FOIA requests with considerable reluctance, and when they saw embarrassing information released to critics like John D. Marks, it only reinforced their commitment to secrecy. The agency's crusade against openness began with the formation of the PRB, which seriously restricted what former employees could say about the intelligence community. The secondary target in Turner's secrecy campaign, of course, was the FOIA amendment of 1974. His deputy fought aggressively to win exemptions for the agency, and although the ACLU and the Organization of American Historians prevailed in that battle, the CIA would mount another offensive a few years later in a much friendlier environment.

If Turner had actually embraced openness while he was DCI, it is possible that he could have done something to change the irrational obsession with secrecy at Langley. But in choosing to become a forceful defender of that culture—sanctioning the lawsuit against Frank Snepp, encouraging Herbert Hetu's bait-and-switch public relations tactics, and allowing Frank Carlucci to lobby against FOIA—Turner helped set the stage for the abuses of power committed by his successor, William Casey.

3 | The Culture of Secrecy Unleashed, 1981–1987

I'll cut your balls off. . . . I'll get my Korean gang after you and
you [won't] look so good when you're hanging by the balls anyway.
—Max Hugel

By the end of the Carter administration, it appeared that Herbert He-tu's policies had staying power. But when William Casey became President Ronald Reagan's DCI, he questioned the need for continuing the public relations campaign at Langley. The CIA had survived the scandals of the 1970s, the Republicans now controlled the White House, and the intelligence community's budget was no longer in jeopardy. As a result, Casey wondered why the agency still found it necessary to publicly defend itself. He soon brought an end to the agency's press briefings, and on July 1, 1981, he shut down the Office of Public Affairs. "The difficulties of the past decade are behind us," he declared.[1] Casey acknowledged that the public relations office served a purpose when it was first created, but he told employees "the time has come for CIA to return to its more traditional low public profile and a leaner—but no less effective—presence on Capitol Hill."[2] Hetu did not welcome Casey's decision,[3] and in August 1981, he left the agency to found Hetu & Lukstat, a public relations firm. The remnants of his office merged with the downsized congressional liaison staff to form a new division under the direction of future CIA chief Robert M. Gates.[4] Contrary to Casey's thinking in 1981, however, the difficulties were only just beginning. In fact, his first year at Langley forced him to completely reverse his views on the value of public relations, and he would ultimately embrace the most aggressive public relations tactics in the history of the CIA. He used public relations to combat the media, to sell the American public on the desirability of covert action in Nicaragua, and to convince the ACLU to endorse the CIA Information Act of 1984.

Max Hugel, a businessman Casey befriended during the Reagan campaign, was a public relations crisis waiting to happen. Hugel had never worked for the CIA before, but Casey let him run the Directorate for Administration, the division in charge of personnel and management. In May 1981, when the clandestine service was in need of a new director, Casey moved Hugel into the position, a maneuver that dumfounded agency insiders. Gates subsequently described Hugel as "the appointment from hell,"[5] recalling that "short Max, with his toupee and mannerisms, his style of speech and dress, was put down by the Agency hierarchy—apart from Bill [Casey]—as soon as he arrived."[6] Officials in the Directorate of Operations did not respect Hugel, and they were determined to undermine him. "Leaks to the press about Hugel's mistakes, mannerisms, and faux pas began nearly immediately," says Gates.[7] It also appears that disgruntled agency employees helped mobilize the powerful network of former intelligence officers. Less than two weeks after Hugel had been selected, Cord Meyer, the author of *Facing Reality,* wrote a scathing assessment of the director's decision, calling it "a breathtaking gamble for which the country will have to pay heavily if Casey has guessed wrong."[8] A week later the *New York Times* printed an editorial titled "The Company Mr. Casey Keeps" that compounded the negative publicity. "Who can be surprised if there are fears of a replay [of past abuses] in an Administration that talks loosely about 'unleashing' the C.I.A.," asked the *New York Times.* "These fears are fanned when an outsider with tenuous credentials is given command of the Company's most free-wheeling division."[9]

Despite the backlash in the media and the frustration of his employees, Casey adamantly defended Hugel. Viewing Hugel as a political lackey, skeptics at Langley were equally stubborn and somewhat merciless. Agency humorists even compared him to Tattoo on the television series *Fantasy Island*: "What does Hugel say each morning to Casey? 'Boss, boss—the plane, the plane!'"[10] Jokes about his height undoubtedly proved embarrassing to Hugel, but the greatest humiliation did not surface until July. *Washington Post* reporters Bob Woodward and Patrick Tyler had been pursuing a story about Hugel's business dealings from the early 1970s. They had received audio tapes from Thomas and Samuel McNell that revealed Hugel had provided Thomas McNell with insider information. The McNell brothers, both former high-rolling brokers on Wall Street, were disreputable and openly despised Hugel. But when Woodward and Tyler played the tapes for Hugel, he admitted that they contained his voice.

The investigation ended with a sensational front-page story in the *Washington Post* on July 14, 1981. According to the article, which contained extensive quotations from the recorded conversations, Hugel told Thomas McNell information about Hugel's company, Brother Limited, that was unavailable to the public: "We originally forecast sales in the U.S. [at] $80 million. . . . We now forecast $70 million, okay, which is a $10 million swing."[11] In a subsequent conversation, Hugel offered details about a recently completed deal between Brother Limited and another company. "I'm telling you confidential stuff, now," he warned, "you understand that?"[12] The tapes also revealed that Hugel had made illegal loans to the McNell brothers, and at one point, he politely advised Thomas McNell to pay the money back, because "if you don't, I'll cut your balls off. . . . I'll get my Korean gang after you and you don't look so good when you're hanging by the balls anyway."[13] Hollywood screenwriters simply could not have written a better script for the scandal. On the morning that the article appeared, Hugel resigned from the CIA.[14] He blamed his demise on "the old-boy network. Some guys on the inside were out to get me. Some were retired guys working from the outside."[15]

With Hugel out of the picture, Congress and the press increasingly scrutinized Casey's own business ventures. "The papers provided the grist," observed Joseph Persico, Casey's biographer, "and the Senate intelligence committee provided the mill."[16] The committee selected Fred Thompson, a prominent attorney and future Republican senator, to investigate the allegations of financial wrongdoing. Casey was one of the people charged in a lawsuit with deceiving the investors of Multiponics, an agricultural company that had gone bankrupt years earlier, and reporters discovered that he had withheld information from the disclosure forms that federal appointees are required to submit. Casey, moreover, initially refused to put his massive portfolio into a blind trust.[17] After Casey testified in detail to the intelligence committee about previous investments, the senators ruled "that no basis has been found for concluding Mr. Casey is *unfit* to serve as DCI."[18]

More than anything else, the extended controversy in 1981 convinced Casey that there was indeed a crucial need for public relations at the CIA. As Persico explains, in 1982 "he went back to the arrangement that had prevailed when he took over the CIA, a separate lobbyist for [Capitol] Hill and a separate Office of Public Affairs for the media."[19] Charles E. Wilson, Hetu's former assistant, initially ran the public affairs division, but Casey ultimately selected George V. Lauder, a member of the clandestine service for over three decades, to take over the public relations campaign in 1983.[20] Lauder had spent years in the Middle East, and although he was an amateur in the realm of public relations, he knew the basics. For instance, CBS repeatedly approached him about the possibly of interviewing Casey. Given Casey's tendency to mumble, Lauder shrewdly declined the offer from *60 Minutes.* "If you had a guy who talks like Bill Casey," he told them, "would you put him on television?"[21]

As the CIA's top public relations man, Lauder obviously communicated with Casey on a wide range of issues. Yet in responding to a FOIA request filed in 2005, the CIA claimed that it was unable to find any correspondence between Lauder and Casey. The agency subsequently turned over sixty documents in Lauder's files when confronted with another FOIA inquiry, but this material only included correspondence with individuals outside of the CIA. In other words, the agency essentially took the position that they could not locate any internal memos written by Lauder while he headed public affairs. In 2011, however, agency officials declassified approximately eight letters from Lauder to Casey without notifying the author.[22] It is difficult to reconstruct how public relations strategies were formulated in the mid-1980s given the paucity of declassified information. Lauder assured a newspaper editor in 1985 that "we [the CIA] do not lie to the American public nor do we engage in 'public relations flimflam to boost' our 'image' in the U.S.,"[23] but the documents that have been declassified do not substantiate this statement. In fact, not only did Lauder and Casey employ public relations "flimflam" to defend the CIA, they also used heavy-handed tactics that were undoubtedly intended to intimidate the media.

Lauder routinely lambasted newspapers for printing articles that portrayed the CIA in a negative light. In October 1984, he complained to an editor at the *New York Times* about two earlier stories that had linked the CIA with "death squad–related activities in El Salvador."[24] Noting that a Senate investigation of the allegations had arrived at different conclusions, Lauder ridiculed the *New York Times* for its failure to issue a retraction: "The *New York Times* says it carries 'all the news fit to print.' Apparently, a story that corrects previous *New York Times* reporting isn't fit to print. I think the *New York Times* owes the Agency and its readers better than that."[25] Despite the CIA's complaints about the articles on El Salvador, it is now clear that the agency supported the country's right-wing government throughout the 1980s. CIA officials almost certainly knew about the violent campaigns that the El Salvadoran military unleashed on the opposition.[26] Two years later Lauder went on the offensive against the editor of the *Christian Science Monitor* after the newspaper ran a story about the downing of a plane in Nicaragua. The article said that the aircraft was on a CIA mission, and not surprisingly, Lauder rejected the accusation. "Mr. [Joseph] Harsch [the author of the story] owes the employees of this Agency an apology for his outrageous defamation of them," he declared.[27] Even though the plane did not belong to the CIA, Lauder failed to mention that the Agency had previously supplied an aircraft that was used to send military equipment to Iran.

Like most public relations men, Lauder insisted that he was not trying to manipulate public opinion. When Vitaly Yurchenko, a Soviet operative, defected to the United States, William Casey used the situation to hype the agency's mystique in the media. In June 1986, the *New York Times* provided details of how the CIA had leaked information to journalists. Yet Lauder claimed "[the] CIA said nothing at all about Yurchenko in other than classified hearings or meetings until he redefected."[28] Lauder acknowledged that the details on Yurchenko's short-lived defection resulted from leaks, but he denied that the agency was responsible for them.[29] This denial was rather unconvincing, especially since few individuals outside the CIA knew much about Yurchenko. Lauder was obviously worried about any accusation that the CIA had engaged in activity that violated Executive Order 12333, which prohibited the CIA from engaging in domestic propaganda. When Washington insiders discovered that Bob Woodward of the *Washington Post* had been meeting with Casey while the reporter was researching *Veil: The Secret Wars of the CIA, 1981–1987*, Lauder sent an angry letter to Woodward: "If you are saying or implying that we are co-collaborators [on the book] you are suggesting that we are in violation of the Executive Order [12333]. . . . We resent both the violations of the ground rules under which we agreed to talk to you and the implication that your product has our approval. It doesn't."[30] Casey, of course, had most likely agreed to meet with Woodward in hopes of shaping how the reporter portrayed the CIA. When this strategy backfired, Lauder attempted to distance the agency from the upcoming publication of *Veil*.

In his correspondence with the press, Lauder frequently lectured editors about the sanctity of classified information. He declared to *American Legion* magazine: "The media must . . . bear the responsibility for acting as a 'fence' for stolen goods and for its involvement in damaging the nation's security."[31] When *USA Today* ran an editorial that criticized the government's excessive use of classification, Lauder suggested that there was nothing wrong with the current system. He warned that lives were at stake: "In short, the press often carelessly tosses about the verbal hand grenades that a leaker hands it. When they explode, killing people and inflicting great damage, the press shrugs and says, in effect, 'well, it's a free country.'"[32] Despite the serious accusations leveled against the media, he failed to offer any specific examples of irresponsible journalism.

Lauder was certainly entitled to share his opinions about the First Amendment, but in at least two situations, he was accused of seeking to undermine the freedom of the press. In October 1985, he challenged the accuracy of an article that William Gertz wrote for the *Washington Times*.[33] Less than two months later, he again contacted Arnaud de Borchgrave, then the editor of the conservative newspaper, claiming that he had been quoted inaccurately by Gertz.[34] De Borchgrave, however, defended Gertz and wondered whether Lauder was trying to pressure the paper into reassigning the young correspondent. Lauder replied that he had no intention of telling de Borchgrave who should be assigned to cover the CIA,[35] but he also made it clear that Gertz was at risk of becoming persona non grata at the agency. "You should know that Gertz is the only journalist in Washington who consistently misrepresents what we tell him," he asserted. "We have arrived at a point where I have had to issue instructions that two of my media relations officers must be on the phone whenever any of us is talking to Gertz so that we will be able to confirm what was and what was not said to him."[36] Lauder informed de Borchgrave that the CIA would no longer grant background interviews to Gertz, and he lamented that the *Washington Times* was not providing friendlier coverage. "The *Washington Post* at least quotes us accurately," he observed.[37]

De Borchgrave allowed Gertz to continue covering the intelligence community, and he never went public with his concern that Lauder was maneuvering to undermine the reporter. Jack Anderson, the renowned investigative columnist, did not keep silent when he experienced a similar confrontation with the CIA's Office of Public Affairs. On the same day that Anderson published an editorial indicating that the CIA might be involved in drug trafficking, Lauder sent the columnist an unusual letter. "Since you have identified your source," he wrote, "you should have no trouble in making the information available. If no such evidence is forthcoming, we will assume that you have none."[38] Lauder requested that Anderson turn over the evidence to the CIA, the Justice Department, and the appropriate congressional committees.[39] Anderson quickly brought the incident to the attention of fellow journalists. "I think the letter smacks of intimidation," he told the *Los Angeles Times,* "but it's not going to be successful."[40] In his reply to Lauder's demands, Anderson quipped that he "would be happy to exchange sources with the CIA at any time."[41] Until CIA officials divulged their informants to Anderson, in other words, he would never reveal his sources of information to them. He realized, of course, that the agency would never agree to such a proposal. His reporting had angered the CIA in the past, and in the early 1970s, the agency even placed him—along with his staffers—under surveillance. Yet, according to Anderson, it was the first time that the CIA had ever approached him directly about a story.[42]

Lauder's confrontation with Anderson was part of a broader CIA effort to downplay the agency's connection to an investment company in Hawaii known as Bishop, Baldwin, Rewald, Dillingham & Wong (BBRDW). Ronald Rewald had established the firm in 1978, and when it collapsed five years later, he attempted to commit suicide in a hotel room. Rewald survived and ultimately went on trial for allegedly defrauding over four hundred investors of approximately $22 million in what was called at the time "a classic Ponzi scheme."[43] Although BBRDW portrayed itself as an investment house that offered a 20 percent rate of return, only a small percentage of the money deposited was actually invested. Rewald embezzled millions of dollars to finance a high-rolling lifestyle of polo matches, luxury cars, and beautiful women.[44] Rewald rejected the accusation that his company had been nothing more than a financial scam, arguing in a lawsuit that BBRDW had been the creation of the CIA. He said that the agency had used the firm to finance arms deals with countries in the Far East and to spy on foreign leaders such as Ferdinand Marcos. He even claimed that the CIA had sent him on a secret mission to steal the designs for a Japanese bullet train.[45] Although CIA officials denied most of Rewald's more sensational charges, they publicly admitted "a slight involvement" with Rewald's firm.[46] Agency lawyers also made sure that the documents in the Rewald case were sealed.[47]

It is possible that Rewald was telling the truth: perhaps the CIA manipulated BBRDW for covert objectives and then allowed him to be the patsy when the scheme imploded. After all, John Peyton, the federal lawyer who prosecuted Rewald, was a former CIA man.[48] Yet the evidence points to a less sinister—but more embarrassing—scenario. Rewald moved to Hawaii in 1977 shortly after he had been convicted of swindling two teachers in Wisconsin, and it appears that he approached the CIA station chief in Honolulu.[49] Explaining that he was an American patriot, he offered to provide jobs in his new company for CIA officers who needed nonofficial cover. The agency admitted that seven officers worked for BBRDW subsidiaries; that Rewald was reimbursed for around $2,700 in expenses; that he signed a secrecy agreement; and that his son spied on foreign students at Brigham Young University's campus in Hawaii.[50] When Jack Kindschi, the Honolulu station chief at the time, retired from the agency in 1980, Rewald hired him as a consultant, paying him an annual salary of $48,000. Kindschi's replacement, Jack Rardin, met with Rewald on several occasions, visited the offices of BBRDW, and agreed to interfere with an IRS investigation of the firm.[51] Reporters in Hawaii also discovered that "as many as 14 CIA [officers] invested more than a total of $300,000 in personal funds in the company."[52] While Kindschi, Rardin, and other agency employees were investing money in BBRDW, Rewald bragged extensively that he worked for the CIA and promised clients that the federal government would insure all of their deposits. Agency officers receive extensive training in the art of deception, but the CIA investors apparently never worried that Rewald, a man with a criminal record, might be trying to scam them.

Ronald Rewald became a household name in Hawaii in July 1983, but the story did not receive much attention on the mainland until the following spring.[53] Then, in September 1984, ABC news reported a new development in the ongoing saga. "Not only was Bishop, Baldwin [Rewald, Dillingham & Wong] involved in selling arms to Taiwan, India and Syria, and promoting financial panic in Hong Kong," said reporter Gary Shepard, "it was also fueling capital flight from two allies, Greece and the Philippines . . . in exchange for intelligence information."[54] ABC claimed in a second report that the CIA had plotted to kill Rewald. The accusation was based on an interview with Scott T. Barnes, who had once been a prison guard in Oahu. According to Barnes, CIA officers instructed him to eliminate Rewald: "'We gotta take him out. . . . You know, kill him,'" they declared.[55] About a week after ABC aired the story, the CIA insisted that the charges were false and requested a retraction.[56] Peter Jennings issued a partial retraction on *World News*

Tonight in November, acknowledging that ABC could not corroborate Barnes's claims.

Dissatisfied with ABC's response, CIA officials filed a petition with the Federal Communications Commission (FCC) on the same day.[57] The agency argued that "ABC deliberately distorted the news and violated the fairness doctrine," and it asked the FCC to "determine what corrective action should be taken by ABC."[58] After investigating the reports, the FCC rejected both the complaint and the CIA's subsequent appeal.[59] But although ABC prevailed in the proceedings, legal experts worried that the precedent established in the case could potentially make the media more reluctant to pursue controversial stories. In essence, the FCC ruled that any government agency had the right to file a complaint against radio or television stations; in the event that the commission sided with the government, broadcasting licenses could be revoked as punishment. "If this [the fairness doctrine] is held to apply to a government agency," observed an ACLU official, "then we are concerned about the chilling effect on investigative reporting."[60] When faced with stories that they perceived as unfair or inaccurate, Lauder and Casey certainly had every right to issue a rebuttal. Yet the CIA's response to the ABC news story reflected a glaring contempt for the First Amendment. The FCC complaint, which undoubtedly left the network with significant legal costs, was not an aberration. It was consistent with the tactics employed against journalists William Gertz and Jack Anderson.

At the same time that Lauder publicly battled the media from inside the Office of Public Affairs at Langley, there was also a covert dimension to Casey's public relations strategy. Robert Parry and Peter Kornbluh have persuasively argued that the DCI actually helped to establish "what appears to be America's first peacetime propaganda ministry."[61] In the summer of 1982, a CIA officer named Walter Raymond Jr. joined President Reagan's National Security Council with Casey's direct approval. Raymond had much in common with David A. Phillips; both men had been educated at the College of William & Mary, and both were propaganda specialists.[62] Parry would later describe Raymond as "a slight, soft-spoken New Yorker who reminded some of a character from a John le Carre spy novel, an intelligence officer who 'easily fades into the woodwork.'"[63] Raymond initially headed the Intelligence Directorate at the National Security Council,[64] which was not an unusual assignment for an intelligence officer. Yet his job description changed tremendously after Reagan signed National Security Decision Directive

77 in January 1983. This directive bolstered and centralized the administration's "public diplomacy" apparatus, defined as "those actions of the U.S. government designed to generate support for our national security objectives."[65] While public diplomacy had been used in the past to build support for the United States overseas, it was now redefined to include the American public. Raymond, who became the director of the Office of International Communications and Public Diplomacy at the National Security Council, outlined a "political action" offensive to covertly influence domestic perceptions of American foreign policy, especially as it pertained to Central America.[66]

Much as Phillips had done in 1975, Raymond eventually resigned from the CIA to ensure "there would be no question whatsoever of any contamination of [public diplomacy in Central America]."[67] He vehemently denied the accusation that agency executives were involved in the public diplomacy crusade: "At no time during my 5 years with the NSC [National Security Council] did I receive any instructions or guidance from Casey or any other senior CIA official."[68] However, as Parry and Kornbluh have shown, Raymond's deposition during the Iran-Contra investigation reveals a completely different story. In fact, he told congressional staffers "he met with then CIA Director William Casey every Thursday between January and July 1983."[69] Raymond, in other words, continued to meet with Casey in the months following his official departure from the CIA in April 1983. When asked during the deposition if he talked about public diplomacy in these meetings, his response was woefully vague. "I wouldn't rule it out that we might have. I cannot remember anything specific on that," he said.[70] Fortunately for historians, Raymond's memos, which were declassified in the congressional report on the Iran-Contra investigation, provide a clearer picture of events than his deposition. On August 29, 1983, for instance, he informed an official on the National Security Council that Casey had phoned him three days earlier to discuss public relations strategies. Raymond apparently recognized that this ongoing communication with the CIA raised constitutional issues, and he alluded to "an effort to get him [Casey] out of the loop."[71]

Raymond may have wanted to establish plausible deniability for the CIA in 1983, but Casey was still in "the loop" three years later. After Congress allowed the CIA to recommence covert action in Nicaragua, Raymond drafted a memo for Casey in August 1986. "It is clear we would not have won the House vote without the painstaking deliberative effort undertaken by many people in the government and outside," he declared.[72] In the same memo, he also noted that he continued to hold a weekly meeting on public diplomacy. Several officials attended these sessions, including "a representative from CIA's Central American Task Force, and key NSC [National Security Council] staffers."[73] Raymond later defended his former boss with the unconvincing claim that Casey was acting "not so much in his CIA hat, but in his advisor-to-the-president hat."[74] The General Accounting Office asserted in 1987 that the Office of Public Diplomacy for Latin America and the Caribbean at the State Department, which Raymond helped launch in the summer of 1983, had engaged in "prohibited, covert propaganda activities designed to influence the media and the public to support the Administration's Latin American policies."[75]

Raymond downplayed his relationship with Lieutenant Colonel Oliver North of the National Security Council in his deposition: "I do know he was in contact with the contras, but beyond that, I was not really involved in the details of his activities."[76] Yet according to North's checklist for the final week of February 1985, he shared responsibility with Raymond for "assign[ing] U.S. intelligence agencies to research, report, and clear for public release Sandinista military actions violating Geneva Convention/civilized standards of warfare."[77] Needless to say, North and Raymond did not request intelligence reports on the human rights abuses and drug trafficking of the contras. Parry and Kornbluh point out that the congressional investigations could have done more to explore the propaganda campaign that Raymond orchestrated in collaboration with North, but Congressman Richard Cheney (R-WY) skillfully worked behind the scenes to prevent that from happening, "arguing that the domestic operations were outside the committees' scope."[78]

If there had been a more detailed investigation, the public would have undoubtedly learned that Casey was not an innocent bystander. In fact, it turns out that he had invited public relations experts to meet with him in the Old Executive Office Building to develop ideas on the best way "to sell a 'new product'—Central America—by generating interest across-the-spectrum."[79] William Greener, then the director of public relations at Philip Morris, was a key participant in the meeting. Given his work for Philip Morris, Greener instinctively recognized that secrecy and public relations were inseparable. For instance, his company knew for decades that cigarettes caused cancer and a long list of other health problems, but instead of acknowledging the facts, executives at Philip

Morris suppressed the data, claiming that the scientific evidence was inconclusive. The CIA implemented a similar strategy during Casey's tenure. Rather than providing a balanced view of events in Nicaragua, Raymond concocted blatant propaganda: "Concentrate on gluing black hats on the Sandinistas and white hats on UNO [the contras' United Nicaraguan Opposition]," he instructed in 1986.[80]

In his determination to win support for the contras in Nicaragua, Casey went so far as to personally embark on a domestic covert operation against Senator Patrick Leahy (D-VT), arguably his most vocal critic on the Senate Select Committee on Intelligence. During Senator Leahy's campaign for reelection, Casey leaked a letter that he had written to Leahy that criticized the senator for allegedly revealing sensitive information about the hijacking of the cruise ship *Achille Lauro*.[81] Casey apparently spoke with Rowland Evans and Robert Novak, and they subsequently wrote an article in *Reader's Digest* in the lead-up to the election. Evans and Novak argued that Leahy's alleged breach of national security "is one of many showing that the current era of Congressional oversight of the CIA is simply not working."[82]

Although Casey could not prevent Leahy from winning a third term, he found it much easier to suppress the views of former CIA officials. In order to combat the criticism from these insiders, he turned to the PRB. Ralph McGehee, who had earlier battled the PRB while Admiral Stansfield Turner headed the CIA, submitted an article to the board in 1981 that alleged the agency was falsifying intelligence on Central America to hype the threat of the Soviet Union. McGehee provided examples from CIA history to illustrate what was happening in El Salvador, but the PRB barred him from mentioning details of previous "disinformation" operations in countries like Indonesia.[83] The harassment continued the following spring when he asked board members to review a revised version of the manuscript that they had already cleared. The PRB now ruled that McGehee had to delete several sections of the book, including his description of a sophomoric prank at Camp Peary in the 1950s, which involved "the booby-trapping of a toilet seat with a military firecracker."[84] The CIA allowed him to reinsert passages that contained information released by Senator Frank Church's committee, and after several more disputes with the board, he finally managed to publish *Deadly Deceits* in 1983.[85]

Admiral Turner encountered similar problems after the PRB examined his memoir. Turner, an ardent critic of the Reagan administration, believed that "between 10 and 15 percent of the time it took me to complete the book was spent in arranging with the CIA for its clearance. . . . It was all most unreasonable and unnecessary."[86] The irony, of course, was that Turner had expanded the powers of the review board back in 1977. "As long as there is almost no check on the arbitrariness of the CIA," he warned, "it is likely that there will be further abuses of the public's right to knowledge about its government."[87] When Frank Snepp learned about Turner's displeasure with CIA censorship, he criticized the former DCI for creating a policy that restricted the First Amendment rights of ex–intelligence officers: "I hate to think of anybody being censored, but I think there is poetic justice in the fact that the architect of the C.I.A.'s censorship should now be feeling the heat."[88]

In addition to worrying about criticism from former insiders like McGehee and Turner, Casey and his advisors were concerned about student protests against covert action in Central America. Nearly seventy student activists at Brown University attracted publicity by initiating a citizen's arrest of CIA recruiters in 1984, which was inspired in part by revelations of the agency's illegal mining of Nicaraguan harbors.[89] Casey thought that public relations could revitalize the agency's recruitment efforts on campuses, and in 1985 he instituted the Officer in Residence Program, a public relations effort that allowed CIA employees to join college faculties for two years to teach classes related to their area of expertise. This program proved especially attractive to universities, because the agency paid for most of the costs. Currently there are between eight and twelve officers in residence at any given time, and more than fifty schools have welcomed CIA officers to their campuses.[90] Although officers in residence must now acknowledge their connection to the CIA and are forbidden to recruit students, the venture obviously began as a strategy to repair the CIA's relationship with the academic community. Harry Fitzwater, the deputy director for administration under Casey, explained in an August 1985 memo that a key objective of the program was to "assist Agency staff recruiting efforts by placing in selected schools experienced officers who can spot promising career candidates, can counsel students as to career opportunities, and can use their knowledge and experience to address questions or concerns students may have regarding the Agency."[91]

Casey also established public relations programs for business executives who operated internationally. His biographer estimates that "between 1984 and 1985, nearly three hundred major American business leaders came to the Agency's executive seminar."[92] When Casey spoke to these visiting executives, he typically explained that Americans "returning from overseas trips have been invaluable not only in providing information but in giving us leads to people willing to make available information which may be critical to our national interests."[93] Casey made little attempt to disguise that he was attempting to secure their cooperation. In soliciting help from corporations, he was even willing to do favors for them. On one occasion, he instructed CIA analysts to research the market for chocolate products in Eastern Europe, and he turned the results over to Mars Candy.[94]

Enhancing the "culture of secrecy" was the most important objective of Casey's legislative agenda, and he understood that public relations could be used to secure the passage of the Intelligence Identities Protection Act and to undercut FOIA.[95] The protection act, which made it illegal to knowingly reveal the name of a covert operative, was an easy sell, and it passed in 1982. Winning relief from FOIA, on the other hand, was much more complicated. Casey recognized that the earlier campaign for an exemption had failed because of outrage from advocates of civil liberties. Admiral Turner, moreover, had allowed his deputy to lobby Congress for the legislation.

Casey initiated a public relations offensive against FOIA; in many of his public appearances, he talked about why the CIA could no longer tolerate it. During a speech in March of 1982, which was later reprinted as an essay in *Presidential Studies Quarterly,* he announced, "The presumption that all Government records should be accessible to the public, unless the Government can justify in detail a compelling national security rationale for withholding them, *unwarrantedly* disrupts the effective operation of an intelligence agency."[96] He did not explain that the CIA spent only a tiny fraction of its budget on FOIA compliance, that there were less than thirty employees assigned to process requests on a full-time basis, and that the agency had never lost a FOIA lawsuit. Casey lashed out against FOIA once again in a speech to the American Legion. "I question very seriously whether a secret intelligence agency and a Freedom of Information Act can coexist for very long," he proclaimed.[97] He told the audience that it was time to "get rid of the Freedom of Information Act."[98] No longer did the CIA want an exemption for their operational files; they now demanded a complete exemption from FOIA. "Instead of nourishing paranoia," the *New York*

Times complained, "Mr. Casey could ease those concerns by explaining to everyone how freedom of information really works."[99]

Yet Casey knew exactly what he was doing. "Nourishing paranoia" helped win support from the American public, a tactic that had proven successful for him as Reagan's campaign manager in 1980. Although he complained that the media "repeatedly distorted" his American Legion speech, he nonetheless reiterated the "inherent incompatibility in applying an openness in government law to intelligence agencies whose missions must be carried out in secrecy."[100] When read between the lines, Casey was essentially saying that he had no problem with FOIA as long as it did not apply to the intelligence establishment. He recycled most of the arguments that Frank Carlucci had first used in 1979, emphasizing, for instance, that Congress was in charge of overseeing the CIA. He did not view FOIA as an instrument of accountability, since he claimed that the CIA was already fully accountable to the intelligence committees. Casey even made reference to Philip Agee's FOIA lawsuit by quoting a federal judge who called the case a "waste of resources."[101]

At the same time Casey was lobbying the public to support changes to FOIA, he was shrewd enough to understand that nothing could be done unless the agency neutralized the ACLU. Although it is difficult to prove, it appears that Casey's demand for a total exemption was a classic bargaining tactic. He had been a successful venture capitalist for most of his adult life, so he knew the importance of demanding more than you expect to receive during negotiations. In essence, when the CIA said that they would be willing to consider an exemption for the operational files, it appeared that they had made a concession. In reality, however, their proposal was comparable to the legislation introduced by Carlucci. The ACLU had effectively blocked the CIA's campaign in 1980, but Casey and agency attorney Ernest Mayerfeld skillfully manipulated the organization. As Angus Mackenzie has documented, Mayerfeld met with Mark Lynch, then an ACLU attorney, in June 1982. Mayerfeld and Lynch established an informal agreement at the meeting: "The ACLU would no longer oppose the exemption, if, in return, the CIA would not seek to be totally exempt from the FOIA."[102] The ACLU, in what is undoubtedly one of the most shameful moments in their history, reversed their earlier position. Rather than fighting the CIA's effort to gain a massive exemption from FOIA, ACLU officials accepted its inevitability. Mayerfeld and Lynch kept in regular contact with each other after their initial compromise in June, and the following March they formalized the deal in the presence of Congressman Romano L. Mazzoli (D-KY).[103]

Reports of the ACLU's negotiations with the CIA first surfaced in May 1983,[104] and on June 18, almost a year after Lynch and Mayerfeld had initially talked about the FOIA exemption, the *Nation* revealed, "the agency has convinced the American Civil Liberties Union to agree to exempt 'operational files' from the Freedom of Information Act. It's a dangerous exemption."[105] ACLU officials, however, denied the accusation, persuading the magazine to issue a "clarification" on July 2.[106] Mackenzie soon discovered that the ACLU's denials were misleading, and he wrote a story about the ongoing negotiations between Lynch and Mayerfeld in late September. Observing that "the A.C.L.U. appears to have swallowed the C.I.A.'s 'trust us' argument," he advised that "[the ACLU] should tell Congress the deal is off, and it should use its influence to kill the legislation."[107] Morton Halperin and Allan Adler of the ACLU's Center for National Security Studies rejected any suggestion that "the A.C.L.U. is being taken for a ride."[108] They talked about a bill in the Senate (S. 1324) introduced by Senator Barry Goldwater (R-AZ), but they made no reference to what was happening in the House of Representatives. Mackenzie has pointed out the ACLU's agreement "was with Congressman Mazzoli in the House. In the clever manner of a Capitol Hill insider, Halperin's denial was literally truthful, while being wholly misleading."[109] Halperin and Adler, in other words, had parsed their words quite carefully.

Goldwater's bill, which had been developed with assistance from the CIA and closely resembled Carlucci's legislation, began a long debate over FOIA's impact on the CIA. Agency officials had continued to argue that FOIA helped explain why some foreigners were reluctant to assist them. When Casey testified in front of a Senate subcommittee, for instance, he claimed that at least two agents had recently quit because "they felt insecure."[110] Yet Senator Leahy pressed Casey to elaborate on how the examples he mentioned related to FOIA, and the DCI conceded that he could not specifically blame the law: "Well, I can't say that. I can't say FOIA [is the reason]."[111] Casey and his subordinates also readily admitted that they already could withhold information from FOIA requesters by invoking a variety of exemptions, something that Victor Navasky learned after he filed a FOIA request in 1976 for a list of all the books that had been published with CIA funding prior to 1967. After the agency rejected his request and subsequent appeal, Navasky took the agency to court. The lawsuit dragged on for over five years, but the CIA ultimately prevailed when the Supreme Court refused to hear the case on appeal in October 1982. The agency maintained that the documents that Navasky wanted were withheld to protect sources—presumably the authors and publishers of the books—and methods (e.g., the fact that the agency engaged in propaganda). Agency lawyers also claimed that releasing the book list, which was over fifteen years old, would undermine national security, and that "its assertion on this matter need not be buttressed by evidence, even shown in camera."[112] Navasky was left to wonder "why the Director wants the C.I.A. exempted from a law that has yet to be seriously enforced against his agency."[113]

The agency had a flawless record in FOIA litigation, and Casey could not provide specific examples of agents who quit because they feared that a FOIA request would lead to their disclosure. When the Senate Intelligence Committee held hearings on the Goldwater bill in June 1983, however, Deputy DCI John McMahon explained, "it is difficult to convince one who is secretly cooperating with us that some day he will not awaken to find in a U.S. newspaper or magazine an article that identified him as a U.S. spy."[114] Rather than dwelling on the benefits that the exemption would provide the agency, McMahon emphasized that the bill would significantly reduce the backlog of FOIA requests at the CIA. This would make it possible for the agency to respond more quickly to journalists, scholars, and other FOIA requesters. Skeptics of the CIA remained unconvinced by McMahon's promises, and they were especially alarmed by the absence of judicial review in the Senate bill. Anna K. Nelson, a history professor who testified on behalf of both the American Historical Association and the Organization of American Historians, warned that the agency might "place ever-increasing numbers of documents in file cabinets marked 'operational,' including those that might be merely embarrassing."[115] Nelson was also one of the few observers to point out that the proposed exemption of operational files would be permanent. No matter how old the files were—whether three years or thirty years—they would be entirely exempt from FOIA requests.[116]

Despite the concerns about the exemption, the Senate passed the bill by voice vote in November. The debate over FOIA then shifted to Congressman Mazzoli's bill in the House.[117] In February 1984, during an appearance in front of a subcommittee of the House Select Committee on Intelligence, McMahon repeated his assurance that the proposed legislation would improve the agency's ability to process FOIA requests.[118] Mazzoli asked him whether the agency could be tempted in the future to adopt a broad definition of operational documents in order to stymie legitimate FOIA requests. "Yes . . . if we were prepared to do something that violated the spirit and the legality of the law, that would be possible," McMahon replied.[119] Yet he promised that this would never happen; like Richard Helms, he believed that agency employees were honorable men, and as a consequence, stated, "my firm belief is that . . . there will not ever again be a repeat of the improprieties of the past."[120]

Shockingly, the ACLU did not challenge the "trust-us" mentality of the CIA. In his prepared statement to the subcommittee, Lynch gave the impression that the legislation under consideration in the House was a good deal. "Only the operational files of the CIA's Directorate of Operations, Directorate of Science and Technology, and Office of Security will be exempt from search and review," he noted. "Thus, operational information located elsewhere in the Agency will be subject to search and review."[121] But this description reflected a glaring ignorance of the CIA's filing system, since few operational documents are found in the Directorate of Administration or the Directorate of Intelligence. It is true that final reports based on information gathered through espionage could still be requested through FOIA, but this was very similar to what the CIA offered in 1979, a deal that the ACLU had justifiably opposed.

Another House subcommittee held hearings on H.R. 5164, a revised version of two previous bills, in May. The ACLU predictably endorsed this bill, since "the delay in responding to requests will be reduced and no meaningful information which is currently released will be lost."[122] Mackenzie took issue with the ACLU's position, and he told the members of the subcommittee about his research on Operation MHCHAOS, the CIA domestic surveillance program in the 1960s and early 1970s. Although the House bill had specified that operational files still must be searched in the event that they were "the specific subject matter of an investigation by the intelligence committees of the Congress, etc.," Mackenzie believed that this language was overly restrictive.[123] In the mid-1970s, both the Church Committee and the Rockefeller Commission had investigated Operation MHCHAOS, but since Congress "did not *specifically* inspect the agency's files on the underground press," the CIA had a loophole to reject any requests pertaining to the program.[124] In fact, Mayerfeld acknowledged that Mackenzie's FOIA lawsuit might be thrown out if the legislation passed.[125] "What the CIA needs is not this legislation to clear up its paperwork, but rather instructions from Congress that it must now comply with the FOIA," Mackenzie told the subcommittee.[126] Ralph McGehee, author of *Deadly Deceits,* had similar concerns about the legislation. He predicted that the Directorate of Operations would be able to claim an exemption for "some 80 to 90 percent" of their records if the bill was approved.[127]

The hearings in May were essentially a formality; only four members of the subcommittee bothered to attend. With the ACLU supporting H.R. 5164, protests from skeptics such as Mackenzie and McGehee could be ignored. The ACLU of Southern California soon complicated the situation by voting in June to fight against any legislation that would offer the CIA an exemption to FOIA. In order to reduce the lengthy backlog of requests at the CIA, the twenty-two-thousand-member ACLU affiliate proposed that Congress should make it more difficult for the agency to engage in "obstructive conduct."[128] One member of the affiliate complained that "the New York and Washington offices of the A.C.L.U. seem to have become a part of the establishment. They have become comfortable with the Washington bureaucrats."[129] The conflict within the ACLU became such a problem that Ira Glasser, the executive director of the organization, ordered a last minute review of the legislation in September.[130] By that time, however, it was too late. When the bill came up for a vote on September 19, Congressman Ted Weiss went to the House floor, imploring his colleagues to oppose it. He had helped block the earlier attempt to exempt CIA operational files from FOIA, but he was a voice crying in the wilderness in the fall of 1984. Only thirty-five representatives joined him in voting against the bill.[131] The following month Casey threw a party on the seventh floor of CIA headquarters to celebrate the CIA Information Act (Public Law 98-477). Three days later, President Reagan signed the law.[132] He described the CIA Information Act as "a small but important first step," anticipating that the relief it provided to the CIA would "become available to other agencies involved in intelligence, who also must protect their sources and methods and who likewise wish to avoid unnecessary and expensive paperwork."[133] During the debate over the FOIA exemptions, critics worried that the Reagan administration would not stop with the CIA. It turned out that their concerns were justified.[134]

In fairness to the ACLU, they honestly believed that the CIA Information Act would dramatically cut down the backlog of FOIA requests at Langley. Once Congress passed H.R. 5164, Casey promised the House Intelligence Committee, "the Agency will establish a specific program designed to substantially reduce, if not entirely eliminate, the current two-to-three-year backlog of Freedom of Information Act (FOIA) requests."[135] He also pledged not to reduce the funding allocated to FOIA compliance for two years.[136] Anyone who has filed a FOIA request with the agency since 1984 can attest that these commitments were not kept. Not only does the backlog remain a problem, McGehee's prophesy about Directorate of Operations files turned out to be accurate. According to James X. Dempsey, an expert on FOIA litigation, "it has become much more difficult, if not impossible, for FOIA requesters to obtain anything involving a program that was once in this directorate."[137] Moreover, one of the provisions in the CIA Information Act requires the CIA to review exempted files every ten years. Congress expected that the exemptions might be removed for some older documents, and although this did happen during the first decennial review, the agency actually undermined the public's right to know by increasing the number of files placed off-limits to FOIA requests in 2005.[138]

Remarkably, despite all of his efforts to undermine historical scholarship on the CIA, William Casey continued to take steps that portrayed the CIA as an open institution. In 1985 he established the Historical Review Program, but in a fitting tribute to his obsession with secrecy, this program did not result in the declassification of any CIA records until 1989, two years after Casey died of brain cancer.[139]

4 | The Rise and Fall of the New Era of Openness at the CIA, 1988–2001

A popular government without popular information or the means of acquiring it is but a prologue to a farce or a tragedy or perhaps both.
—James Madison (1822)*

Secrecy in government is fundamentally anti-democratic, perpetuating bureaucratic errors. Open debate and discussion of public issues are vital to our national health.
—Justice Hugo Black (New York Times v. United States, 1971)†

There's a big difference between openness and P.R.; what we've got here is P.R.
—Steven Aftergood‡

Public relations at the CIA did not die with William Casey. If anything, his successors improved and expanded the public relations initiative. William H. Webster used public relations to rehabilitate the agency's image in the aftermath of Iran-Contra; in 1992, with the Cold War over, Robert M. Gates promised a new era of openness to assuage the concerns of CIA critics; R. James Woolsey and John Deutch reached out to Hollywood to ensure a more positive portrayal of the CIA in popular culture; and George Tenet embraced public relations to protect the agency's legendary mystique. Like Admiral Stansfield Turner in the late 1970s, all of these DCIs portrayed the CIA as an open institution. Gates and Woolsey even expressed a willingness to declassify CIA records on covert operations. But in the final analysis, the "culture of secrecy" at Langley prevailed. The reforms at the CIA between 1987 and 2017—most notably the declassification of millions of pages of documents—were primarily the result of intervention from historians, Congress, and the White House.

After Casey resigned in early 1987, it appeared for a time that his loyal deputy, Robert M. Gates, would be the next DCI. However, because of the ongoing controversy surrounding Iran-Contra, Gates withdrew his name from consideration and FBI Director William H. Webster got the job instead. The new DCI continued to utilize public relations during the final years of the Cold War. As Admiral Turner had done a decade earlier, Webster brought an outside public relations specialist to Langley. Bill Baker, who had perfected his craft at the FBI, reinvigorated the CIA's public affairs division before handing the position over in 1989 to James Greenleaf, a fellow G-man.[1] In 1991, according to an internal report, public affairs officials fielded 3,369 telephone calls from the media, delivered 174 background briefings, and scheduled 164 interviews with high-ranking CIA officials.[2] Webster helped repair the damage that Casey had inflicted on the CIA's image, and unlike his predecessor, he managed to keep himself out of the headlines.

But as Webster distanced himself from Casey's recklessness, the CIA continued its irrational obsession with secrecy. In 1989, for instance, the State Department's historical division released a volume of the *Foreign Relations of the United States* (*FRUS*) series that focused on American foreign policy in Iran between 1952 and 1954. Since the CIA refused to release documents on the toppling of Muhammad Mossadegh in 1953, the *FRUS* volume on Iran did not even mention the event.[3] Diplomatic historians were outraged by the omission, arguing that America's role in the shah's coup had been previously disclosed by Kermit Roosevelt, the CIA man who helped execute the mission. Warren Cohen, the chairperson of the historical advisory committee at the State Department, resigned in protest the following February. Cohen characterized the volume on Iran as "a fraud," and he described the inherent danger of "an overly elaborate, costly declassification process that encourages distortion and coverup."[4]

Senators Claiborne Pell (D-RI), David Boren (D-OK), and Jesse Helms (R-NC) responded with a legislative proposal to bring greater oversight to the publication of *FRUS*.[5] Senator Helms summarized the bipartisan concern about the government's declassification procedures when he complained: "Too much about our foreign policy is hidden for too long from public scrutiny."[6] Congress eventually passed Public Law 102-138 in 1991 to change how the State Department compiled and published *FRUS*. As historian Warren Kimball has explained, the legislation established a new advisory committee that had the power to "kick open the doors, look at the records, and then raise holy hell when it concluded that the bureaucrats were withholding 30-year-old secrets without a legitimate 'national security' reason."[7] Not only did Public Law 102-138 establish a thirty-year rule for document declassification, it also *required* government agencies like the CIA to share information with the State Department's history staff. The law was a stunning rebuke to the CIA's clandestine mind-set.

When Webster stepped down in 1991, President George H. W. Bush boldly decided to replace him with Gates. The confirmation process was brutal. A group of Gates's colleagues testified that he intentionally politicized intelligence while running the agency's analytical division between 1982 and 1986. According to Melvin Goodman, a retired CIA analyst, Casey and Gates had selectively used analysis to support "operational commitments" in Central America, Afghanistan, and the Middle East, while simultaneously manipulating the evidence to present a more pessimistic interpretation of the Soviet Union.[8] CIA veteran Harold Ford substantiated Goodman's accusations, arguing that Gates's actions went "beyond professional bounds and clearly constitute a skewing of intelligence, not in the fields of military and strategic issues, but chiefly concerning Soviet political matters and the Soviets and the Third World."[9] Gates, in other words, only interfered with CIA analysts in certain situations. As former CIA analyst Jennifer L. Glaudemans explained at the hearings, "politicization is like fog. Though you cannot hold it in your hand or nail it to the wall, it is real. It does exist. And it does affect people's behavior."[10] Gates adamantly denied the accusations, and the Senate ultimately confirmed his nomination.

Even before the controversy over the alleged politicization began, however, Gates promised the senators on the intelligence committee that he intended to make the CIA more accessible to Congress and the American public. He acknowledged that Langley continued to have an image problem, and from his perspective, "changing perceptions first requires greater openness by the Agency."[11] As the opposition to his nomination mounted, Gates repeated his promise of increased openness, even writing Senator Sam Nunn (D-GA) a letter in which he described his strategy for leading the CIA into the post–Cold War world.[12] There was obviously an element of self-interest involved in Gates's proposals for the future; in fact, he admitted to committee members that the agency had to evolve in order to justify its existence: "CIA and U.S. intelligence must change, and be seen to change, or confront irrelevance and growing sentiment for their dismantlement."[13]

On November 18, 1991, just six days after he was sworn in as DCI, Gates sent a memo to his director of public affairs, Joseph R. DeTrani, requesting the establishment of a task force to examine the agency's existing policies on openness. Gates wanted the group to complete its study by December 20, asking them to formulate "additional proposals for making more information about the Agency available to the American people and to give greater transparency to our organization."[14] DeTrani wasted no time in assembling what became known as the Task Force on Greater CIA Openness. Four days later he reported to Gates that a task force of seven CIA officials had been formed with himself as chairperson, noting that the group planned "to meet with John Scali of ABC, Jack Nelson of the *Los Angeles Times*, David Ignatius of the *Washington Post*, and Jerry Seib of the *Wall Street Journal*, and others."[15]

The task force first met on November 25, and during this session, they started to brainstorm ideas. Although it remains unclear whether DeTrani and his colleagues were aware of the recommendations that a similar ad hoc group had offered to William Colby sixteen years earlier, they developed suggestions that sounded much the same. For instance, the task force advised that it would be useful to seek outside assistance in defending the CIA. Not only should the agency "get our customers to speak for us on the value of our work/product," task force members wanted to "do more with and through professional organizations."[16] They also believed that the agency must "aggressively respond to 'cheap shots' by the media with op-ed pieces or letters to the editor and if they aren't printed, work [the response] into public statement by DCI."[17]

The task force solicited comments on their project from both insiders and outsiders. During the first week of December, they held discussions with agency employees, and at their second meeting, the group listened intently to an invited guest named George Tenet, then staff director for the Senate Select Committee on Intelligence. DeTrani told Gates in a detailed memo that Tenet provided them with several "admonitions"; of the ten that DeTrani listed, the first was undoubtedly the most significant: "Keep the mystique—we could lose if we are perceived as an ordinary bureaucracy (in resource game and in public image)."[18] Instead of demystifying their clandestine activities, in other words, Tenet encouraged them not to sacrifice the CIA's mystique. This recommendation unwittingly highlighted the fundamental contradiction of CIA public relations since the "Year of Intelligence" in that the agency had consistently viewed openness in terms of self-preservation

rather than the public's right to know. "Give the public a better understanding of what [the CIA does], the quality of [CIA] people and
the risks they take," Tenet advised. "Keep openness institutional rather
than issue-oriented."[19] In keeping with this sycophantic tone, he observed, "Doug MacEachin, Bob Blackwell and George Kolt are the 'best
show in town' on the Soviet Union and should be seen and heard more
widely."[20] Tenet further advised the agency to reach out to academics by
possibly reevaluating classification rules and "packaging information on
former denied areas to get some credit for past efforts."[21] As the staff director of the Senate's oversight committee, Tenet had a responsibility to
ensure the CIA's accountability to Congress. Yet his recommendations
were dominated by a focus on public relations, eerily foreshadowing his
tenure at the CIA.

In the week following Tenet's visit, officials on the task force kept a
busy schedule. They journeyed to *Washington Post* headquarters for a
meeting; they listened to presentations from CIA officials; and they had
conversations with scholars, retired DCI Richard Helms, and reporters
such as Wolf Blitzer and Doyle McManus.[22] After gathering at least twice
to discuss their findings, the group submitted their final report to Gates
on December 20 for his review. On the second page of this document,
the authors borrowed several of Tenet's ideas without attributing them
to him, advising Gates to "preserve the mystique."[23] The following page
of the report was reminiscent of the "Telling the Intelligence Story"
memo that had been sent to Colby in 1975. "We have an important
story to tell," the task force announced, "a story that bears repeating.
We are the most open intelligence agency in the world which is proper
in our form of democracy."[24] Yet despite this preexisting openness, they
worried, "many Americans do not understand the intelligence process
and the role of intelligence in national security policymaking. Many
still operate with a romanticized or erroneous view of intelligence from
the movies, TV, books and newspapers."[25] In essence, the report suggested that only the positive elements of the CIA mystique were worth
protecting.

The Task Force on Greater CIA Openness described for Gates a variety of "steps we can take which will benefit us and the American people," offering him a total of thirty recommendations to either approve
or reject.[26] The media should be a top priority for the Office of Public
Affairs, the task force concluded, and they believed it would be beneficial for the CIA to "provide more background briefings, when practical,

to a greater number of print and electronic media journalists" and to encourage the media to interview top CIA officials.[27] Their report then mentioned the possibility of allowing reporters to do "individual profiles" on CIA employees to "help personalize the world of intelligence in broad circulation newspapers or magazines," which might also demonstrate "the growing number of women and minorities in each directorate and increasingly in more senior positions."[28] Gates accepted almost all of the ideas for improving media relations, telling DeTrani that "careful records should be kept of such contacts [with the press]."[29] In responding to proposals outlined in another section of the report, Gates supported the production of more public relations–type material, expressed an interest in making television appearances, and agreed that "the Agency's briefing program for the full range of potential audiences should be expanded as opportunities arise."[30]

For anyone familiar with the history of CIA public relations, it is obvious that the majority of recommendations in the report were not new. The task force apparently thought they had developed a new idea when they advised Gates to invite CEOs to Langley for seminars, but in reality, Casey and other DCIs had previously encouraged such visits.[31] Moreover, the speaker's bureau that Herbert Hetu initiated over a decade earlier was revived prior to Gates's arrival, and according to the task force, agency employees had made over sixty public appearances in 1991. Accepting the report's advice, Gates called for the program to be expanded.[32] In addition to reviewing the recommendations that were approved in January 1992, it is important to consider those that were rejected. Generally speaking, Gates viewed the program as a chance to sell the agency's image to a wide audience. He concurred with the task force: "Our objective is to make CIA and the intelligence process more visible and understandable rather than to seek inevitably incomplete or unattainable openness on specific substantive issues."[33] When translated into practice, this mentality helps to explain why Gates did not approve a recommendation to encourage the intelligence committees to "issue an unclassified annual report on the performance of the Intelligence Community."[34] Gates wanted better public relations, not accountability.

Less than a week after Gates issued his assessment of the task force's report, Elaine Sciolino broke the story on the front page of the *New York Times*.[35] DeTrani sent a memo to Gates about the article on the following day. "Given the fact that Sciolino insisted on running this story now despite my best efforts to convince her to hold off," he wrote, "I think the story is about as good as we could have hoped for."[36] DeTrani was most likely hoping to keep the task force's existence under wraps until Gates could publicly announce the CIA's new policy on openness. In a speech to the Oklahoma Press Association on February 21, 1992, about five weeks after Sciolino's article, Gates formally outlined his strategy. At the beginning of the talk, he jokingly compared his situation to the scene in *Indiana Jones and the Last Crusade* (1989) where Jones must cross to the other side of a deep canyon on faith alone. "I will now step out into that chasm [of credibility] on faith," he said, "the faith that what I have to say will persuade you of our seriousness of purpose and action."[37] Although Gates acknowledged that there had been previous attempts at greater openness, he noted that "all of this took place against a backdrop of overall continuing and undifferentiated secrecy. . . . This is going to change."[38] He focused on three aspects of the task force report in his speech—the media, academia, and declassification policies—and assured the audience that "these measures, taken together, represent a real shift on CIA's part toward greater openness and sense of public responsibility."[39]

By proclaiming greater openness at the CIA, Gates won excellent publicity for the agency. His promise to declassify more documents was especially well received at the time. Yet the praise quickly turned into embarrassment when agency officials refused to show the press a copy of the Task Force Report on Greater CIA Openness.[40] The Center for National Security Studies at the ACLU soon filed a FOIA request for the document, but the FOIA office ruled that "it must be withheld in its entirety."[41] Gates would later contend that the report had been withheld initially "because some of the people who signed it were under cover."[42] This explanation was somewhat misleading. On March 18, Gary Foster, DeTrani's replacement at the public affairs office, told a congressional committee that in addition to the names of the signers, other information in the report had to remain classified. He claimed that the unclassified sections "wouldn't mean much to anybody."[43] Gates, however, ultimately overruled Foster, and in early April, he declassified the internal study and his memo of January 6, choosing simply to redact the relevant names while allowing most everything else to become public.

After looking over the recommendations of the task force, an ACLU official dismissed the report as little more than "an internal discussion of how we [the CIA] can get people to like us."[44] Steven Aftergood, editor of the *Secrecy & Government Bulletin*, now titled *Secrecy News*, had previously quipped that the CIA was "invulnerable to irony."[45] Why else would the agency classify as secret a study on greater openness to the public? CIA officials most likely were worried about disclosing aspects of the report that evaluated previous public relations efforts. In the report's section on the media, for example, the authors of the study boasted: "PAO [public affairs office] now has relationships with reporters from every major wire service, newspaper, news weekly, and television network in the nation. This has helped us turn some 'intelligence failure' stories into 'intelligence success' stories."[46] They observed that "in many instances, we have persuaded reporters to postpone, change, hold, or even scrap stories that could have adversely affected national security interests or jeopardized sources and methods."[47] The report also mentioned that the public affairs office routinely mailed material to around seven hundred professors, held biannual events at Langley for college administrators, and was currently in the process of "building a database of information about Agency contacts with academia."[48]

Three days before Gates announced the new policy in Tulsa, DeTrani issued an update on what had been accomplished so far. He informed his boss that a video entitled *In America's Interest* was nearing completion; that briefings for the press had been expanded (twenty-eight during the month of January); and that planning was underway for CEOs to tour the CIA.[49] DeTrani's office also hosted several guest speakers, including an astonishing visit from Norman Mailer.[50] Even though Mailer had once accused the CIA of manipulating the stock exchange and eviscerating American radicalism, he published a book about the agency in 1991 called *Harlot's Ghost* that depicted the agency as "a company of the elegant, secretly gathered to fight a war so noble that one could and must be ready to trudge for years through the mud and the pits."[51] During his promotion of the epic novel, which totaled over 1,200 pages, Mailer did not hesitate to share his personal views of the CIA. "I could have been in the CIA," he remarked. "And I probably would have been pretty good at it."[52] He also condemned his participation in the Fifth Estate during the 1970s, telling *Vanity Fair*, "I cringe when I think of the name now."[53] Mailer visited CIA headquarters, delivered a speech inside the Bubble, and met with top CIA officials in Robert M. Gates's conference room. CIA employees were thrilled with the speech, offering Mailer "standing ovations several times."[54] Mailer announced that the agency should assassinate Saddam Hussein, and he emphasized the importance of espionage in the aftermath of the Cold War. "Now that the cold war is over," he observed, "the C.I.A. can get out of the bear trap of ideology and begin to provide serious and needed intelligence on the rest of the world."[55]

In addition to the obvious public relations component of Gates's new policy, scholars were promised a radically different approach to the declassification of CIA records. The task force had outlined a proposal to "establish a senior-led, Agency-wide group to review the Agency's policy and practices related to declassification and release of records under the Historical Review and FOIA programs . . . with a view to accelerating the process," and they followed this with a recommendation to declassify "historical materials on specific events, particularly those which are repeatedly the subject of false allegations, such as the 1948 Italian Elections, 1953 Iranian Coup, 1954 Guatemalan Coup, 1958 Indonesian Coup and the Cuban Missile Crisis in 1962."[56] In his speech to the Oklahoma Press Association, Gates confessed: "The results of our historical review program have been quite meager—the consequences of low priority, few resources, and rigid agency policies and procedures heavily biased toward denial of declassification."[57] Gates, however, selected his words very carefully that evening. He announced "a new approach" to increase the number of records declassified, but in the same sentence, he added an important caveat: the program would abide by the CIA Information Act of 1984.[58] This meant that operational records would be exempt from the review process.

Of all the records that the task force listed for possible declassification, Gates only approved the release of documents pertaining to the Cuban Missile Crisis. CIA officials organized a conference at Langley on the missile crisis to commemorate its thirtieth anniversary, and during this event, the agency "issued a handsomely printed volume of documents tracing the history of the crisis."[59] As James X. Dempsey has observed, however, it was not accidental that the CIA selected the missile crisis as the subject of its inaugural symposium; after all, the agency's handling of the nuclear standoff is widely considered to be one of its finest moments.[60] Given the obvious public relations concerns about accentuating the positive, the agency hierarchy rejected a plan to hold a conference on Team B, the group of conservative Cold Warriors who challenged CIA analysis of the Soviet Union in 1976.[61] Such an event would inevitably raise questions about the politicization of intelligence, a topic that Gates and his subordinates most likely wanted to avoid.

R. James Woolsey, who served as President Bill Clinton's first DCI from February 1993 through January 1995, attempted to cultivate the support of the American public using the same techniques as Gates. In order to more effectively convey the CIA message during television interviews and other public appearances, he even hired a public relations consultant to provide pointers on public speaking.[62] He told Congress that he would continue the openness initiative, promising a "warts and all" approach to the declassification of older documents.[63] In September 1993, he testified about plans to release documents on several covert operations from the Cold War. The CIA would move forward with Gates's "plans to declassify records on the Bay of Pigs operation, the coups against President Arbenz of Guatemala and against Prime Minister Mossadeq in Iran, and operations in the Dominican Republic and the Congo," said Woolsey. Another six operations would also be added to the list: "France and Italy in the 1940s and 1950s; support to anti-Sukarno rebels in Indonesia in 1958; support to Tibetan guerillas in the 1950s and early 1960s; operations against North Korea during the Korean War; and operations in Laos in the 1960s."[64]

But despite these assurances, Woolsey's primary concern was the improvement of public relations. While previous DCIs had reached out to the media and academia, Woolsey understood that the CIA also needed to focus attention on the entertainment industry. In 1994 he agreed to enter negotiations with Television Production Partners (TPP), a production company financed by advertising firms that was interested in developing a series based on the CIA. Interestingly, plans for a CIA television show had been kicking around for nearly three decades. During his retirement, Allen Dulles hoped that CBS might develop a series on the CIA similar to *The F.B.I.* (1965–1974), a fictional show about the bureau that J. Edgar Hoover enthusiastically supported.[65] The proposal resurfaced during the "Year of Intelligence," and although William Colby was intrigued by the idea, George H. W. Bush reportedly had no interest in pursuing the project after his arrival at the CIA in 1976. CBS began to develop a similar program in the summer of 1980 with the support of AFIO.[66]

It remains unclear whether Woolsey was aware of these earlier projects, but even if he did know about them, he clearly wanted to take a new approach. The agreement the agency signed with TPP at the end of 1994 reflects Woolsey's desire to directly involve the CIA in the production process. It gave the CIA the authority to "review and approve or deny all stories and scripts produced. In exchange for this extraordinary control, CIA . . . granted TPP the right to use the CIA name and seal in the production and to state that the stories are fictional accounts based on actual CIA files."[67] According to Dennis Boxx, then public affairs director at Langley, "this project presents an unprecedented opportunity for CIA to influence the portrayal of this Agency and US intelligence in a potentially high-profile and successful television series reaching millions of Americans. It has been briefed to and has the support of both congressional oversight committees."[68] In order to adequately evaluate the scripts for the show, Boxx proposed the establishment of an internal review board that "may include an Associate Deputy Director from each directorate as well as the General Counsel and the Director of Public Affairs [Boxx]."[69]

The CIA has only declassified two memos pertaining to the agreement with TPP,[70] but it appears that John Deutch, President Clinton's second DCI, did not share Woolsey's enthusiasm for the project.[71] Like Woolsey, however, Deutch was quite interested in shaping the CIA's image in popular culture. CIA officials on the seventh floor approached a case officer named Chase Brandon with the idea of starting the first film liaison office at the agency. After initially declining the offer, Brandon, who had family connections to the film industry, subsequently reconsidered and made the decision in 1996 to come out of the cold and into the spotlight.[72] He remained in the position for more than a decade.[73] When he left the CIA, Brandon allegedly "took with him every telephone number and piece of paper related to his job [as film liaison]."[74] If this allegation is indeed true, Brandon most likely violated federal law. The incident vividly demonstrates how secrecy and public relations are intertwined.

Brandon began his career at the agency in the early 1970s, shortly before the CIA entered the contentious "Year of Intelligence." "[The] CIA and I were both born in 1947," he proudly explained in 2005, "and I was recruited into its organizational ranks when we were both 25 years old."[75] Brandon holds a PhD in linguistics and spent over two decades in the Directorate of Operations. The details of his clandestine work for the CIA are obviously classified, but it is known that he participated in paramilitary operations in El Salvador and other Central American locations during the 1980s. By the mid-1990s, the agency hierarchy had selected him to run the CIA station in Houston. Brandon remained undercover while serving as the Houston station chief, and he appears to have worked closely with oil companies that had interests in Latin America. In fact, he sometimes distributed business cards that indicated he was the vice president of Patriot Petroleum in Baytown, Texas.[76] Patriot Petroleum, of course, was simply a CIA front company.

Between 1996 and 2007, Brandon participated in a long list of movies and television shows. He described his philosophy of the liaison job by paraphrasing a famous line from *Field of Dreams* (1989): "If I give them a phone number, they will call."[77] By implementing a strategy he called the "three legs of a stool approach" (i.e., documentaries, movies, and television shows), Brandon attempted to "showcase good qualities" of CIA employees in hopes of improving the CIA's public image.[78] When determining whether to offer CIA assistance to a project, he examined outlines and scripts to make sure that they were "fair and balanced."[79] He openly admitted withholding support from proposals that might have portrayed the agency in a negative light:

> If there is something wrong or maliciously ugly about us, they can correct the part that's factually wrong or temper whatever is maliciously ugly, and maybe they can film here. But if they have clichés about us as rogue assassins, I'm sorry, but we're not going to let them come film here and use our people, because that's not what we are.[80]

Dan Neil, a *Los Angeles Times* columnist, says that Brandon essentially replaced "tradecraft" with "image craft," arguing that "Brandon's job dangerously stokes two of America's most outsized appetites, for fantasy and authority."[81] Neil believed that the CIA should simply not get involved with "producers who want to make quasi-propaganda."[82]

The issue of assassination is especially sensitive for CIA officials, and when the film *In the Line of Fire* was released in the summer of 1993, they found it horrifying that the deranged assassin, played by John Malkovich, was scripted as a former CIA man. Brandon, for instance, turned down the producers of *The Bourne Identity* (2002), a film starring Matt Damon as a deadly CIA assassin on the run from Langley bosses who are trying to kill him. "By page 25 [of the screenplay]," Brandon recalls, "I lost track of how many rogue operatives had assassinated people. I chucked the thing in the burn bag."[83] Brandon also avoided projects that suggested the CIA toppled foreign governments. "There is always some ugly representation of us as a conspiratorial government-overthrow apparatus," he complained.[84] The film liaison office was apparently interested in falsifying the historical record, for in truth, the agency had destabilized and overthrown the elected leaders of numerous countries over the years.

According to the late Angus Mackenzie, "for the average outsider, being taken into the CIA's confidence can be breathtaking."[85] Mackenzie recognized that CIA officials often used the basic strategies of agent recruitment for public relations purposes. Interestingly, Brandon was once an instructor at "the Farm," the CIA's not-so-secret training facility at Camp Peary on the outskirts of Williamsburg, Virginia.[86] Winning a person's trust was something that came naturally to him. Recognizing that Hollywood celebrities are often distrustful of the CIA, he frequently invited writers, actors, and directors to visit Langley. He skillfully used these VIP tours to promote the agency's mystique. For instance, after Patrick Stewart journeyed through the halls of the CIA in December 1997, he admitted, "this visit has certainly shifted my perceptions and made me review my attitudes toward the Agency and my conditioning from previous reading about you [most notably, Harvey Weinstein's book on MKULTRA]."[87] Since he and his fiancée planned on forming a production company, Stewart promised that he would be willing to consider "projects that give a more positive view of the good work of your organization."[88] In fact, he was so impressed with the agency that he even offered to make a subsequent visit to deliver a lecture in the Bubble on acting in espionage films.[89] Will Smith, Robert DeNiro, Ben Affleck, Dean Cain, and Dan Aykroyd are just a handful of other actors who have toured the CIA with Brandon.[90] Like Stewart, Affleck commented on how normal the CIA seemed during his visit to prepare for the role of Jack Ryan in *The Sum of All Fears* (2002): "It wasn't some kind of cloak-and-dagger operation, but more like an office with a very diverse group of people—highly competent and very smart people—who are dedicated, patriotic Americans."[91] Of course, neither Affleck nor Stewart appears to have considered that their tour of Langley was undoubtedly carefully managed from start to finish.

Having once encouraged agency officials to maintain their mystique, it is not surprising that George Tenet ardently supported the film liaison office when he became DCI in 1997. He soon took an interest in a project that Brandon had undertaken with Robert Cort, a successful Hollywood producer who briefly worked as a CIA analyst in the early 1970s. Cort had written a story about a fictional CIA operation, and Roger Towne, the screenwriter of *The Natural* (1984), was enlisted to prepare an adaptation. Actor Tim Matheson, best known to moviegoers as Eric "Otter"

Stratton in *Animal House* (1978), signed on as the film's director. As plans for the television movie began to crystallize, Matheson, Cort, and David Madden, the co-producer, visited Langley where Tenet personally welcomed them. Matheson explained that he fully intended "to capture on film the professionalism, dedication, and patriotism which CIA truly represents and which the American public little understands."[92]

Matheson and the producers made arrangements for several of the actors in the movie to receive similar tours. Tom Berenger, who in the film portrays a CIA officer sent to North Korea on a covert operation, went to Langley for two days, meeting with Tenet and at least one top official in the Directorate of Operations. Ron Silver, the actor selected for the role of DCI, also visited CIA headquarters to prepare for the film. Silver said that Tenet provided him with invaluable advice: "There's no way I could have ever prepared as thoroughly for this role without talking to Mr. Tenet. His responsibilities are enormous and I deeply appreciate the time and insights he gave me—both will better enable me to portray the DCI in this movie."[93] Then, on June 20, 1998, two months after the start of principal photography, Matheson spent the entire Saturday at CIA headquarters filming scenes in the lobby, hallways, and rear entrance. Over fifty CIA employees participated as "extras," because it would have been too time-consuming for the Office of Security to obtain clearances for civilians.[94]

When the editing of the Showtime movie was complete, Tenet arranged for *In the Company of Spies*[95] to premiere at the CIA in October 1999. Not only did agency officials literally roll out the red carpet for the event, they also positioned klieg lights near the entranceway to welcome about five hundred invited guests.[96] Tenet had claimed only a year earlier that the agency simply could not afford to continue its voluntary declassification program, but he somehow managed to find room in the budget for the extravaganza. Tenet commended the production team, happily noting that "they were great to work with. They portray us in a good light, and I want the American people to know the values we believe in. Our work is secret and it will always be secret. But every now and then, we should take the opportunity to portray ourselves. A little bit of fun—there's nothing wrong with that."[97] The DCI had good reason to be thrilled with what he saw on the screen inside the Bubble that evening, and for the rest of his tenure, he commonly described *In the Company of Spies* as "our movie."[98] At the beginning of the film, a senator thanks Ron Silver's character for his honest testimony in front of the Senate Intelligence Committee. "We are, after all, entering a new era of openness and accountability," he observes.[99] The movie perpetuates the idea that the public only learns about the CIA's failures. After the mission in North Korea is perfectly executed, the president is overawed with the CIA's brilliance: "By God, when the agency is good, it's spectacular. And no one even knows!"[100] CIA critics, however, were less than impressed with the movie's message. "For people who get their information from government documents, not from television and the movies, there has actually been a reduction in accountability," said Steven Aftergood. "They're going to have to do better than TV movies."[101]

Given the success of *In the Company of Spies*, Brandon continued to assist television producers. *The Agency*, a show that offered a fictionalized view of Langley operations, premiered on CBS in 2001. The production team received guidance from CIA officials, and they were allowed to film inside agency headquarters in April 2001. CBS apparently retained creative control over the episodes, but the evidence also suggests that the CIA's willingness to provide assistance to the network helped ensure that they were portrayed positively. In a letter thanking agency personnel for their support, the production manager boasted that a scene from the pilot, which was filmed on the first floor of Langley, "could be a recruiting movie for the CIA."[102] Brandon must have been thrilled with this compliment.

Brandon served as a consultant to ABC's *Alias* (2001–2006), a television show about an agency operative named Sydney Bristow (played by Jennifer Garner). Bristow is a full-time graduate student, but when she is not writing papers, she wears tight outfits, hunts down the enemies of the United States, and then punishes them with spin-kicks. Brandon acknowledged that Garner's character was far-fetched, but he believed that Bristow displays many of the qualities that the agency looked for in potential recruits. Most importantly, he said, Bristow is "rock solidly patriotic."[103] In 2003 he recruited Garner for a CIA recruitment video; this advertisement appealed to the patriotism of young Americans:

I'm Jennifer Garner. I play a CIA officer on the ABC TV series *Alias*. In the real world, the CIA serves as our country's first line of defense in the ongoing war against international terrorism. [The] CIA's mission is clear and direct: safeguard America and its people. And it takes smart people with wide-ranging talents and diverse backgrounds to carry out this mission . . . people with integrity, common sense, patriotism and courage. . . . Today, the collection of foreign intelligence has never been more vital for national security.[104]

Having established connections in Hollywood, Brandon pursued movie projects as well. He helped Towne write another screenplay about the agency, sharing information about his experiences as an instructor at Camp Peary. *The Recruit* (2003) centers on the recruitment and training of James Clayton (played by Colin Farrell), a computer genius who graduated from MIT at the top of his class. When Walter Burke (played by Al Pacino), a veteran CIA officer, attempts to sign him up, Clayton is initially uninterested, mocking the CIA as "a bunch of fat, old white guys who fell asleep when we needed them most."[105] Clayton, however, believes that his father was working for the CIA, not an oil company, when he died in a plane crash in 1990. He reconsiders Burke's offer in hopes of learning what actually happened to his dad, and he begins his training at "the Farm." One might argue that Burke's proclamations are directed at both the actors *and* the audience: "Our failures are known," he says, "our successes are not."[106] He also reminds the recruits that "our cause is just," and that enemies of the United States are "all around us."[107]

Reviewers were not kind to *The Recruit.* A. O. Scott jokingly described the movie as an "Al Pacino crazy mentor picture," noting that "what Mr. Pacino provides is an acting lesson, one that Mr. Farrell would do well to heed."[108] Stephen Hunter of the *Washington Post* went so far as to argue that the movie "clinically illustrates *everything wrong with the modern American motion picture.*"[109] Although Brandon conceded that the final cut was "not nearly as good as the story was originally," he claimed that *The Recruit* was "hugely popular" at the CIA.[110] In fact, he said that since the movie was released, all of the recruitment classes were required to watch it during training.[111]

The CIA does not sign contracts with filmmakers they are assisting; on the contrary, the film liaison office prefers to establish "a gentlemen's agreement."[112] When he discovered a problem in a script, Brandon simply presented filmmakers with alternative options. For instance, during a conference call with Universal Studios about *Meet the Parents* (2000), he said that the production team asked him what the CIA's kidnapping and torture manuals might look like, because they wanted Ben Stiller's character to find them on a desk to establish that his soon-to-be father-in-law was a CIA operative. Uncomfortable with the idea, Brandon proposed that they make the CIA connection by showing "a panoply of photographs" of Robert DeNiro's character with several international figures.[113] The Universal Studios executives loved the suggestion, and they decided to write it into the screenplay.

As Tenet expanded the scope of the agency's public relations crusade, he showed little interest in releasing historical records. He essentially viewed the declassification process as an extension of its public relations efforts; since documents had the potential to undermine the CIA's mystique, they needed to be withheld from the public. In May 1997, during his Senate confirmation hearing, Tenet warned about the perils of too much historical inquiry: "The new challenges rushing toward us make it dangerous, frankly, to keep looking over our shoulders."[114] Later that month the *New York Times* ran a story about a speech that George Herring had delivered at a historical conference.[115] Herring, a well-respected diplomatic historian and an expert on the Vietnam War, belonged to the agency's Historical Review Panel from 1990 until 1996 when he was asked to step down. Reflecting on his experiences, he felt "a nagging sense of frustration and a persisting anger at having, on occasion, been used."[116] After the panel first met in August 1990, he revealed, it did not meet again for another four years. Herring was outraged that the CIA projected an image of openness throughout the committee's lengthy hiatus: "Now I'm from Kentucky, and I'm not supposed to be swift, but it didn't take too long even for me to realize that I was being used to cover the agency's ass while having no influence. The fact was that . . . the CIA panel had no chair, met at the whim of the Agency, exerted no real influence, and at times was used as window dressing."[117] He described Gates's openness initiative as "a brilliant public relations snow job" that established "a carefully nurtured myth that was not at all easy for me to dispel."[118]

Tenet and his advisors responded to Herring's attack with a demonstration of their public relations tactics. Nick Cullather, who joined the CIA's history staff about five months after Gates announced the openness initiative, wrote a classified history of Operation PBSUCCESS, the covert venture that led to the overthrow of President Jacobo Arbenz in 1954. Although Cullather had completed the study before leaving the agency in 1993, it remained locked away inside Langley along with thousands of pages of primary documents on the operation. Suddenly, two days after the Herring story appeared in the *New York Times*, the CIA notified Cullather about the impending declassification of his project.

The CIA had been promising to release the documents on Operation PBSUCCESS since 1992, but nothing was declassified until Herring slammed the agency for its intransigence. Rather than turning over all the files to the National Archives, the CIA initially retained almost everything. In fact, Cullather estimates "less than one percent of the total collection" emerged in 1997.[119] A large percentage of the remaining documents was finally released in 2003 as part of the *FRUS* series.

By releasing Cullather's study, the CIA hoped to deflect the criticism directed at the agency's declassification process. Yet it remained obvious that the agency had not honored the promises that it made in 1992 and 1993. In attempting to explain the failure of the openness initiative, CIA officials claimed many of the documents had been destroyed. Less than two weeks after the article on Herring's speech, the *New York Times* reported that most of the records documenting the coup against Prime Minister Mossadegh were long gone.[120] But in April 2000, a front-page article in the newspaper revealed that the CIA had been distorting the truth. Approximately one thousand pages of the material on the covert operation in Iran remained. James Risen, the story's author, also received a classified history of the operation that had been completed by Donald Wilber in early 1954.[121] Wilber, one of the CIA operatives involved in the coup, had been frustrated by the lack of attention given to his study, writing in his memoir, "if this history had been read by the planners of the Bay of Pigs, there would have been no such operation."[122]

Interestingly, although Gates had pledged in February 1992 to declassify documents on the Bay of Pigs invasion, nothing had been released by 1996. The National Security Archive, a nongovernmental organization housed at George Washington University, filed multiple FOIA requests for the records, and after stalling for two years, in February 1998 the CIA finally released the internal report on the operation written by Lyman Kirkpatrick, the inspector general of the CIA between 1952 and 1963.[123] The Kirkpatrick Report presented a scathing assessment of the Bay of Pigs, and the CIA burned most of the copies. If the report ever became public, officials worried about what would happen to the mystique that Allen Dulles had so painstakingly created during the 1950s. "In unfriendly hands," warned the deputy DCI in December 1961, "[the Kirkpatrick Report] could become a weapon unjustifiably [used] to attack the entire mission, organization, and functioning of the Agency."[124]

In July 1998, about five months after the release of the inspector general's report, Tenet shut down all declassification projects at the CIA not mandated by law.[125] Cullather perceptively described Tim Weiner's article in the *New York Times* on Tenet's decision as "an obituary for the openness program."[126] Since the CIA was unwilling to voluntarily release information, Congress found it necessary to pass the Nazi War Crimes Disclosure Act in 1998. The CIA had long downplayed the use of former Nazis during the Cold War, but the documents released in response to the law proved the skeptics had been correct.[127] In June 2006, the media reported that the agency had been told in 1958 the alias of Adolf Eichmann and that he was hiding in Argentina. Even though they knew that Israel had been searching for Eichmann, agency officials did not turn over the information. It took the Mossad another two years to capture him.[128] Researchers also learned more about Heinz Felfe, an ex-Nazi that the CIA trusted to run counterintelligence in West Germany. Felfe had actually been a classic double agent, betraying American secrets and personnel to the Soviets.[129]

Within a year of the Nazi War Crimes Disclosure Act, President Clinton's National Security Council ordered the intelligence agencies to "review for release . . . all documents that shed light on human rights abuses, terrorism and other acts of political violence during and prior to the Pinochet era in Chile."[130] The CIA released around six hundred documents in June 1999, but it initially refused to declassify records on the American effort to destabilize Chile in the years prior to the 1973 coup against Salvador Allende. As Peter Kornbluh bluntly observed at the time, "[CIA officials] have decided to sabotage this commitment to openness with the same degree of success they used to sabotage the economy in Chile. The CIA is directly challenging the president of the United States and the integrity of this White House–mandated project."[131]

Despite the fact that the CIA was now mandated to participate in the *FRUS* series, Tenet allowed his subordinates to obstruct historians at the State Department. According to Page P. Miller, a scholar who has carefully examined the CIA's interference with *FRUS*, "the most troubling, unresolved barrier to ensuring publication of an accurate and comprehensive account of U.S. foreign policy remains the CIA's lack of cooperation."[132] The CIA refused to turn over documents on the agency's operations in Japan for the *FRUS* volume on Northeast Asia (1961–1963). The advisory committee, frustrated by Langley's continued intransigence, warned readers in the preface of the volume, "this published compilation does not constitute a 'thorough, accurate, and reliable documentary record of major United States foreign policy decisions,' the standard set by Public Law 102-138."[133]

In 2000, four years after the release of the Northeast Asia volume, the CIA once again interfered with the publication of the series. CIA officials successfully blocked for three years the release of the volume covering American foreign policy in Greece in the mid-1960s, and a few officers even claimed that the revelations would lead to a resurgence of Greek terrorism.[134] The following spring the CIA used similar tactics to prevent the distribution of a *FRUS* compilation on Indonesia. Yet the Government Printing Office had already sent copies to several libraries. The documents on Indonesia did not contain any information that could damage national security, but they did reveal how the American government had turned over lists that helped Indonesian officials track down and violently eliminate left-wing opposition in the country.[135] A retired State Department official lamented the CIA's power to withhold its history: "It's basically a case of the CIA putting pressure on State and the State's bureaucratic culture being wimpy. CIA usually gets its way."[136]

In truth, the CIA is now a far more open institution than it was in 1992, but this openness resulted more from external forces than the policies of Gates and Woolsey. Executive Order 12958, which President Clinton issued in April 1995, attempted to mandate the release of government records over twenty-five years old.[137] This order began with good intentions, but it soon became clear that the agency wanted exemptions for over 60 percent of its records.[138] The most important result of Executive Order 12958 was the establishment of the CIA Records Search Tool (CREST) at the National Archives II in College Park, Maryland. CREST is a database that contains over eleven million pages of declassified CIA material. For nearly two decades, researchers could only access CREST using four computers located on the third floor of the National Archives building in College Park.[139]

Beginning in January 2017, CREST became available online. According to the agency's website, the "CIA recognized that such visits [to the National Archives] were inconvenient and presented an obstacle to many researchers."[140] In reality, the decision to place CREST online was directly connected to a lawsuit that MuckRock filed in June 2014. MuckRock, a nonprofit organization established in 2010, is a "collaborative news site that brings together journalists, researchers, activists, and regular citizens to request, analyze, and share government documents, making politics more transparent and democracies more informed."[141] When the CIA attempted to stall the lawsuit, Michael Best, an independent researcher, initiated an ambitious Kickstarter campaign to purchase a Fujitsu scanner and other equipment. After printing records from CREST, Best planned on scanning them. "Once digitized, the documents will be uploaded to the Internet Archive where everyone will be able to access and download them for free," he explained.[142] Best exceeded his fundraising goal of $10,000, and since his plan was perfectly legal, the CIA ultimately backed down. Even though the online accessibility of CREST is undeniably a positive development, it is important to keep in mind that the agency continues to withhold literally millions of pages in its archives older than twenty-five years.

A basic axiom of CIA public relations is that the agency's failures are known while its successes are secret. But the documents released so far have routinely undermined the agency's mystique; the evidence that has emerged from the archives on CIA operations in countries such as Iran, Guatemala, and Chile has vividly shown that missions once viewed as successes frequently had tragic, long-term consequences. As agency officials point out, they have the power to keep secrets for reasons of national security. The National Security Act of 1947 also requires the DCI to protect intelligence sources and methods. No observer would question that there are very good reasons for classifying documents. Too often, however, the CIA has invoked "sources and methods" to keep embarrassing information out of the hands of scholars.

As Thomas Powers explained in *The Man Who Kept the Secrets*, the forces of secrecy at Langley have repeatedly distorted the agency's history:

> CIA people are cynical in most ways, but their belief in secrets is almost metaphysical. In their bones they believe they know the answer to that ancient paradox of epistemology, which asks: If a tree falls in the forest without witness, is there any sound? The CIA would say no. It would agree with historian David Hackett Fisher that history is not what happened but what the surviving evidence says happened. If you can hide the evidence and keep the secrets, then you can write the history.[143]

This study illustrates that not enough has changed at the CIA since Powers made this observation in 1979.

5 | "We Either Get Out and Sell, or We Get Hammered"

The Spinning of Torture, 2002–2017

I want to be absolutely clear with our people, and the world: the United States does not torture.
—President George W. Bush (September 2006)

We tortured some folks.
—President Barack Obama (August 2014)

When Khaled el-Masri arrived at the border of Macedonia on December 31, 2003, he thought that his vacation was about to begin. Within a matter of minutes, however, the vacation turned into a nightmare. The border guards were apparently under the impression that Khaled el-Masri, a German citizen, was Khalid al-Masri, a suspect in the attacks of September 11, 2001. Macedonian officials detained el-Masri for more than three weeks before turning him over to the CIA. Shortly after being rendered to Afghanistan, he was bluntly informed that the rule of law no longer applied: "Where you are right now there is no law, no rights, no one knows you are here, and no one cares about you."[1] His interrogators believed that he was "a senior Qaeda operative who was trained in Jalalabad, Afghanistan," and accused him of knowing Mohamed Atta, the lead hijacker of American Airlines Flight 11.[2] El-Masri received multiple beatings throughout his ordeal. Although he was aggressively questioned about 9/11, he maintained his innocence; as he later explained in the *Los Angeles Times,* "I told the truth: that I had no connection to any terrorists, had never been in Afghanistan and had never been involved in any extremism. I asked repeatedly to meet with a representative of the German government, or a lawyer, or to be brought before a court. Always, my requests were ignored."[3] CIA records from January 2004 confirm that el-Masri insisted to his captors "[the CIA] has the wrong person."[4]

El-Masri was finally released on May 29, 2004.[5] The *New York Times* reported his allegations in January 2005, and in the months that followed, the CIA's covert program to detain suspected terrorists in secret prisons began to unravel.[6] Senator Jack Rockefeller (D-WV), the vice chairman of the Senate Select Committee on Intelligence, announced on February 3 a proposal "to conduct a comprehensive Committee investigation of the CIA's detention, interrogation and rendition activities, including a review of the legality and effectiveness of CIA interrogations."[7] CIA officials were determined to block the investigation, and they developed a plan to "shut Rockefeller up."[8] Not surprisingly, public relations would be at the center of this plan. On April 13, John P. Mudd, the deputy director of the Counterterrorist Center at the CIA, provided one of the most revealing descriptions of the agency's obsession with public relations that has ever been written: "We either get out and sell, or we get hammered, which has implications beyond the media. [C]ongress reads it, cuts our authorities, messes up our budget. [W]e need to make sure the impression of what we do is positive."[9] From Mudd's perspective, the CIA "must be more aggressive out there. [W]e either put out our story or we get eaten. [T]here is no middle ground."[10] Although the detention program was classified, CIA officials decided to provide information to reporters. Mudd observed, "when the w post/ny times [*Washington Post/New York Times*] quotes 'senior intel. official[s],' it's us . . . authorized and directed by opa [Office of Public Affairs]."[11]

The top officials at the CIA apparently agreed with Mudd's advice, and they set in motion an elaborate public relations offensive that lasted for several years. Much of the information relating to the CIA's strategy remains classified, but it is clear that the program went through two phases. In the first phase, the primary objective of the CIA was to prevent a congressional investigation of the CIA's secret prisons. The Senate Intelligence Committee discovered that agency officials provided "classified information on the CIA's Detention and Interrogation Program to select members of the media to counter public criticism, shape public opinion, and avoid potential congressional action to restrict the CIA's detention and interrogation authorities and budget."[12] James Pavitt, the deputy director for operations between 1999 and 2004, feared that the American people would learn about what the CIA had done in those prisons; as he explained to the Office of the Inspector General in 2003, disclosure of the covert program was "the CIA's worst nightmare."[13] Documents from the office reveal that DCI George Tenet shared Pavitt's assessment: "Tenet believes that if the general public were to find out about this program, many would believe we are torturers."[14] Mudd and his superiors must have been relieved when—shortly after Mudd's "get out and sell" message—the intelligence committee voted to reject the investigation that Senator Rockefeller had proposed.[15]

CIA officials became increasingly frustrated and concerned about revelations in the media. A key turning point was Dana Priest's exposé of the CIA's foreign prisons, which appeared on the front page of the *Washington Post* on November 2, 2005. Priest revealed that over "100 suspected terrorists have been sent by the CIA into the covert system, according to current and former U.S. intelligence officials and foreign sources."[16] Her sources were excellent: the Senate Intelligence Committee later determined that the number of detainees was 119 (see table 5.1). Perhaps most disturbingly, Priest noted, "virtually nothing is known about who is kept in the facilities, what interrogation methods are employed with them, or how decisions are made about whether they should be detained or for how long."[17] Top officials at the agency had attempted to convince the *Washington Post* not to publish Priest's article, but they were ultimately unsuccessful.[18] Less than a week after the *Washington Post* ran the story, the CIA had to shut down their secret prison in Romania (see table 5.2).[19]

Despite the uproar that Priest's article created in late 2005, the CIA was able to hold off an investigation for over three years. But everything changed in 2009. The Senate—with the Democrats now in the majority—launched an inquiry into the detention and interrogation program. Senator Dianne Feinstein (D-CA), who chaired the Senate Intelligence Committee throughout the investigation, says that between 2009 and 2012 "a small group of Committee staff reviewed the more than six million pages of CIA materials, to include operational cables, intelligence reports, internal memoranda and emails, briefing materials, interview transcripts, contracts, and other records."[20] The final report, which the Senate finalized and approved in 2012, is over 6,700 pages and still classified. An executive summary was released in December 2014.

Once it became clear that the congressional investigation was inevitable, the CIA's public relations campaign entered its second phase. While the first phase had focused primarily on influencing reporters, the second phase was considerably more ambitious and remarkably similar to CIA public relations in the mid-1970s. As noted in the first chapter, David A. Phillips retired from the agency in May 1975 and he skillfully orchestrated a counter-offensive against critics of the CIA.

Table 5.1 Number of detainees entering the CIA's Detention and
Interrogation Program by year

Year	Number of Detainees
2002	38
2003	53
2004	22
2005	4
2006	1
2007	1

Source: Committee Study of the Central Intelligence Agency's Detention and Interrogation Program (2014), Appendix 2.

Table 5.2 CIA prisons

Location	Color Indication in SSCI[a] Executive Summary	Dates Operated
Thailand	Green	March 2000–December 2002
Afghanistan (Salt Pit)	Cobalt	September 2002–2004
Poland (Quartz)	Blue	December 2002–September 2003
Afghanistan	Gray	2003
Romania	Black	2003–2005
Afghanistan	Orange	2004–2006
Lithuania	Violet	2005–2006
Afghanistan	Brown	2006–2008

[a]Senate Select Committee on Intelligence.
Source: Adam Goldman and Julie Tate, "Decoding the Secret Black Sites on the Senate's Report on the CIA Interrogation Program," *Washington Post,* 9 December 2014.

In an interesting historical twist, José A. Rodriguez Jr. joined the CIA around eighteen months after Phillips's retirement. Rodriguez rose quickly through the ranks, ascending in 1995 to the top of the Latin American Division in the Directorate of Operations, the same position that Phillips had once held.[21] After the attacks on September 11, 2001, Rodriguez took over the Counterterrorist Center and finished his career as the deputy director for operations.

Upon retiring from the CIA in January 2008, Rodriguez emerged as the central figure in the second phase of the CIA's public relations offensive. Like Phillips, Rodriguez utilized skills that he had learned during his CIA career. Rodriguez teamed up with Bill Harlow, the director of the Office of Public Affairs at Langley under George Tenet. The only person with a greater impact on that office was Herbert Hetu. Journalists Michael Isikoff and David Corn describe Harlow in *Hubris* as "a moody, brooding part-time novelist, [who] probably played the media better than any government press officer in town."[22] Harlow had already helped Tenet write his memoir, and he would provide similar assistance to Rodriguez.[23] The book that resulted from their collaboration is not a traditional CIA memoir; in fact, the central objective of *Hard Measures* is to defend the CIA's detention and interrogation program. It is common for retired CIA officers to express strong opinions in their memoirs, but Rodriguez provides an extremely misleading account of what happened inside the agency's secret prisons that crosses the line into the realm of propaganda.

Since the executive summary of the Senate investigation was not released until 2014, *Hard Measures,* which was a *New York Times* best seller, controlled the narrative for over two years. Rodriguez argues that the secret prisons received excellent supervision; that the detainees were well treated; and that the critics of the programs were misinformed. Rodriguez called it "the most effective and carefully managed program I was involved with in my thirty-one years at the CIA. But I also say that without doubt it remains the most maligned, misunderstood, and mischaracterized mission in the Agency's mystery-clouded history."[24] In his account of the clandestine program, for example, the detainees had phenomenal healthcare: "Whether they cooperated or not, we took exceptionally good care of them. The detainees had access to outstanding medical, dental, and even vision care. . . . The medical care they received far exceeded that which was available to their captors."[25]

After reviewing millions of pages of CIA records, the Senate investigation developed a vastly different assessment of the program than Rodriguez: "The CIA's management and operation of its Detention and Interrogation Program was deeply flawed throughout the program's duration, particularly so in 2002 and early 2003."[26] Including Khaled el-Masri, at least twenty-six of the 119 detainees were "wrongfully held."[27] The CIA did not keep adequate records of prisoners held in Afghanistan at the beginning of the program, which reveals a fundamental lack of oversight from CIA headquarters.[28] The CIA station in Afghanistan reported to Langley in December 2003, "we have made the unsettling discovery that we are holding a number of detainees about whom we know very little. The majority of detainees [in Afghanistan] have not been debriefed for months and, in some cases, for over a year. . . . In a few cases, there does not appear to be enough evidence to continue incarceration, and, if this is in fact the case, the detainees should be released."[29] El-Masri would be rendered to Afghanistan the following month, a decision that strongly suggests the CIA was not learning from its mistakes.

The Senate investigation also determined that "the conditions of confinement for CIA detainees were harsher than the CIA had represented to policymakers and others."[30] For instance, the prisoners held at the Salt Pit, one of the CIA's four secret prisons in Afghanistan, "were kept in complete darkness and constantly shackled in isolated cells with loud noise or music and only a bucket to use for human waste."[31] The CIA officer in charge of interrogation admitted to the Office of the Inspector General that the Salt Pit "is good for interrogations because it is the closest thing he has seen to a dungeon."[32] To make the situation even worse, the CIA interrogators were not properly vetted and did not receive sufficient training: "Numerous CIA officers had serious documented personal and professional problems—including histories of violence and records of abusive treatment of others—that should have called into question their suitability to participate in the CIA's Detention and Interrogation Program, their employment with the CIA, and their continued access to classified information."[33] In fairness, there were officials at the CIA who recommended a more thorough selection process for the interrogators. The legal staff at the Counterterrorist Center argued that it was essential for lawyers to get involved. Yet Rodriguez vehemently opposed the plan: "I do not think that CTC/LGL [Counterterrorist Center/Legal] should or would want to get into the business of vetting participants, observers, instructors or others that are involved in this [detention and interrogation] program. It is simply not [their] job."[34]

If Rodriguez had been more willing to allow oversight of the secret program, it is possible that at least some of the abuses could have been prevented. The CIA officer in charge of the Salt Pit facility did not have any training or experience in interrogations, and more shockingly, his own colleagues had previously warned that he demonstrated "a lack of honesty, judgment, and maturity."[35] One supervisor at the agency noted that the officer had "issues with judgment and maturity, [and his] potential behavior in the field is also worrisome."[36] These concerns would be prophetic. While running the Salt Pit, the CIA officer was directly involved in the interrogation of a detainee named Gul Rahman, on whom he implemented a variety of interrogation techniques without prior approval from Langley; Rahman, a suspected terrorist, underwent "48 hours of sleep deprivation, auditory overload, total darkness, isolation, a cold shower, and rough treatment."[37] It is unclear how many times Rahman was forced under a cold shower, but one CIA witness explains that the detainee "was so cold that he could barely utter his alias . . . [and then he was] moved to one of the four sleep deprivation cells where he was left shivering for hours or overnight with his hand chained over his head."[38] Another witness described a concerted effort to break Rahman. "They dragged him outside [of his cell], cut off his clothes and secured him with Mylar tape," said the contractor. "They covered his head with a hood and ran him up and down a long corridor adjacent to his cell. They slapped him and punched him several times."[39]

In November 2002, the CIA officer in charge of the Salt Pit ordered his subordinates to shackle Rahman inside his cell. Naked from the waist down, Rahman was found dead the next day.[40] Not only was he never punished for the incident, the CIA officer apparently received a $2,500 bonus four months later for "consistently superior work."[41] Rodriguez does not even mention Gul Rahman's name in *Hard Measures*, but when the Office of the Inspector General interviewed him in August 2003,[42] Rodriguez attempted to distance himself from what had happened inside the Salt Pit. This interview directly contradicts the argument that the detention and interrogation program was well supervised. Rodriguez, then director of the Counterterrorist Center, did not provide more oversight of the facility, for, in his words, he had "other higher priorities."[43]

In falsely claiming that the CIA program was properly managed, Rodriguez consistently maintained that there was overwhelming support for aggressive interrogation at the agency; "the people involved, almost to a man and woman, have told me that they were extraordinarily proud of what we did," he says in his memoir.[44] John Rizzo, who served in the CIA's legal division for over three decades, went even further in his memoir: "Every, and I mean every, career CIA employee who was involved in it believed in it wholeheartedly and unswervingly."[45] The assertions of Rodriguez and Rizzo are simply false. From the beginning of the program, CIA officials questioned the legality and the morality of the interrogation tactics. The CIA's chief interrogator, who had been involved in waterboarding, told his superiors at the Counterterrorist Center (presumably Rodriguez) that he would "no longer be associated in any way with the interrogation program due to serious reservation[s] about the current state of affairs."[46] His e-mail on January 22, 2003, described the program as "a train wreck waiting to happen and I intend to get the hell off the train before it happens."[47]

Other CIA officers involved in waterboarding held similar concerns. Abu Zubaydah was the first detainee in the CIA program, and in August 2002, he was also the first prisoner to be waterboarded. The interrogators of Zubaydah were most likely chosen for their toughness; yet internal CIA records reveal that "several on the team [were] profoundly affected [by the interrogation] . . . some to the point of tears and choking up."[48] On the following day, CIA officials worried that as many as three interrogators would request transfers because they no longer wanted to participate.[49] But did Rodriguez know about these concerns in the field? Based on the available information, he was fully aware. In fact, he did not respond kindly when he learned about the criticism. He issued a clear directive to his interrogators on August 12, 2002: "[I] strongly urge that any speculative language as to the legality of given [interrogation] activities or, more precisely, judgment calls as to their legality vis-à-vis operational guidelines for this activity agreed upon and vetted at the most senior levels of the agency, be refrained from in written traffic (email or cable traffic). Such language is not helpful."[50] It is important to keep in mind that Rodriguez had graduated from law school at the University of Florida before joining the CIA, and he also survived the Iran-Contra scandal during the 1980s.[51] Given his background, it seems logical that Rodriguez understood the important role that documents would have in any future investigation. The available evidence strongly indicates that he wanted to manipulate the historical record as early as 2002, ten years before the publication of *Hard Measures*. One CIA interrogator admitted to the Office of the Inspector General in 2003 that nothing critical was put into writing; from his experience in the program, the "cables reflect things that are 'all rosy.'"[52]

In addition to arguing that the program was closely supervised, Rodriguez maintains that the interrogation used at the secret prisons was not torture. In his opinion, "the treatment that a small handful of terrorists received at our hands was unpleasant. It was unpleasant for them and, not insignificantly, unpleasant for us. But we went to great lengths to make sure that it was legal, safe, and effective."[53] He points out that the interrogation methods were "approved by the highest levels of the U.S. government, certified as legal by the Department of Justice, and briefed to and supported by bipartisan leadership of [the] congressional intelligence oversight committees."[54] The entire legal justification for the so-called enhanced interrogation techniques (EITs) can be traced to the Office of Legal Counsel at the Department of Justice. In the summer of 2002, John Yoo, then a thirty-five-year-old deputy assistant attorney general, prepared an eighteen-page memo for his boss, Assistant Attorney General Jay S. Bybee. The memo authorized the use of ten EITs in the questioning of Abu Zubaydah, who was held at a CIA prison in Thailand: "(1) attention grasp, (2) walling, (3) facial hold, (4) facial slap (insult slap), (5) cramped confinement, (6) wall standing, (7) stress positions, (8) sleep deprivation, (9) insects placed in a confinement box, and (10) the waterboard."[55] Yoo provided detailed descriptions of each technique in the memo. When waterboarding a prisoner, he noted:

> The individual is bound securely to an inclined bench, which is approximately four feet by seven feet. The individual's feet are generally elevated. A cloth is placed over the forehead and eyes. Water is then applied to the cloth in a controlled manner. As this is done, the cloth is lowered until it covers both the nose and mouth. Once the cloth is saturated and completely covers the mouth and nose, air flow is slightly restricted for 20 to 40 seconds due to the presence of the cloth.[56]

As the detainee's oxygen level decreased, he would experience "the perception of drowning. The individual does not breathe any water into his lungs."[57] Assistant Attorney General Bybee signed the memo on August 1, 2002. The techniques were subsequently used on an additional thirty-eight detainees.

When defending the EITs, Rodriguez quotes extensively from Bybee's memo.[58] "Although we were authorized to conduct waterboarding as described [in the memo]," he observes, "in fact our officers in the field used far *less* water for far shorter periods of time than they were allowed."[59] This statement is extremely misleading. Just weeks after Bybee signed the memo, CIA interrogators in Thailand used a style of waterboarding that did not comply with the Justice Department's description of the technique. To ensure the safety of Zubaydah, it is clear that he was not supposed to ingest water; yet on at least one occasion, he "became completely unresponsive, with bubbles rising through his open, full mouth."[60] During the waterboarding of Khalid Sheikh Mohammed (KSM) seven months later, the interrogators again exceeded the guidelines. KSM ingested so much water that his "abdomen was somewhat distended and he expressed water when the abdomen was pressed."[61] The medical expert who witnessed the interrogation noted the brutality of what was happening: "In the new technique we are basically doing a series of near drownings."[62]

Internal CIA records make it abundantly clear that agency officials were aware that detainees subjected to EITs could be severely hurt or even killed. In the event that harsh interrogation killed Zubaydah, for instance, the CIA planned on cremating his body.[63] Zubaydah did not die, but at some point during his detention, he lost his left eye.[64] Rodriguez had claimed that the detainees had access to excellent healthcare, but the documents tell a different story. According to one directive to the field in 2002, "the interrogation process takes precedence over preventative medical procedures."[65] When Senator Bill Nelson (D-FL) volunteered to be waterboarded in order to personally assess the technique, CIA officials refused to provide him the demonstration. They were concerned that Senator Nelson might have a heart attack "during the experiment," says Rodriguez.[66]

Rodriguez also maintains that the EITs were only used when a detainee refused to cooperate, and once the decision was made, the interrogation process would be gradual and closely monitored. "If a terrorist cooperated with us from the start," he alleged, "none [no EITs] would be employed. If he was nonresponsive, the most benign tactics were used first, and only after the detainee showed that he continued to be noncompliant and after specific written authorization from Agency headquarters would a more aggressive technique be used."[67] Like so many of his assertions, there is no truth to this claim. The Senate investigation found that there were many prisoners who were never given the opportunity to cooperate. In 2003, for example, "at least six detainees were stripped and shackled nude, placed in the standing position for sleep deprivation, or subjected to other CIA enhanced interrogation techniques prior to being questioned by an interrogator. . . . Five of these detainees were shackled naked in the standing position with their hands above their head immediately after their medical check."[68] Interrogators inside the secret prisons had a great deal of control over the process; in fact, "at least 17 CIA detainees . . . were subjected to one or more CIA enhanced interrogation techniques without CIA

Headquarters approval."[69] The CIA has officially acknowledged water-boarding only three detainees. However, there is strong evidence that indicates that the number may have been higher. A photograph taken at the Salt Pit shows that a waterboard was present at the secret prison even though the CIA claims that none of the prisoners there were inter-rogated using the technique; according to the description in the execu-tive summary, "the waterboard device in the photograph is surrounded by buckets, with a bottle of unknown pink solution (filled two-thirds of the way to the top) and a watering can resting on the wooden beams of the waterboard."[70]

Although the media has focused extensively on waterboarding, it is often overlooked that the CIA developed another technique known as water dousing. Unlike waterboarding, the Department of Justice never approved water dousing. Prisoners at the Salt Pit "were often held down, naked, on a tarp on the floor, with the tarp pulled up around them to form a makeshift tub, while cold or refrigerated water was poured on them. Others were hosed down repeatedly while they were shackled naked, in the standing sleep deprivation position."[71] A CIA interroga-tor who used water dousing described the technique, and he e-mailed headquarters in 2003 to warn them. "If one is held down on his back, on the table or on the floor, with water poured in his face I think it goes beyond dousing and the effect . . . could be indistinguishable from the water board," the interrogator noted. "I have real problems with putting one of them on the water board for 'dousing.' Putting him in a head down attitude and pouring water around his chest and face is just too close to the water board, and if it is continued [it] may lead to problems for us."[72] The CIA officer in charge of the Salt Pit used water dousing extensively. This is the same officer who was directly involved in the death of Gul Rahman; according to one witness, he "poured cold water directly on [another detainee's] face to disrupt his breathing."[73] The cloth covering the detainee's face was only removed after the prisoner "turned blue."[74]

Rodriguez says nothing about water dousing in *Hard Measures*, but he does devote an entire chapter to KSM. He contends, "the harsh treat-ment [of KSM], which I believe to have been 'necessary roughness,' lasted for only days."[75] What happened to KSM, the forty-fifth detainee to enter the CIA's detention program, was more complicated than Rod-riguez acknowledges. After KSM was captured in Pakistan on March 1, 2003, he was quickly rendered to the Salt Pit in Afghanistan. Just minutes after the interrogation of KSM began, CIA officers implemented approved as well as unapproved EITs. In addition to rectal rehydration, "KSM was subjected to facial and abdominal slaps, the facial grab, stress positions, standing sleep deprivation . . . nudity, and water dousing."[76]

The CIA soon transferred KSM from the Salt Pit to the agency's secret prison in Poland.[77] CIA contractors commenced with additional EITs: "nudity, standing sleep deprivation, the attention grab and insult slap, the facial grab, the abdominal slap, the kneeling stress position, and walling."[78] On the day that KSM arrived in Poland, the contractors also threatened his children. CIA headquarters clearly sanctioned the aggressive tone of the interrogation: "I want to know what he [KSM] knows, and I want to know it fast," declared then Director of the Directorate of Operations James Pavitt.[79] Between March 10 and March 24, CIA interrogators waterboarded KSM on fifteen separate occasions. The total number of applications of water to the mouth would reach 183. CIA officials, however, were disappointed with the lack of results. On March 14, the deputy director of the agency's clandestine interrogation program acknowledged that KSM was not breaking; the waterboard "has proven ineffective."[80] Four days later the CIA experimented with sleep deprivation, keeping KSM awake for over seven days. For most of these 180 hours, he was kept standing, although there were at least four waterboarding sessions.[81] During the final waterboarding session on March 24, the CIA characterized KSM as "composed, stoic, and resigned."[82]

For reasons that remain unclear, the CIA stopped using EITs against KSM the following day. Defenders of the harsh interrogation methods correctly point out that these techniques were successful in getting KSM to talk. The available evidence demonstrates that KSM manipulated his interrogators from the beginning of his detention, providing information that was false and misleading. Less than a week after his capture, KSM told CIA officers about a person that he trusted to guard his family. The interrogators were thrilled with the tip, and CIA officers used the information to capture two men in 2003. Both of these men were innocent. Although the CIA eventually freed them, the agency imprisoned Shaistah Habibullah Kahn for around seven months and Sayed Habib for over a year.[83]

After waterboarding KSM on March 22, the CIA once again believed that they had scored a major victory in the war on terrorism. KSM appeared compliant, informing his interrogators that he was "ready to talk."[84] He confessed direct involvement in a terrorist plot inside the United States: he had dispatched an operative to Montana with the objective of recruiting African American Muslims.[85] At the time of his "confession," KSM had been extensively waterboarded and had not slept for several days. The CIA should have recognized that they were being played, but according to Jane Mayer, the intelligence community went "on a wild-goose chase for black Muslim Al Qaeda operatives in Montana."[86] Not surprisingly, they never found any evidence of a sleeper cell in Montana, and KSM later recanted the entire story.

Rodriguez has argued that the EITs were effective in making the CIA's detainees compliant. Given the evidence that has emerged about the program, it would be more accurate to say that EITs produced the illusion of compliance. In the words of an unidentified CIA official, "What KSM's doing is fairly typical of other [CIA] detainees. . . . [They] are doing what makes sense in their situation—pretend cooperation."[87] KSM certainly provided information, but it was often false or designed to manipulate. In June 2003, over two months after the EITs had ended, officials at Langley worried, "KSM is withholding, exaggerating, misdirecting, or outright fabricating information on CBRN [chemical, biological, radiological, and nuclear] issues."[88] During his detention, KSM intentionally provided wrong names to the CIA and misidentified terror suspects in photographs. A top CIA official lamented in October 2003 that KSM was "obstructing our ability to acquire good information," since he "misidentifie[s] photos when he knows we are fishing."[89] The official also complained that KSM "misleads us on telephone numbers."[90]

The interrogation of KSM has been a central theme in CIA public relations. In the immediate aftermath of the successful raid in Abbottabad, Pakistan, that killed Osama bin Laden on May 2, 2011, Rodriguez and other CIA officials developed a myth that has become entrenched in popular culture. *Time* magazine published an article on May 4 based on an interview with Rodriguez. "Information provided by KSM and Abu Faraj al-Libbi about bin Laden's courier was the lead information that eventually led to the location of [bin Laden's] compound and the operation that led to his death," he declared.[91] The *Wall Street Journal* printed an editorial from Michael B. Mukasey on May 6 titled "The Waterboarding Trail to bin Laden." Mukasey, President George W. Bush's last attorney general, falsely claimed that the discovery of bin Laden's compound "began with a disclosure from Khalid Sheikh Mohammed (KSM), who broke like a dam under the pressure of harsh interrogation techniques that included waterboarding. He loosed a torrent of information—including eventually the nickname of a trusted courier of bin Laden."[92] General Michael Hayden, the CIA director between 2006 and 2009, made similar assertions in television interviews at this time.[93] In *Hard Measures,* which was published about a year after bin Laden's assassination, Rodriguez continued to maintain that the Seal Team Six operation in May 2011 "started with information a detainee provided after receiving EITs bolstered by information that KSM and Abu Faraj al-Libi [*sic*] (who both became compliant after receiving EITs) gave us, whether they meant to or not."[94]

It is abundantly clear that former CIA and White House officials developed a coordinated public relations strategy after bin Laden's death; one of their main talking points, which was repeated extensively, was straightforward: the CIA's EITs led to the identification of bin Laden's courier, and the courier ultimately led the CIA to bin Laden's compound in Abbottabad.[95] The Office of Public Relations at the CIA took a position that was almost identical to the one former officials had taken. In fact, Leon Panetta, the CIA director between 2009 and 2011, has revealed that he informed the agency's public relations director about the top secret plan to raid bin Laden's compound over a month before the operation was executed.[96] As Seal Team Six prepared to raid bin Laden's compound, public relations officials at the CIA were busy with their own plans. They recognized that the raid—if successful in killing or capturing bin Laden—could be used to enhance the agency's image. Most of the details of the public relations campaign remain classified, but it is known that the strategy had three primary points. The first, and arguably most important, was to emphasize "the critical nature of [the] detainee reporting in identifying Bin Ladin's courier."[97]

Within hours of the raid, the Office of Public Affairs targeted the media as precisely and effectively as Seal Team Six had targeted bin Laden's compound. Mark Mazzetti, a national security reporter at the *New York Times,* appears to have been one of the CIA's primary targets. On May 2, 2011, Mazzetti was the lead author of an article that directly followed the CIA's prepackaged script. "Behind the Hunt for Bin Laden" describes the prolonged silence in the Situation Room the previous evening that finally ended with perhaps the most famous quote in recent presidential history: "We got him," President Obama declared.[98] Just a few sentences later, Mazzetti and his colleagues presented the CIA's public relations campaign as the true account of how bin Laden was found.

According to the article, EITs led the CIA to compound: "It wasn't until after 2002, when the agency began rounding up Qaeda operatives—and subjecting them to hours of brutal interrogation sessions in secret overseas prisons—that they finally began filling in the gaps about the foot soldiers, couriers and money men Bin Laden relied on."[99] Mazzetti accepted the CIA's version of events just as Judith Miller had previously accepted the Bush administration's false claim that Saddam Hussein possessed weapons of mass destruction.

The Office of Public Relations would soon expand their public relations campaign, focusing extensively on popular culture. Panetta was directly involved in this effort. In April 2010, he met Kathryn Bigelow, the acclaimed Hollywood director who, a month earlier, had received an Academy Award for *The Hurt Locker* (2008). Mark Boal, a former journalist, won an Academy Award for the film's screenplay. Bigelow explained to Panetta that she was collaborating again with Boal on a movie that told the story of bin Laden's escape from Tora Bora after the American invasion of Afghanistan in 2001. Panetta agreed to provide assistance to the filmmakers.[100] Boal had almost finished the screenplay for the movie when bin Laden was killed, and he ultimately decided to begin an entirely new script about how the CIA tracked him down.

On May 10, 2011, the Office of Public Relations received a letter from Boal formally requesting assistance from the CIA.[101] The letter led to a conference call on May 17, and three days later Boal met with Panetta's chief of staff and George Little, the director of public affairs. Based on the documents that have been declassified, it appears that the CIA received similar requests from other filmmakers. Public relations officials, however, recognized that they should give priority to Bigelow's film. Marie E. Harf, then the CIA spokesperson, e-mailed Little on June 7 to voice her strong support for the movie. "I know we don't 'pick favorites' but it makes sense to get behind the winning horse. . . . Mark and Kathryn's movie is going to be the first and the biggest. It's got the most money behind it, and two Oscar winners on board," Harf explained.[102] Boal visited CIA headquarters again the same week that Harf sent this e-mail. During his visit, Boal had meetings with Panetta's chief of staff, the director of the Counterterrorist Center, the deputy director of the center, and other CIA officers. He also met with Michael Morell, the deputy director of the CIA.[103]

Boal returned to the CIA on June 24. In addition to meeting with Counterterrorist Center officers, he was also invited to attend a ceremony honoring the members of Seal Team Six who had participated in the bin Laden operation. Boal's appearance at the event would later lead to an internal investigation. When the Office of the Inspector General questioned him, Panetta said that he did not know Boal had been invited to the ceremony, and he also claimed "he never met Boal and, therefore, would not be able to identify him."[104] The Office of the Inspector General "found no information that affirmatively identified who authorized Boal's invitation to the UBL Operation Awards Ceremony."[105] However, the evidence strongly indicates that Panetta lied to the investigators, for in May 2010, he sat at the same table with Boal and Bigelow at the White House Correspondents' Dinner.[106] The investigation concluded that "Panetta disclosed classified information during his speech at the 24 June 2011 UBL Operation Awards Ceremony," but the Department of Justice declined to pursue the case.[107]

Kathryn Bigelow visited CIA headquarters on July 15 for almost three hours. She received several tours, and she also met with Morell.[108] From Harf's perspective, the visit "went really, really well." During Bigelow's meeting with Morell, which lasted forty minutes, he reportedly "gushed to [K]athryn about how much he loved [*The Hurt Locker*]."[109] The following week the filmmakers spent several more hours at the CIA, meeting with two CIA officers and "the translator who was on the raid."[110] Several CIA officials also had off-site meetings with the filmmakers in Washington, DC and Los Angeles. The Office of the Inspector General determined that these officials were collectively treated to at least eleven meals, and that a few individuals even received gifts. One CIA officer received a bottle of tequila valued at $169.99.[111]

The CIA provided Boal with unprecedented access to information; for instance, when Boal's assistant e-mailed Harf with a question about the floor plan of the compound in Abbottabad, he received a quick response. "I checked with our folks," Harf replied, "and that floor plan matches up with what we have. It looks legit to us."[112] Boal e-mailed Little on July 20 to "say thanks and thanks again for pulling for us at the agency. It made all the difference."[113] He also extensively praised Harf; "as you know Harf logged many, many extra miles on this project with total finesse," said Boal, "and she has our complete confidence going forward."[114] Once Boal completed the screenplay, he contacted the Office of Public Affairs, and in four separate telephone conversations, he read them the script.[115] While it is unclear if the filmmakers had agreed earlier to share the script with the CIA in exchange for the assistance, the evidence demonstrates that the agency was able to convince them to make changes. The initial screenplay included a scene at "a rooftop party in Islamabad where an officer, after drinking, fires a celebratory burst of AK-47 gunfire into the air."[116] Public affairs officers were less than thrilled, informing Boal that "mixing drinking and firearms is a major violation and actions like this do not happen in real life. We requested this be taken out of the film."[117] If Boal had investigated further, he would have learned that such violations have actually happened. (For instance, CIA officer Lou Conein, who helped overthrow the president of South Vietnam in 1963, had a passion for alcohol and firearms—once opening fire on his own car when it failed to start at the Saigon Airport.)[118] Boal, however, agreed to this request, and he also complied when asked to remove dogs from an interrogation scene.[119]

Given the extent of the CIA's involvement with Boal and Bigelow, it was only a matter of time before journalists discovered the connection. Maureen Dowd briefly outlined the collaboration in her *New York Times* column on August 6, revealing how "Boal got welcomed to the upper echelons of the White House and the Pentagon and showed up recently—to the surprise of some military officers—at a C.I.A. ceremony celebrating the hero Seals."[120] Dowd had asked Mazzetti to fact check the story, but she obviously did not anticipate that he would leak a copy to Harf; adopting the CIA's strategy of plausible deniability, Mazzetti informed Harf that "this [Dowd's column] didn't come from me . . . please delete after you read."[121] The e-mail exchange between Mazzetti and Harf illustrates Mazzetti's cozy relationship with the Office of Public Affairs and helps to explain why he so uncritically accepted the CIA's assessment of the use of EITs in the hunt for bin Laden. National security reporters are expected to receive leaked government documents; in a disturbing reversal of roles, however, Mazzetti leaked information to the CIA. Although it was a blatant violation of journalistic ethics, Mazzetti's superiors at the *New York Times* took no disciplinary action against him.

Dowd's column in August 2011 ignited a firestorm long before the movie was filmed. Conservative critics pointed out that the movie would be released in October 2012, and from their perspective, the Obama administration was manipulating the filmmakers to secure a victory in the November election. However, *Zero Dark Thirty* was not released until December 2012, which undermined the conspiracy theories. Moreover, when the film was finally released, it became clear that Boal told the story of the Seal Team Six operation almost entirely through the eyes of CIA officials. The opening minutes of the film are arguably the most horrifying in American film history; the audience can see only a black screen, but they hear a cacophony of actual emergency response calls from September 11, 2001. There is an overwhelming sense of panic: screams are heard, and there is desperation in the voices. Although the words are unintelligible at first, a woman can be heard pleading with an operator: "There is no one here yet, and the floor is completely engulfed," she yells. "We're on the floor, and we can't breathe. . . . I'm going to die, aren't I. . . . I'm going to die. . . . I'm going to die. Please God."[122] The caller then explains what is happening: "It's so hot I'm burning up."[123] Before this moment, the 911 operator had been attempting to calm the woman; yet she now recognizes the tragedy that is unfolding, exclaiming, "Oh my God."[124]

The next sound heard in the film is a metal door swinging open at a CIA prison. Dan, the CIA interrogator (played by Jason Clarke), is angry, and Kathryn Bigelow clearly encourages the audience to share this rage, since the detainee allegedly funded the 9/11 attacks. "If you lie to me," Dan coldly warns the terrorist, "I'm going to hurt you."[125] Later in the movie, he is even more direct with another prisoner: "Can I be honest with you? I'm bad fucking news. I'm not your friend. I'm not gonna help you. I'm going to break you. Any questions?"[126] Although Bigelow depicts the brutality of the EITs, she portrays them as extremely effective. The interrogation of the first detainee unfolds in two segments, each lasting less than eight minutes. Dan, with the assistance of Maya (played by Jessica Chastain), quickly breaks him, and he provides the name of bin Laden's courier.

The film reveals the difficulty of locating the courier. Bigelow skillfully shows the desperation at the CIA, including footage of terrorist attacks in Khobar, Saudi Arabia, in May 2004; London in July 2005; and Islamabad, Pakistan, in 2008; as well as the unsuccessful plot to bomb Times Square in May 2010. These events build the film's momentum, and Maya emerges as the heroine who dedicates her life to stopping terrorists. Just over an hour into the film, Boal inserts a monologue that effectively reenergizes the audience. A top CIA official named George (played by Mark Strong) is furious at the lack of results: "We are failing. We're spending billions of dollars, people are dying. . . . They attacked us on land in '98, by sea in 2000, and from the air in 2001. They murdered 3,000 of our citizens in cold blood . . . and what the fuck have we done about it? . . . Bring me people to kill."[127] Maya follows orders, and within twenty minutes, bin Laden's compound is located. The final sequence of the film vividly captures the Seal Team Six raid in May 2011; when the team returns to Afghanistan, Maya identifies the body as bin Laden's.

Zero Dark Thirty is one of the most extensively reviewed films in recent history. Frank Bruni of the *New York Times* offered a succinct assessment of the film's narrative structure: "No waterboarding, no Bin Laden."[128] By beginning the film on September 11, 2001, Bruni notes, it is "set up as payback."[129] Writing in *New York Magazine*, David Edelstein called the film "an unholy masterwork."[130] Like Bruni, Edelstein took notice of the favorable depiction of the CIA. "*Zero Dark Thirty* is the most neutral-seeming 'America, fuck yeah!' picture ever made," he opined.[131] In her review of the film, Manohla Dargis conveyed the powerful impact of the torture scenes, arguing, "they linger, casting a long, dreadful shadow over everything that comes after."[132]

When initially promoting *Zero Dark Thiry*, the filmmakers maintained that the film was historically accurate. Boal, of course, was a journalist before he became a screenwriter, and he explained to Charlie Rose that he wrote the screenplay "the same way I would have reported an article."[133] During the same interview with Rose, Bigelow lavished praise on Boal for the research that went into the script. "In my humble opinion Mark [Boal] did an extraordinary job of reporting this," she said. According to the film's production notes, "Boal's inspiration was the New Journalism of the 1960s, when major American writers learned to apply the techniques of literature to the description of real events. In this sense, *Zero Dark Thirty* attempts to move the genre of literary reportage forward, offering the audience a unique kind of movie: the reported film."[134]

But from the perspective of Senators Dianne Feinstein, Carl Levin (D-MI), and John McCain (R-AZ), Boal had done a terrible job reporting the story. At the beginning of their letter to the head of Sony Pictures on December 19, the senators point out that *Zero Dark Thirty* "opens with the words 'based on first-hand accounts of actual events' and there has been significant media coverage of the CIA's cooperation with the screenwriters."[135] The evidence gathered during the Senate investigation of the CIA's detention and interrogation program directly contradicted the film's narrative. "Regardless of what message the filmmakers intended to convey," they explain, "the movie clearly implies that the CIA's coercive interrogation techniques were effective in eliciting important information related to a courier for Usama [*sic*] Bin Laden. We have reviewed CIA records and know that this is incorrect."[136] They worried that the movie had "the potential to shape American public opinion in a disturbing and misleading manner."[137] In essence, the screenplay rewrote the history of the CIA's detention and interrogation program based on false and misleading information; according to the senators, "the filmmakers and your production studio are perpetuating the myth that torture is effective. You have a social and moral obligation to get the facts right."[138]

The letter to Sony Pictures accelerated the media firestorm in the weeks leading up to the movie's nationwide release. Rather than admitting mistakes, Bigelow and Boal vigorously defended the film, but they began to distance themselves from earlier comments comparing the screenplay to journalism. Bigelow authored an editorial that appeared in the *Los Angeles Times,* emphasizing that the torture scenes in the movie did not indicate "endorsement."[139] In her opinion, "confusing 'depiction' with 'endorsement' is the first step toward chilling any American artist's ability and right to shine a light on dark deeds, especially when those deeds are cloaked in layers of secrecy and government obfuscation."[140] More remarkably, she ignores the opening thirty minutes of *Zero Dark Thirty:* "Torture was . . . employed in the early years of the hunt. That doesn't mean it was the key to finding Bin Laden."[141] Yet the central argument of her movie is that torture led to the identification of bin Laden's trusted courier. Interestingly, she made no reference to the assistance the filmmakers received from the CIA. The overall tone of the editorial reveals how effectively the CIA had manipulated the filmmakers; in fact, the final paragraph echoed the CIA's public relations campaign, in which Bigelow argues that "Bin Laden wasn't defeated by superheroes zooming down from the sky; he was defeated by ordinary Americans who fought bravely even as they *sometimes* crossed moral lines, who labored greatly and intently, who gave all of themselves in both victory and defeat, in life and in death, for the defense of this nation."[142]

Just one day after the editorial was published, Matt Taibbi, a contributing editor at *Rolling Stone* magazine, slammed Bigelow in a scathing review. Knowing the cooperation between the filmmakers and the CIA, he observed, "It seems an eerie coincidence that she [Bigelow] was 'honest' about torture in pretty much exactly the way a CIA interrogator would have told the story, without including much else."[143] Taibbi believed it was delusional to claim that the film was not an endorsement of torture. "There's no way to watch *Zero Dark Thirty* without seeing it as a movie about how torture helped us catch Osama bin Laden," he concluded.[144] He also perceptively explained how the CIA had corrupted the film: "What happened with Boal and Bigelow is what you might call 'access drift'—when you really, really love the drama of the story you're hearing, you start leaning in the direction of your sources even if the truth doesn't quite cooperate."[145] In essence, the CIA had successfully manipulated the filmmakers largely by encouraging closeness with agency officials.

Given the controversy surrounding *Zero Dark Thirty*, journalists attempted to assess the accuracy of the screenplay. Peter Maass argued in the *Atlantic* that the movie "represents a new genre of embedded filmmaking that is the problematic offspring of the worrisome endeavor known as embedded journalism."[146] To better understand how the screenplay was written, Maass contacted Boal. The screenwriter's response was evasive and troubling:

> It's not a documentary. . . . I'm not going to go scene by scene or line by line, because first of all I think I've got to have some authorial privilege. . . . My standard is not a journalistic standard of "Is this a word-for-word quote?" I'm not asking to be held to that standard and I'm certainly not representing my film as that. The standard is more, "Is this more or less in the ballpark?"[147]

Yet Boal had told Charlie Rose a week earlier that he developed the script using the same techniques that he previously used as a journalist. Rather than castigating the filmmakers, however, Maass praised aspects of the movie while taking aim at the CIA. He described *Zero Dark Thirty* as "a dazzling film. But what's more dazzling—and frustrating—is the government's skill, time and time again, in getting its story told so uncritically."[148] Although his assessment was more favorable than Taibbi's review, Maass nonetheless criticized the hagiographic portrayal of the CIA; from his perspective, "the film fails to consider the notion that the CIA and the intelligence industry as a whole, rather than being solutions to what threatens us, might be part of the problem."[149] After spending almost three hours in a dark theater, he explained, "we're getting the myth of history before getting the actual history."[150]

Pulitzer Prize–winning journalist Steve Coll provided what is perhaps the best analysis of *Zero Dark Thirty*. Unlike most of the authors who reviewed the film, Coll showcased a detailed understanding of the agency's recent history, and he positioned the movie within that context. Coll noted that the torture scenes illustrated "precisely how the CIA's coercive interrogation regime was constructed to break prisoners, according to José Rodriguez Jr."[151] Other reviewers had discussed the torture scenes, but Coll was more perceptive. "Arguably," he says, "the film's degree of emphasis on torture's significance goes beyond what even the most die-hard defenders of the CIA interrogation regime, such as Rodriguez, have argued."[152] The filmmakers did not adequately research the CIA's use of torture, and as a result, the interrogation scenes are flawed. Given the available evidence, he concludes, "Boal and Bigelow have conflated the pseudoscience of the CIA's clinical, carefully reviewed 'enhanced techniques' such as waterboarding with the out-of-control abuse of prisoners by low-level military police in places such as Abu Ghraib and Guantánamo."[153] In his final analysis Coll writes, "*Zero Dark Thirty* ultimately fails as journalism because it adopts shortcuts that most reporters would find illegitimate."[154]

In addition to the reviews from film critics and journalists, Rodriguez offered a candid appraisal of the movie in the *Washington Post*. Like Coll, he identified obvious mistakes in the interrogation scenes. CIA interrogators never used dog collars, and according to Rodriguez, they also did not use large water pitchers when waterboarding detainees. "Instead of a large bucket," he says, "small plastic water bottles were used on the three men [on whom the CIA admitted waterboarding], who were on medical gurneys."[155] Despite these points of criticism, Rodriguez was impressed with the film: "I had to smile at one scene in which a White House official demands more information from the CIA, only to be asked how the agency is supposed to obtain it when the detention and interrogation program has been taken away. The screenwriter seemed to catch the nuance that the [Obama] administration has made the CIA's job much harder."[156] Although he maintained that Boal had oversimplified the search for bin Laden, Rodriguez agreed that harsh interrogation was of critical importance in the manhunt. From his vantage point, "I saw nothing in *Zero Dark Thirty* that I believed to be classified—unless one considers secret the notion that enhanced interrogation techniques played a role in getting bin Laden. The Senate committee seems to want to punish the agency for telling that truth."[157] Rodriguez strongly recommended the movie, describing it as "well worth seeing."[158]

Most reviewers were captivated by Maya, the CIA officer in the film who relentlessly tracks down bin Laden against all odds. By any standard of measurement, Jessica Chastain's performance is mesmerizing. Roger Ebert observed that "Chastain shows again how versatile an actress she is. Apart from Meryl Streep, who else has appeared in new movies with such a range and ability to convince?"[159] Coll was intrigued that Maya's character was "based on a real-life CIA employee whom Boal reportedly met."[160] In the film, Maya is visibly uncomfortable with the torture of detainees, but she eventually comes to understand that these harsh methods are necessary. Bigelow brilliantly develops the character to argue that while torture is brutal, unpleasant, and even horrifying, it was necessary to find bin Laden. As Matt Taibbi explains, "the idea that audiences weren't supposed to identify with 'Maya the torturer' is ludicrous."[161]

Maya is based on an actual CIA officer named Alfreda F. Bikowsky.[162] Unlike the fictional Maya, however, Bikowsky was never squeamish about enhanced interrogation. Not only was she directly involved in the waterboarding of both Zubaydah and KSM, CIA colleagues believe that she took pleasure in brutalizing the prisoners. For instance, she believed that KSM, who she nicknamed "Mukie," was telling the truth about a terrorist plot in Montana. "Mukie is going to be hatin' life on this one," she declared in an e-mail.[163] KSM, of course, was the mastermind of September 11, 2001, and Bikowsky's eagerness to exact retribution appears connected to the CIA's failure to stop the attacks. Her subordinate at the Counterterrorist Center had failed to share information with the FBI about two of the hijackers. According to NBC, moreover, Bikowsky was directly responsible for the detention of Khaled el-Masri in 2004. Even though her colleagues quickly recognized that el-Masri was innocent, she initially blocked his release.[164]

Bikowsky was instrumental in developing the strategy that the CIA used to defend the detention and interrogation program. In fact, she wrote an e-mail in 2004 about KSM's interrogation that was incredibly misleading. The Senate investigation concluded that this document "would serve as a template on which future justifications for the CIA [detention and interrogation] program and the CIA's enhanced interrogation techniques were based."[165] After analyzing internal CIA records, the Senate determined that her "representations were almost entirely inaccurate."[166] It remains unclear how closely Bikowsky coordinated her efforts with Rodriguez, but when he retired from the agency in 2008, there is no question that his public defense of the program closely followed Bikowsky's strategy. Top CIA officials used her arguments to persuade many politicians that the EITs had been effective and saved lives.

When Mark Boal began visiting CIA headquarters, a female CIA officer, who was almost certainly Bikowsky, realized that she had an unprecedented opportunity to shape popular culture. Beginning in May 2011, she had at least five meetings with Boal at the CIA, and she also met him more than four times at other locations. Remarkably, a representative from the CIA's Office of Public Affairs did not always accompany her.[167] In the summer of 2011, she had several meetings with Boal in his suite at the Jefferson Hotel in Washington, DC. After she reviewed the screenplay for *Zero Dark Thirty* in November 2011, she "spent about eight hours shopping and dining with Boal."[168] During this shopping trip, "she saw something designed by Prada and commented that she liked the designer. Boal said he knew the designer personally and offered her tickets to a Prada fashion show."[169] She declined this offer, but she did accept a pair of Tahitian pearl earrings from Bigelow after meeting her at the Ritz-Carlton Hotel in Georgetown.[170] Although the CIA contends that no classified material was provided to Boal, CIA officials heavily redacted the information that she shared with him. A CIA report says that she explained to the filmmakers "how the UBL operation team got from point A to point B."[171] Following this sentence, nearly half a page of material is entirely withheld.

When it was first revealed that the filmmakers provided gifts to CIA officials, commentators focused on the possibility that Boal and Bigelow were bribing government officials for classified information.[172] In reality, of course, CIA officials were manipulating the filmmakers in order to defend the CIA's program. Much like the CIA's disseminated propaganda during the Cold War through cooperative reporters, Bikowsky used the film to convey a false narrative about the discovery of bin Laden's compound. While Boal probably viewed himself as an unbiased journalist, the evidence tells a different story.

Zero Dark Thirty, which grossed $132.8 million and received nominations for five Academy Awards, including Best Picture and Best Original Screenplay, was the culmination of a massive public relations strategy that the CIA deployed after bin Laden's assassination. However, it is important to remember that former CIA officers contributed to the public relations effort in their publications and public appearances. In the same year that *Zero Dark Thirty* was released, José A. Rodriguez's *Hard Measures* became a *New York Times* best seller. Rodriguez presented false and misleading information to whitewash the recent history of the CIA. To borrow a phrase from Sam Adams, the tenacious CIA analyst who battled the Pentagon during the Vietnam War, *Hard Measures* is "a monument of deceit."[173] It is mythology masquerading as nonfiction.

Conclusion

We have been moved further into a PR society and, sadly, public relations has become a key part of government and our politics.
—Walter Pincus ("A Farewell to the *Washington Post*," December 2015)

The underlying conclusion of this study is that public relations and government secrecy are two sides of the same coin. After closely examining the history of the CIA between the mid-1970s and the present, I have found overwhelming continuity in the agency's public relations strategy; that agency officials have used public relations to defend and perpetuate the "culture of secrecy" at Langley; and that the CIA has been remarkably effective in controlling its history. Researching the CIA is incredibly challenging. I have extensively used FOIA and the CREST system at the National Archives in College Park, Maryland, to provide the definitive account of CIA public relations. While it is hardly surprising to say that CIA officials have used public relations to improve the agency's public image, I believe that most Americans would be shocked by the scope of these efforts. I argue that there are five pillars of CIA public relations that are used aggressively—often with considerable success.

Pillar #1:
The CIA has a mystique, and agency officials use this mystique to win support from Congress and the American people.

The National Security Act established the CIA in 1947, and the law clearly prohibits the agency from engaging in domestic operations. However, the CIA has repeatedly targeted the American public with propaganda since the early years of the Cold War. Allen Dulles, the DCI between 1953 and 1961, orchestrated an extensive public relations effort in the 1950s to ensure that the CIA remained unaccountable to Congress; two decades later William Colby used similar tactics to prevent the abolition of covert operations. By promoting the CIA's mystique, both Dulles and Colby successfully beat back challenges to the "culture of secrecy." It will be recalled that George Tenet advised CIA officials in 1991 to "keep the mystique—we could lose if we are perceived as an ordinary bureaucracy (in resource game and in public image)."[1] Less than six years later, Tenet would become President Bill Clinton's DCI. Tenet and his public relations director, Bill Harlow, astutely cultivated the agency's mystique to protect the CIA in the aftermath of the Cold War.

Pillar #2:
The CIA emphasizes the heroism and patriotism of agency employees to deflect criticism.

There is no denying that CIA operatives have chosen an extremely dangerous profession. A total of 125 CIA employees have died in the line of duty since 1947, and they are each commemorated with a black star on the Memorial Wall at Langley.[2] CIA officials like to portray the agency as remarkably successful, but when a mission fails, the mystique of the CIA is inevitably challenged. By keeping the focus on heroism, the CIA diverts attention away from accountability for major failures. This strategy is an essential feature of crisis public relations. How the CIA has told the story of John T. Downey and Richard G. Fecteau, two of the most significant heroes in the history of the CIA, is illustrative of this public relations tactic. In November 1952, while on an air mission over China, the young CIA officers were shot down and captured. The Chinese held Fecteau until 1971, while Downey was released in 1973.[3] The CIA has celebrated the heroism of Downey and Fecteau, the hardships that they endured, and their loyalty to the agency. In a ceremony at CIA headquarters in 1998, DCI Tenet awarded them the Director's Medal, explaining that their odyssey was "one of the most remarkable in the history of the Central Intelligence Agency."[4] The CIA later provided funding to make a documentary film about their failed mission.[5] By focusing on the heroism of Downey and Fecteau, the CIA has obscured the glaring incompetence that led to their capture. After the Chinese Communists took power in 1949, the CIA attempted to overthrow them by developing "domestic antigovernment guerrilla operations. This was to be accomplished by small teams of Chinese agents, generally inserted through airdrops, who were to link up with local guerrilla forces, collect intelligence and possibly engage in sabotage and psychological warfare, and report back by radio."[6] The strategy was doomed to failure, but it would be repeated in other countries. A CIA officer familiar with the mission has revealed that the agency had evidence in the summer of 1952 indicating that the Communists had turned the Chinese agents that Downey and Fecteau were sent to retrieve. "After Downey and Fecteau's flight failed to return," says Nicholas Dujmovic, "the unit chief called the officer back and told him not to talk about the matter, and he followed instructions—much to his later regret."[7] The CIA has repeatedly benefited from telling the story of Downey and Fecteau, but no one has been held accountable for this avoidable tragedy.[8]

Pillar #3:
Since secrecy is essential for the activities of the CIA, agency officials argue that they must conceal evidence of successes. "Our failures are known, our successes must be kept hidden" has been the mantra of CIA public relations for almost four decades.

Tricia Jenkins calls this "the CIA's favorite talking point."[9] She points out that the mantra is "conveniently impossible to disprove, since it allows the Agency to claim that it regularly averts national [security] threats without the organization ever having to disclose the threat level of those attacks, the frequency of these successes, or even the veracity of the claim at all."[10] The emphasis on secrecy helps enhance the agency's mystique; Americans are given the impression that although the victories of the CIA are spectacular, they will never be revealed.

Pillar #4:
The CIA contends that the agency abides by the United States Constitution, taking orders from the president.

Allen Dulles developed the fourth pillar after the Bay of Pigs, but the strategy expanded in response to a famous quote from Senator Frank Church. On July 19, 1975, Senator Church announced to the media, "the CIA may have been behaving like a rogue elephant on a rampage."[11] It is important to remember that top CIA officials feared that Church's investigation of the intelligence community in 1975 might lead to the demise of covert operations. David A. Phillips helped lead the counter-offensive against Senator Church, and a key talking point of this public relations campaign was to reject the "rogue elephant" metaphor.[12] This talking point is no longer as central to CIA public relations as it once was, but it remains important.

Pillar #5:
CIA officials consistently portray the agency as accountable to Congress and American citizens.

Richard Helms, the DCI between 1966 and 1973, perfected this argument in an address to the Society of Newspaper Editors, famously explaining that "the nation must to a degree take it on faith that we too are honorable men devoted to her service."[13] Helms declared that CIA employees "are, after all, a part of this democracy, and we believe in it. We would not want to see our work distort its values and its principles. We propose to adapt intelligence to American society, not vice versa."[14] Interestingly, Helms did not inform his audience that the CIA had been spying on opponents of the Vietnam War, which was a direct violation of the National Security Act of 1947. In the aftermath of the Cold War, the fifth pillar evolved into what DCI Robert M. Gates described as a "new era of openness." More recently, General Michael Hayden delivered a speech in June 2007 to the Society for Historians of American Foreign Relations in which he spoke of the CIA's "social contract with the American people."[15] Hayden argued that the agency's right to operate in secrecy was "not a grant of power, but a grant of trust. Each day, we have to earn that trust—as our democratic system demands—by acting as our fellow citizens expect us to: skillfully, boldly, and always in keeping with the laws and values of our Republic. That's our social contract."[16] As Gates had done in February 1992, Hayden expressed a willingness to release documents of historical value. Declassifying records, he explained, "is in CIA's interest: We want our history and our role in key decisions to be written accurately and fairly."[17] He neglected to mention that the CIA won the nonprofit National Security Archives' Rosemary Award in 2006 for the worst FOIA compliance of any federal agency.

Despite the public relations campaign about openness and accountability, the evidence overwhelmingly demonstrates that the "culture of secrecy" remains entrenched at the CIA. Starting in the late 1990s, the

CIA, along with a handful of other government agencies, secretly reclassified documents at the National Archives. DCI George Tenet claimed that the CIA could not afford declassification expenses, but he had no problem finding a way to finance the reclassification project. This program accelerated after President George W. Bush[18] took office in 2001, and audits revealed that over fifty thousand pages were reclassified in the following years.[19] Rather than telling researchers what was happening, the CIA signed a secret Memorandum of Understanding (MOU) with the National Archives in 2001 that instructed archives staff to embrace the principle of plausible deniability. "NARA [National Archives and Records Administration] will not attribute to CIA any part of the review or the withholding of documents from this exposed collection," said the MOU.[20]

Matthew M. Aid, an expert on the National Security Agency, became suspicious when he noticed that documents formerly available to researchers at the National Archives had been withdrawn. He also discovered that the CIA had removed documents from the CREST database.[21] Thanks to his determination and investigatory skills, the *New York Times* broke the story in February 2006. Subsequent reports demonstrated that the CIA had reclassified documents for reasons unrelated to national security or sources and methods. In fact, many of the CIA records removed were dated from the early years of the agency. Personnel from Langley believed they had the right to reclassify material that detailed an unsuccessful Cold War mission to distribute propaganda in Eastern Europe using balloons; an inaccurate prediction that China would not enter the Korean War; and an angry response from the DCI about the negative publicity that resulted from his analysts being unable to anticipate anti-American protests in Colombia in 1948.[22] In 1999, the official in charge of the Office of Information Management at the CIA had proudly explained that the declassification of the Korean War document was evidence of Langley's greater openness to scholars; Langley would not withhold material simply because it might prove embarrassing, he declared.[23] Needless to say, the covert reclassification team at the National Archives obviously disagreed. The reclassification scandal revealed that the agency's rhetoric about valuing declassification, which had been perpetuated by the CIA since 1992, was public relations flimflam.

In addition to reclassifying documents, the CIA has also destroyed internal records. Just one week after Dana Priest revealed the CIA's secret

detention and interrogation program in November 2005, José A. Rodriguez, then the director of the National Clandestine Service, ordered the
shredding of over ninety videotapes that showed the use of enhanced
interrogation techniques on two al-Qaeda prisoners.[24] Gina C. Haspel,
Rodriguez's chief of staff, had drafted the order. (In February 2017,
Haspel was appointed deputy director of the CIA.)[25] When the story
leaked in December 2007, Hayden unconvincingly argued that the
tapes were eliminated to protect the identities of agency operatives.[26]
The investigative reporting of Scott Shane and Mark Mazzetti has shown
that, in reality, the agency wanted to protect its image: "Every action in
the prolonged drama of the interrogation videotapes was prompted in
part by worry about how its conduct might be perceived—by Congress,
by prosecutors, by the American public and by Muslims worldwide."[27]
The deputy to the CIA's executive director explained in an e-mail that
Rodriguez feared what would happen "if the tapes ever got into public
domain. . . . Out of context they would make us look terrible; it would
be 'devastating' to us."[28]

Rodriquez's decision to destroy the tapes would ultimately lead to
the Senate Intelligence Committee's lengthy investigation of the detention and interrogation program. At the beginning of this investigation
in 2009, the CIA agreed to establish an electronic database of agency
records called the Rendition, Detention, and Interrogation network
(RDINet). Once the CIA released files to the Senate side of the network,
staffers were allowed to review the records. However, on at least two
occasions in 2010, CIA employees removed documents that had been
previously turned over to the Senate. On March 11, 2014, Senator Dianne Feinstein delivered a shocking speech on the floor of the Senate,
accusing the CIA of searching the e-mails of Senate staffers and remov-
ing an agency document known as the Panetta Review.[29] "I have grave
concerns that the CIA's search may well have violated the separation
of powers principles embodied in the United States Constitution," she
declared.[30] Speaking at the Council on Foreign Relations, CIA director
John Brennan denied any wrongdoing: "As far as the allegations of CIA
hacking into Senate computers—nothing could be further from the
truth. We wouldn't do that. . . . That's just beyond the scope of reason."[31]
Brennan, however, was not telling the truth, for he had already ordered
an internal investigation. This investigation, which was completed in
July 2014, concluded that "five Agency employees, two attorneys and
three information technology (IT) staff members, improperly accessed

or caused access to the SSCI [Senate Select Committee on Intelligence] Majority staff shared drives on the RDINet."[32] Contrary to Brennan's denials, CIA employees had indeed searched the e-mails of Senate staffers; moreover, three of the employees involved "demonstrated a lack of candor about their activities during interviews by the OIG [Office of Inspector General]."[33]

When he learned about the findings of the internal inquiry, Senator Mark Udall (D-CO), a member of the Senate Intelligence Committee, called on Brennan to resign. "The C.I.A. unconstitutionally spied on Congress by hacking into the Senate Intelligence Committee computers. This grave misconduct not only is illegal but it violates the U.S. Constitution's requirement of separation of powers," he observed.[34] The CIA received even worse publicity in early December when the Senate finally released the 525-page executive summary of its detention and interrogation report. Although it would be reasonable to assume that the negative headlines badly damaged the CIA's image, this was not the case. The Pew Research Center conducted a survey about four weeks after the release of the executive summary, and the results were revealing. Compared to March 2010, when the CIA had a favorability rating of 52 percent in January 2015, 54 percent of those surveyed held a favorable view of the agency. While Democrats had a less favorable view of the CIA overall, Republicans and Independents both rated the CIA higher than in 2010.[35]

To be clear, evaluating opinion polls presents a serious challenge for historians. The obvious question is whether there is any evidence to suggest that the CIA's public relations efforts have influenced its approval ratings over the years. In October 1975, at the height of the "Year of Intelligence," 53 percent of Americans polled gave the CIA a positive rating.[36] In other words, the CIA had about the same level of public support in 2015 as it did four decades earlier. There are two possible interpretations of this statistic. According to the first interpretation, public relations is irrelevant; approval ratings are impossible to control and tend to fluctuate unpredictably over time. Yet from a different perspective, the CIA has benefited from public relations since 1975.

This study contends that the Office of Public Affairs has helped to maintain the CIA's image even during crisis situations. By focusing on the positive and diverting the public's attention from the negative, CIA officials have protected both covert operations and the "culture of secrecy." In reviewing a book about American public diplomacy in France after World War II, Christopher Endy pointed to the power of ambivalence. He noted the book's acknowledgment that public diplomacy did not change French opinions of the United States, prompting Endy to ask an insightful question: "What if ambivalence was all the United States needed to obtain its goals? Ambivalence, after all, was not a coherent call to reject U.S. influence."[37] A similar argument can be made about the CIA's public relations efforts.

In the final analysis, Americans do not always trust the CIA, but they have been convinced of the agency's mystique; this mythology, which is not supported by the historical evidence, has protected the agency's "culture of secrecy." A key result of this culture has been, in the words of historian Jonathan Nashel, the creation of a vast "warehouse of hidden histories" inside Langley.[38] If these "hidden histories" are ultimately revealed, how will they change our understanding of American foreign relations since 1947? Warren Kimball complained in 1998 that the CIA's unwillingness to abide by their legal obligations to declassify older records for State Department historians made it increasingly likely that the *FRUS* series could become "an official lie."[39] Needless to say, this "official lie" almost always supports the orthodox interpretation of American foreign policy while concealing the darkness at the heart of the American empire: the coups that have toppled democratically elected leaders and replaced them with authoritarian regimes, the interlocking relationships between the intelligence establishment and American multinational corporations, and the frequent manipulation of foreign elections.

Four decades have passed since Senator Frank Church courageously attempted to reform the intelligence establishment. He died in 1984 at the age of fifty-nine, but for advocates of openness, he is not forgotten. Had Church lived to see the United States in the twenty-first century, he would most likely shake his head in disgust. Yet he might also encourage us once again to consider the final paragraph of his committee's report on assassination plots:

> Despite our distaste for what we have seen, we have great faith in this country. The story is sad, but this country has the strength to hear the story and to learn from it. We must remain a people who confront our mistakes and resolve not to repeat them. If we do not, we will decline; but, if we do, our future will be worthy of the best of our past.[40]

I share his optimism, and I share his unwavering belief that the system can be reformed. But since this reform can only happen with support from Congress and the White House, the American people must demand it. As Edward R. Murrow wisely said, "Our history will be what we make it. If we go on as we are, then history will take its revenge, and retribution will not limp in catching up with us."[41]

It is time to confront the "culture of secrecy." It is time for another Church Committee.

Acknowledgments

When I moved to Williamsburg, Virginia, in August 2001 to begin the graduate program in history at the College of William & Mary, I never imagined that I would ultimately write a history of the CIA. I planned on studying nineteenth-century social history, but just a few weeks into the master's program, the attacks of September 11 left me with difficult questions about American foreign policy that I was unable to answer. It was around this time that I first met Professor Ed Crapol. I told him during office hours one afternoon that I was interested in examining American encounters with terrorism in the 1980s. He expressed interest in assisting with the thesis, and he kindly agreed to stay on as my dissertation advisor after his retirement in 2004. It is hard for me to imagine having written either my master's thesis or my doctoral dissertation without his guidance and support. I want to thank Ed for all the assistance that he has provided over the years, and I am forever grateful to him for introducing me to William Appleman Williams and the "Wisconsin School" of diplomatic history.

I am extremely grateful that Hiroshi Kitamura, Betsy Konefal, and Jonathan Nashel served on my dissertation committee. Hiroshi arrived at William & Mary shortly after I completed my comprehensive exams, and his optimism about my research motivated me to move forward— even when I was unsure where I was heading. His detailed comments on my dissertation in the fall of 2007 were incredibly helpful. Betsy's feedback helped me to think more carefully about the complexity of government secrecy, and Jonathan offered excellent advice. I always look forward to seeing his name in my e-mail inbox.

I owe a tremendous intellectual debt to several faculty members at William & Mary. Melvin Ely, Cindy Hahamovitch, Leisa Meyer, Scott Nelson, Abdul-Karim Rafeq, Carol Sheriff, Helen C. Walker, and Jim Whittenburg all helped me to better understand what it means to be a "teacher-scholar." In addition to the faculty mentioned above, I must acknowledge the late Paul S. Boyer. During his tenure as the James Pinckney Harrison Visiting Professor at the college in 2002–2003, his course on the atomic age inspired me to think creatively about the Cold War.

Beginning in 2005, the Office of the Provost at William & Mary provided me with three consecutive summer grants that were of great assistance. I am very grateful to Louise Kale, emerita director of the Historic Campus, for giving me the opportunity to work at the Christopher Wren Building in the summers of 2004 and 2005. I also want to thank Roz Stearns and Betty Flanigan for their many years of service to the History Department. They are both retired now, but they probably deserve their own acknowledgments section. I apologize to Betty for jamming the Risograph machine on so many occasions.

I wish to thank the many librarians and archivists who have assisted this project. According to my records, the Interlibrary Loan Office at Swem Library promptly responded to at least thirty requests from me during my time at William & Mary. Alan F. Zoellner, the government information librarian at Swem, provided crucial assistance, especially during the final round of revisions. I benefited as well from the assistance of staff members at both the National Archives II in College Park, Maryland, and the Library of Congress. The late John E. Taylor gave me a terrific introduction to the CIA records at the National Archives II when I first visited in June 2005. When I was a lecturer at the University of Tennessee, Chattanooga, Dean Theresa Liedtka enthusiastically supported my grant to expand the university's collection in the field of intelligence studies as the library staff prepared to move into a new, world-class facility. Irene Handy, Sue Moss, and Carly Winfield—librarians at my current institution—have consistently gone above and beyond the call of duty. Carly has repeatedly tracked down elusive articles and books through interlibrary loans.

Ransom Clark has compiled an impressive online bibliography of CIA history at http://intellit.muskingum.edu/cia_folder/ciatoc.html, which has helped me tremendously. His bibliography is well organized and painstakingly annotated. The nonprofit National Security Archive in Washington, DC, which was established in 1985, uses the Freedom of Information Act to obtain government records, and their electronic briefing books on the intelligence establishment are phenomenal. Anyone interested in government secrecy should visit the National Security Archive's website: https://nsarchive.gwu.edu/.

Of all the scholars that I have cited in the endnotes, there are six that I should mention at the outset even though I have met only one in person. Kathryn S. Olmsted's *Challenging the Secret Government* and Rhodri Jeffreys-Jones's *The CIA and American Democracy* were critical resources at every stage of this project. Peter Kornbluh's *The Pinochet File* is a masterful work of history, and it should be read by every student of American foreign relations. I only hope that my study expands on Angus Mackenzie's *Secrets: The CIA's War at Home*. Thomas Powers brilliantly explored the clandestine mind-set in *The Man Who Kept the Secrets*, a study that had an immense impact on how I understand the "culture of secrecy" at the CIA. All scholars of the CIA owe a huge debt to John Prados, who graciously agreed to serve as the chair and commentator on a conference panel that I organized in 2005.

I might have survived without my fellow graduate students, but it would have been much less fun. The list is a long one: Gordon Barker, Emily Moore, Ryan Booth, Dave Brown, Stacey Schneider, Josh Beatty, John Weber, Buddy Paulett, Ellen Adams, Celine Carayon, Evan Cordulack, Jim David, Jack Fiorini, Margaret Freeman, Sarah Grunder, Sean Harvey, Caroline Hasenyager, Sarah McLennan, John Miller, Caroline Morris, Liam Paskvan, Ed Pompeian, Kristen Proehl, and Andrew Sturtevant. I apologize if I have overlooked anyone.

After leaving William & Mary in 2008, I held a series of academic appointments before joining the faculty of Richard Bland College of William & Mary in August 2015. I made many friendships on this long, stressful journey: at Furman University—John Barrington, Lloyd Benson, Monica Black (now at the University of Tennessee, Knoxville), Nellie Boucher (now at Amherst College), Erik Ching, Tim Fehler, Matthew Gillis (now at the University of Tennessee, Knoxville), Jonas Kauffeldt (now at the University of North Georgia), Savita Nair, David Spear, Marian Strobel, Courtney Tollison, and Diane Vecchio; at Stetson University—Paul Croce, Eric Kurlander, Emily Mieras, Kimberly Reiter, Paul Steeves, and Margaret Venzke; and at the University of Tennessee, Chattanooga—Catharine Franklin (now at Texas Tech University), James Guilfoyle, Amy Huesman, Lindsay Irvin, and Michelle White.

I owe a huge debt of gratitude to Dean Vern Lindquist. Vern took a chance on me when no one else would. Since starting at Richard Bland College, time previously spent on job applications has been dedicated in part to forging new friendships with Tiffany Birdsong, Celia Brockway, Eric Earnhardt, Rachel Finney, Shawn Holt, Mike Lehman, Lisa Lindquist, David Majewski, Eric Miller, Jill Mitten, Barbara Morgan, Jena Morrison, Warren Nesbitt, Linda Pittman, Matt Smith, Vanessa Stout, Alexandra Youmans, and Dan Zelinski. I am extremely proud to have played a small role in hiring Dan Franke and Adam Zucconi in

2016. Dan and Adam are terrific colleagues, and they have been a constant source of encouragement.

While I was the Lewis L. Glucksman Fellow at William & Mary in 2006, I had the opportunity to develop an upper-level course on the history of the CIA. I have taught this course on ten occasions, and I want to thank the hundreds of students who have signed up; their questions, comments, and papers have confirmed the adage that you never fully understand something until you have to teach it.

Special thanks to everyone at the University Press of Kansas. Joyce Harrison, the editor in chief, responded with tremendous enthusiasm when I first contacted her in January 2017. I am in awe of her organizational skills. Kelly Chrisman Jacques, the managing editor, skillfully shepherded the manuscript through the many stages of production.

When I was in middle school, my parents dragged me against my will to Colonial Williamsburg. I now forgive them. I don't know how I can ever repay them for all they have done for me in the last forty years. This book is dedicated to them.

In June 2014, when I was pretty much convinced that my academic career was over, Sarah Elise Stephan walked into my life quite unexpectedly. She gave me renewed hope, and that is always the most important thing for a writer. The next book will be for her.

Notes

Preface: The "Family Jewels"

1. "Gerald R. Ford's Remarks upon Taking the Oath of Office as President," Gerald R. Ford Presidential Library and Museum, accessed 29 May 2017, https://www.fordlibrarymuseum.gov/library/speeches/740001.asp.

2. Ibid.

3. Seymour Hersh, "Huge C.I.A. Operation Reported in U.S. against Antiwar Forces, Other Dissidents in Nixon Years," *New York Times*, 22 December 1974.

4. John Prados, *The Family Jewels: The CIA, Secrecy, and Presidential Power* (Austin: University of Texas Press, 2013), 214.

5. The position of DCI actually predated the CIA; the position was eliminated in April 2005 with the creation of the director of national intelligence (DNI).

6. "Memorandum for All CIA Employees," 9 May 1973, accessed 29 May 2017, http://nsarchive.gwu.edu/NSAEBB/NSAEBB222/schlesinger_jewels.pdf.

7. Ibid.

8. For the definitive history of the document and its legacy, see Prados, *The Family Jewels*, 9–21. Prados believes that "'the Family Jewels' really serves as a metaphor: Family Jewels designate a certain category of operations . . . that become[s] sensitive as exuberance exceeds proper boundaries. Family Jewels are eternal. Only their specific content changes over time." Ibid., 3.

9. Ibid., 19.

10. Cynthia M. Nolan, "Seymour Hersh's Impact on the CIA," *International Journal of Intelligence and Counterintelligence* 12, no. 1 (1999): 18–34.

11. "Report to the President by the Commission on CIA Activities within the United States," chap. 11 in *Special Operations Group* (Washington, DC: Government Printing Office, 1975), 130.

12. Loch K. Johnson, "The Church Committee Investigation of 1975 and the Evolution of Modern Intelligence Accountability," *Intelligence and National Security* 23 (April 2008): 200.

13. For a succinct overview of the Pike Committee, see Gerald K. Haines, "The Pike Committee Investigations and the CIA," *Studies in Intelligence* (Winter 1998–1999): 81–92. For a more detailed assessment, see Kathryn S. Olmsted, *Challenging the Secret Government: The Post-Watergate Investigations of the CIA and FBI*, chap. 6 (Chapel Hill: University of North Carolina Press, 1996). The document was later published. *CIA: The Pike Report* (Nottingham, UK: Spokesman Books, 1977).

14. Loch K. Johnson, *A Season of Inquiry: The Senate Intelligence Investigation* (Lexington: University Press of Kentucky, 1985), 211–226.

Introduction: "A Fundamental Public Relations Problem"

1. "DCI Speech to CIA: Today and Tomorrow," 4 March 1976, 3, CIA Records Search Tool (CREST) System, National Archives at College Park, College Park, MD.
2. Cynthia M. Nolan, "Seymour Hersh's Impact on the CIA," *International Journal of Intelligence and Counterintelligence* 12, no. 1 (1999): 21.
3. Kathryn S. Olmsted, *Challenging the Secret Government: The Post-Watergate Investigations of the CIA and FBI* (Chapel Hill: University of North Carolina Press, 1996), 140, 224n122.
4. "DCI Speech to CIA: Today and Tomorrow," 4 March 1976, 3.
5. Peter Kornbluh, ed., *Bay of Pigs Declassified: The Secret CIA Report on the Invasion of Cuba* (New York: New Press, 1998), 2.
6. Simon Willmetts, "The Burgeoning Fissures of Dissent: Allen Dulles and the Selling of the CIA in the Aftermath of the Bay of Pigs," *History* 100 (April 2015): 171.
7. Ibid., 187–188.
8. Tity de Vries, "The 1967 Central Intelligence Agency Scandal: Catalyst in a Transforming Relationship between State and People," *Journal of American History* 98, no. 4 (March 2012): 1076.
9. Ibid., 1075.
10. Rhodri Jeffreys-Jones, *The CIA and American Democracy,* 3rd ed. (New Haven: Yale University Press, 2003), 153–164. Nicholas Katzenbach, then undersecretary of state, chaired the investigation commission, and according to Jeffreys-Jones, "the salient feature of the Katzenbach reform was its cosmetic, stopgap character." Ibid.,163.
11. De Vries, "The 1967 Central Intelligence Agency Scandal," 1076. For more on the scandal, see Angus Mackenzie, *Secrets: The CIA's War at Home* (Berkeley: University of California Press, 1997), 15–25; John Prados, *Safe for Democracy: The Secret Wars of the CIA* (Chicago: Ivan R. Dee, 2006), 369–375; and Hugh Wilford, *The Mighty Wurlitzer: How the CIA Played America* (Cambridge, MA: Harvard University Press, 2008), 1–5, 237–248.
12. Thomas Powers, *The Man Who Kept the Secrets: Richard Helms and the CIA* (New York: Alfred A. Knopf, 1979), 298.
13. Kornbluh, *Bay of Pigs Declassified,* 10.
14. Ibid., 15.
15. Ibid.
16. Mackenzie, *Secrets,* 17–21.
17. De Vries, "The 1967 Central Intelligence Agency Scandal," 1086.
18. John D. Marks, "On Being Censored," *Foreign Policy* 15 (Summer 1974): 107.

19. Victor Marchetti and John D. Marks, *The CIA and the Cult of Intelligence* (New York: Alfred A. Knopf, 1974; repr., New York: Dell, 1980), 12.

20. Ibid., 16. For an excellent overview of Marchetti's story, see Christopher Moran, *Company Confessions: Secrets, Memoirs, and the CIA* (New York: St. Martin's, 2015), 113–122. Moran has written the definitive history of CIA memoirs. He persuasively argues that "memoirs by renegades and whistle-blowers [in the 1970s] fundamentally challenged the celebratory story of US Cold War foreign policy, and provided further grist to the mill of nascent revisionism in this area" (Moran,112).

21. Seymour M. Hersh, "C.I.A. Chief Tells House of $8-Million Campaign against Allende in '70–'73," *New York Times,* 8 September 1974; Seymour M. Hersh, "Censored Matter in Book About C.I.A. Said to Have Related Chile Activities," *New York Times,* 11 September 1974, 14.

22. The title of the story on the CIA answered the question posed on the front cover. See "The CIA: Time to Come In from the Cold," *Time,* 30 September 1974, 16–24.

23. Seymour Hersh, "Huge C.I.A. Operation Reported in U.S. against Antiwar Forces, Other Dissidents in Nixon Years," *New York Times,* 22 December 1974.

24. For the three best books about the "Year of Intelligence," see Loch K. Johnson, *A Season of Inquiry: The Senate Intelligence Investigation* (Lexington: University Press of Kentucky, 1985); Olmsted, *Challenging the Secret Government;* and Frank J. Smist Jr., *Congress Oversees the United States Intelligence Community, 1947–1994,* 2nd ed. (Knoxville: University of Tennessee Press, 1994). For an outstanding examination of William Colby's role in the investigations, see John Prados, *Lost Crusader: The Secret Wars of CIA Director William Colby* (New York: Oxford University Press, 2003), 297–330. For more specialized studies of the Church Committee, see Loch K. Johnson, "The Church Committee Investigation of 1975 and the Evolution of Modern Intelligence Accountability," *Intelligence and National Security* 23 (April 2008): 198–225; Frederick A. O. Schwarz Jr., "The Church Committee and a New Era of Intelligence Oversight," *Intelligence and National Security* 22 (April 2007): 270–297; and Frederick A. O. Schwarz Jr. and Aziz Z. Huq, *Unchecked and Unbalanced: Presidential Power in a Time of Terror* (New York: New Press, 2007), 21–62. For a succinct overview of the Pike Committee, see Gerald K. Haines, "The Pike Committee Investigations and the CIA," *Studies in Intelligence* (Winter 1998–1999): 81–92. The National Security Archive has compiled several electronic briefing books related to the "Year of Intelligence." See "White House Efforts to Blunt 1975 Church Committee Investigation into CIA Abuses Foreshadowed Executive-Congressional Battles After 9/11," 20 July 2015, *National Security Archive Briefing Book No. 522,* eds. John Prados and Arturo Jimenez-Bacardi, accessed 2 June 2017, http://nsarchive .gwu.edu/NSAEBB/NSAEBB522-Church-Committee-Faced-White-House -Attempts-to-Curb-CIA-Probe/; "Gerald Ford White House Altered Rockefeller Commission Report in 1975; Removed Section on CIA Assassination Plots," 29 February 2016, *National Security Archive Briefing Book No. 543,* eds. John Prados and Arturo Jimenez-Bacardi, accessed 2 June 2017, http://nsarchive.gwu.edu

/NSAEBB/NSAEBB543-Ford-White-House-Altered-Rockefeller-Commission
-Report/; and "The White House, the CIA and the Pike Committee, 1975,"
2 June 2017, *National Security Archive Briefing Book No. 596*, eds. John Prados
and Arturo Jimenez-Bacardi, accessed 2 June 2017, http://nsarchive.gwu.edu
/NSAEBB/NSAEBB596-Pike-Committee-and-White-House-clashed-over-access
-to-CIA-secrets/.

25. Baker quoted in Frederick A. O. Schwarz Jr., *Democracy in the Dark: The
Seduction of Government Secrecy* (New York: New Press, 2015), 173.

26. Angleton quoted in Johnson, *A Season of Inquiry*, 266. Although they
do not always mention the Church Committee, former CIA officers often complain about perceived restrictions on agency operations. For instance, see Robert Baer, *See No Evil: The True Story of a Ground Soldier in the CIA's War on Terrorism*
(New York: Three Rivers, 2002). Baer maintains:

> What happened to the CIA didn't happen just by chance. The CIA was sys-
> tematically destroyed by political correctness, by petty Beltway wars, by ca-
> reerism, and much more. At a time when terrorist threats were compound-
> ing globally, the agency that should have been monitoring them was being
> scrubbed clean instead. . . . Defanged and dispirited, the CIA went along
> for the ride. And then on September 11, 2001, the reckoning for such vast
> carelessness was presented for all the world to see. (Baer, xviii–xix)

27. Stephen F. Knott, *Secret and Sanctioned: Covert Operations and the American
Presidency* (New York: Oxford University Press, 1996), 172.

28. Ibid., 184–185.

29. Ibid., 156–159. For an excellent critique of Knott's analysis, see Loch K.
Johnson, *Bombs, Bugs, Drugs, and Thugs: Intelligence and America's Quest For Security* (New York: New York University Press, 2000), 208–211.

30. Knott, *Secret and Sactioned*, 178–179.

31. *The 9/11 Commission Report: Final Report of the National Commission on
Terrorist Attacks upon the United States* (New York: W. W. Norton, 2004), 419. See
also Schwarz Jr., and Huq, *Unchecked and Unbalanced*, 61.

32. Johnson, *A Season of Inquiry*, 2.

33. Ibid., 249.

34. Olmsted, *Challenging the Secret Government*, 169.

35. Jeffreys-Jones, *The CIA and American Democracy*, 214–215.

36. Johnson, *Bombs, Bugs, Drugs, and Thugs*, 206.

37. Ibid.

38. Loch K. Johnson, "The Church Committee Investigation," 198–199.
Johnson maintains that members of the oversight committees typically fall into
one of four categories: ostriches, cheerleaders, lemon-suckers, or guardians.
Ibid., 211–214, 219–220.

39. Ibid., 199.

40. Marchetti and Marks, *The CIA and the Cult of Intelligence*, 6.

41. Ibid.

42. Victor Marchetti, "Propaganda and Disinformation: How the CIA Manufactures History," *Journal of Historical Review* 9 (Fall 1989): 319.

43. Two of these documents are reproduced in the second chapter of Tricia

Jenkins, *The CIA in Hollywood: How the Agency Shapes Film and Television* (Austin: University of Texas Press, 2012), 40–43.

44. "Perhaps because its efforts in film and television are relatively new," says Jenkins, "only a very small amount of scholarship has examined the CIA's collaborations, motivations, and methodologies in this field." Jenkins, *The CIA in Hollywood*, 1. Jenkins was apparently unable to consult my dissertation, which included extensive material on the CIA's involvement in Hollywood. See David S. McCarthy, "The CIA & the Cult of Secrecy," (PhD diss., College of William & Mary, 2008).

45. Mordecai Lee, *Congress vs. the Bureaucracy: Muzzling Agency Public Relations* (Norman: University of Oklahoma Press, 2011), 4.

46. Ibid. It is important to point out that the book only mentions the CIA once (Ibid., 123).

47. "Briefing Book Prepared by Public Affairs Office for Admiral Turner," 19 September 1977, Document No. CK3100202484-CK3100202532, Tab E, 2, Declassified Documents Reference System [DDRS]. This database is now titled U.S. Declassified Documents Online.

48. Richard P. Longaker, *The Presidency and Individual Liberties* (Ithaca, NY: Cornell University Press, 1961), 175.

49. Ibid., 181; see also Philip H. Melanson, *Secrecy Wars: National Security, Privacy, and the Public's Right to Know* (Washington, DC: Brassey's, 2001), 183.

Chapter 1. *"Telling the Intelligence Story"*

1. George H. W. Bush, DCI Speech to CIA: Today and Tomorrow, 4 March 1976, 4, CREST System, National Archives at College Park, College Park, MD.

2. Ibid.

3. "The Suspicion Business," *Three Days of the Condor*, chapter 11, directed by Sydney Pollack (1975; Hollywood, CA: Paramount Pictures, 1999), DVD.

4. Vincent Canby, "Redford a C.I.A. Eccentric in 'Three Days of the Condor,'" *New York Times*, 25 September 1975.

5. "Telling Stories," *Three Days of the Condor*, chapter 16, DVD.

6. Ibid.

7. Ibid.

8. Ibid.

9. Ibid. When this book was nearly finished, Simon Willmetts published a magisterial history of Hollywood films about the Office of Strategic Services and the CIA. For his assessment of *Three Days of the Condor*, see Simon Willmetts, *In Secrecy's Shadow: The OSS and CIA in Hollywood Cinema, 1941–1979* (Edinburgh, UK: Edinburgh University Press, 2016), 248–253; see also David S. McCarthy, "The CIA & the Cult of Secrecy," (PhD diss., College of William & Mary, 2008), 82–91.

10. William F. Buckley Jr., "The Case of Redford vs. the C.I.A.," *New York Times*, 28 September 1975.

11. Ibid.

12. Benjamin Stein, "Let's Tar and Feather the CIA," *Wall Street Journal*, 2 October 1975.

13. Ibid.

14. "DCI Speech to CIA: Today and Tomorrow," 4 March 1976, 4, CREST System, National Archives at College Park, College Park, MD.

15. Carl Bernstein, "The CIA and the Media," *Rolling Stone*, 20 October 1977, accessed 14 June 2017, http://www.carlbernstein.com/magazine_cia_and_media.php.

16. Loch K. Johnson, "The CIA and the Media," *Intelligence and National Security* 1 (May 1986): 145.

17. Hugh Wilford, *The Mighty Wurlitzer: How the CIA Played America* (Cambridge, MA: Harvard University Press, 2008), 7.

18. Ibid., 226.

19. David P. Hadley, "A Constructive Quality: The Press, the CIA, and Covert Intervention in the 1950s," *Intelligence and National Security* 31, no. 2 (2016): 246.

20. Ibid., 264.

21. Carl Bernstein, "The CIA and the Media."

22. Ibid. For more on the Alsop interview, see Wilford, *The Mighty Wurlitzer*, 225–226.

23. Carl Bernstein, "The CIA and the Media."

24. Wilford, *The Mighty Wurlitzer*, 227.

25. Tim Weiner, "Role of C.I.A. in Guatemala Told in Files of Publisher," *New York Times*, 7 June 1997. For more on the incident, see Nick Cullather, *Secret History: The CIA's Classified Account of Its Operations in Guatemala, 1952–1954* (Stanford, CA: Stanford University Press, 1999), 94; John Prados, *The Family Jewels: The CIA, Secrecy, and Presidential Power* (Austin: University of Texas Press, 2013), 194; Eric Pace, "Sydney Gruson, 81, Correspondent, Editor and Executive for 'The New York Times,' Dies," *New York Times*, 9 March 1998; and Hadley, "A Constructive Quality," 254. The Guatemalan government had expelled Gruson on February 2, 1954, but he was allowed to return in May. CIA officials were apparently most concerned about Gruson's investigative skills; declassified records show that Dulles was misleading Arthur H. Sulzberger about the reporter's politics. According to one CIA assessment, "a comparison of Gruson's reports on Guatemala with current reporting by other special correspondents does not set his work apart as showing strong 'leftist' or 'pro-Guatemalan' bias in the extent to which he quotes Guatemalan official statements or dwells upon the resurgence of 'anti-Yankee' sentiment in the area." See "Reporting on Guatemala by 'New York Times' Correspondent Sydney Gruson," 27 May 1954, 3, CREST System, National Archives at College Park, College Park, MD.

26. Rhodri Jeffreys-Jones, *The CIA and American Democracy*, 3rd ed. (New Haven: Yale University Press, 2003), chap. 5.

27. Dulles quoted in Christopher Moran, *Company Confessions: Secrets, Memoirs, and the CIA* (New York: St. Martin's, 2015), 84–85.

28. Ray S. Cline, *Secrets, Spies, and Scholars: Blueprint of the Essential CIA* (Washington, DC: Acropolis, 1976), 119; see also Jonathan Nashel, "The Rise of the

CIA and American Popular Culture," in *Architects of the American Century: Individuals and Institutions in Twentieth-Century U.S. Foreign Policymaking*, ed. David F. Schmitz and T. Christopher Jespersen (Chicago: Imprint, 1999), esp. 66–73.

29. Jeffreys-Jones, *The CIA and American Democracy*, 78; David M. Barrett, *The CIA & Congress: The Untold Story from Truman to Kennedy* (Lawrence: University Press of Kansas, 2005), 171–172.

30. Mansfield quoted in Barrett, *The CIA & Congress*, 173.

31. Ibid., 174.

32. According to one observer's diary entry, "[Dulles] said that we did not like this proposal [from Senator Mike Mansfield] in its present form, but that we did not want to appear to fight it." Ibid., 172.

33. Peter Grose, *Gentleman Spy: The Life of Allen Dulles* (Boston: Houghton Mifflin, 1994), 416; Thomas Powers, *The Man Who Kept the Secrets: Richard Helms and the CIA* (New York: Alfred A. Knopf, 1979), 100, 375n20, 376n24; Hadley has also examined the impact of the articles. See Hadley, "A Constructive Quality," 252–253.

34. Jonathan Nashel, *Edward Lansdale's Cold War* (Amherst: University of Massachusetts Press, 2005), 98.

35. Richard and Gladys Harkness, "The Mysterious Doings of CIA," *Saturday Evening Post*, 30 October 1954.

36. Ibid., 20–21.

37. Ibid., 21.

38. Ibid., 162.

39. Cullather, *Secret History*, 106–107.

40. Richard and Gladys Harkness, "The Mysterious Doings of CIA," *Saturday Evening Post*, 6 November 1954.

41. Ibid.

42. Richard and Gladys Harkness, "The Mysterious Doings of CIA," *Saturday Evening Post*, 13 November 1954.

43. Ibid.

44. Ibid.

45. Grose, *Gentleman Spy*, 416; Barrett, *The CIA & Congress*, 223–233; Jeffreys-Jones, *The CIA and American Democracy*, 79–80.

46. Nashel, *Edward Lansdale's Cold War*, 166.

47. Seth Jacobs, *America's Miracle Man in Vietnam* (Durham: Duke University Press, 2004), 110; Nashel, *Edward Lansdale's Cold War*, 163–171, esp. 164–166.

48. For the definitive history of FBI public relations, see Matthew Cecil, *Branding Hoover's FBI: How the Boss's PR Men Sold the Bureau to America* (Lawrence: University Press of Kansas, 2016); see also Cecil, *Hoover's FBI and the Fourth Estate: The Campaign to Control the Press and the Bureau's Image* (Lawrence: University Press of Kansas, 2014).

49. "History of CIA Public Affairs," Public Affairs Advisory Group Fact Sheet, 2, CREST System, National Archives at College Park, College Park, MD.

50. For example, see Ruth Montgomery, "CIA's 'No-Comment' Man," *New York Journal American*, 1 December 1963, CREST System, National Archives at College Park, College Park, MD.

51. Simon Willmetts, "The Burgeoning Fissures of Dissent: Allen Dulles and the Selling of the CIA in the Aftermath of the Bay of Pigs," *History* 100 (April 2015): 169n11.

52. Sheffield Edwards, "Public Relations Policy for CIA," 21 December 1951, 1, CREST System, National Archives at College Park, College Park, MD.

53. Ibid.

54. Ibid.

55. Ibid., 2.

56. Ibid.

57. As Simon Willmetts correctly points out, "Dulles's penchant for publicity . . . stood in marked contrast to the approach of his former Agency." Willmetts, "The Burgeoning Fissures of Dissent," 172.

58. Hadley, "A Constructive Quality," 264.

59. "Col. S.J. Grogan Was CIA Official," obituary, *Washington Post*, 19 April 1978.

60. Bernstein, "The CIA and the Media."

61. Ibid.

62. DeLillo quoted in Willmetts, "The Burgeoning Fissures of Dissent," 173.

63. Grose, *Gentleman Spy*, 539; James Srodes, *Allen Dulles: Master of Spies* (Washington, DC: Regnery, 1999), 552. According to Tad Szulc, "Hunt himself quietly collaborated with Dulles in drafting the former CIA Director's book, although the Agency nowadays denies this with vigor." See Szulc, *Compulsive Spy: The Strange Career of E. Howard Hunt* (New York: Viking, 1974), 21. Szulc also says that future DCI "[Richard] Helms kept copies of Hunt's spy novels around his office and often gave or lent them to friends and visitors." Ibid., 105.

64. Willmetts, "The Burgeoning Fissures of Dissent," 178.

65. "Memorandum For: The DCI," memorandum, 11 July 1963, 2, CREST System, National Archives at College Park, College Park, MD.

66. Ibid., 6.

67. Ibid., 5; see also Willmetts, "The Burgeoning Fissures of Dissent," 178–179.

68. David Wise and Thomas B. Ross, *The Invisible Government*, (1964; repr., New York: Vintage, 1974), viii; see also Evan Thomas, *The Very Best Men: Four Who Dared* (New York: Simon & Schuster, 2006), 319.

69. Joseph B. Smith, *Portrait of a Cold Warrior* (New York: Ballantine, 1976), 425.

70. Ibid. For a good overview of the incident, see Prados, *The Family Jewels*, 203–205.

71. John D. Marks, "On Being Censored," *Foreign Policy* 15 (Summer 1974): 100.

72. Ibid., 101.

73. Ibid., 101–102; Eric Pace, "Cuts That C.I.A. Sought in Book Touch on Official Slips," *New York Times*, 15 April 1974.

74. Marks, "On Being Censored," 106.

75. Ibid., 107.

76. Seymour M. Hersh, "C.I.A. Aides Assail Asia Drug Charge," *New York*

Times, 22 July 1972; Richard R. Lingeman, "The C.I.A. as Book Reviewer," *New York Times Book Review,* 3 September 1972.

77. Prados, *The Family Jewels,* 208.

78. For more on this bizarre story, see Gary Fishgall, *Against Type: The Biography of Burt Lancaster* (New York: Scribner, 1995), 286; David A. Phillips, *The Night Watch* (New York: Ballantine, 1977), 312; and Willmetts, *In Secrecy's Shadow,* 232–235.

79. *The Directors: Sydney Pollack,* directed by Robert J. Emery (1997; New York: Fox Lorber CenterStage, 1999), DVD.

80. John Prados, *Lost Crusader: The Secret Wars of CIA Director William Colby* (New York: Oxford University Press, 2003), 330.

81. Phillips, *The Night Watch,* 372; for more on the divisions inside the CIA at the time, see Prados, *Lost Crusader,* 310–311.

82. Prados, *Lost Crusader,* 311.

83. Colby quoted in Phillips, *The Night Watch,* viii, 372.

84. William Colby and Peter Forbath, *Honorable Men: My Life in the CIA* (New York: Simon & Schuster, 1978), 21.

85. Ibid.

86. "Telling the Intelligence Story," Task Group Memo to DCI, 30 October 1975, 1, CREST System, National Archives at College Park, College Park, MD. See also Moran, *Company Confessions,* 153–154.

87. "Telling the Intelligence Story," 1.

88. Ibid. Six topics were mentioned in the attachment: "the operations center," "personality interviews," "current intelligence," "academic skills," "counterintelligence," and "backgrounders." Ibid., Tab A.

89. Ibid., 1.

90. Ibid., 2.

91. Ibid.

92. Ibid.

93. Colby and Forbath, *Honorable Men,* 379.

94. Ibid., 378.

95. Ibid.

96. Ibid. Phillips says that "we had hundreds of visitors to our building: college classes, high school students, and businessmen. The last college group I saw in the halls was from the Malcolm X College." See Phillips, *The Night Watch,* 312.

97. Colby and Forbath, *Honorable Men,* 378.

98. Phillips, *The Night Watch,* vii; Christopher Moran, "The Last Assignment: David Atlee Phillips and the Birth of CIA Public Relations," *International History Review* 35, no. 2 (2013): 337–355. In an otherwise noteworthy article, Moran is mistaken in his description of the scholarship on public relations: "The historiographical orthodoxy about public relations by the CIA is that it commenced in a post–cold-war context, as the Agency tried to convince the public, but also Congress, of the need to maintain a well-funded, permanent foreign intelligence service to combat new threats to the nation's security." Ibid., 351. Kathryn S. Olmsted actually discussed Phillips in her 1996 study of the "Year of

Intelligence." See Olmsted, *Challenging the Secret Government: The Post-Watergate Investigations of the CIA and FBI* (Chapel Hill: University of North Carolina Press, 1996), 146–147.

99. The Directorate of Operations became known as the National Clandestine Service in 2005.

100. Harry Rositzke, "Controlling Secret Operations," *New York Times*, 7 October 1974.

101. Ibid.

102. Ray S. Cline, "The Value of the C.I.A.," *New York Times*, 1 November 1974. Cline argued that America intervened in foreign politics to protect democracy, a proud tradition that he said could be traced back to the Agency's role in Italian elections during the early years of the Cold War. He proclaimed that "the principal supporters of President Salvadore Allende Gossens' administration intended to establish a dictatorship of the revolutionary left, abolish Congress and neutralize or destroy the entire managerial and middle class." Ibid., 39. Not surprisingly, Cline failed to mention that Allende had been democratically elected in September 1970, and he presented no concrete evidence to explain how events in Chile were connected to the national security of the United States. In September 1974, Seymour Hersh revealed details about CIA involvement in Chile. Ibid.

103. Phillips, *The Night Watch*, 346.

104. Ibid., 345.

105. *The Selling of the Pentagon*, produced and written by Peter Davis (New York: Carousel Film & Video, 1971), VHS; Garth S. Jowett, "The Selling of the Pentagon," *Museum of Broadcast Communications*, accessed 21 February 2006, http://www.museum.tv/archives/etv/S/htmlS/sellingofth/sellingofth.htm; the origins of the documentary can be traced to Senator J. W. Fulbright (D-AR). J. W. Fulbright, *The Pentagon Propaganda Machine* (New York: Liveright, 1970); Jack Gould, "TV: C.B.S. Explores Pentagon Propaganda Costs," *New York Times*, 24 February 1971; Jack Gould, "The Unselling of the Pentagon," *New York Times*, 7 March 1971; see also William C. Berman, *William Fulbright and the Vietnam War: The Dissent of a Political Realist* (Kent, OH: Kent State University Press, 1988), 142.

106. Colby quoted in Phillips, *The Night Watch*, 345.

107. Ray Cline to David A. Phillips, 27 March 1975, part 1: container 7, folder 3, Papers of Ray Cline, Library of Congress Manuscript Division.

108. David A. Phillips, ARIO form letter, 15 March 1975, part 1: container 7, folder 3, Papers of Ray Cline, Library of Congress Manuscript Division; "C.I.A. Aide Quitting to Defend Agency," *New York Times*, 22 March 1975; Phillips, *The Night Watch*, 348–349.

109. Jean M. White, "Intelligence Gathering: Insiders Meet on the Outside," *Washington Post*, 18 September 1976; Phillips, *The Night Watch*, 366.

110. Joseph Novitski, "CIA Aide Quits, Will Head Drive," *Washington Post*, 10 May 1975.

111. Maggie Kennedy, "With Speeches Spy Comes Out of Cold," newspaper clipping, 4 November 1976, *Dallas Times Herald*, container 5, folder 3, Papers of David A. Phillips, Library of Congress Manuscript Division.

112. Olmsted, *Challenging the Secret Government*, 147.

113. Phillips, *The Night Watch*, 364, 376.

114. Ibid., 364. For an excellent overview of Agee, see Moran, *Company Confessions*, 122–141.

115. Angus Mackenzie, *Secrets: The CIA's War at Home* (Berkeley: University of California Press, 1997), 65.

116. Phillips, *The Night Watch*, 376.

117. David A. Phillips, "This Is About (shh)," *New York Times*, 25 May 1975.

118. Ibid.

119. Ibid.

120. Phillips, *The Night Watch*, 351.

121. Ibid., 140.

122. Ibid., 290.

123. Ibid., 311.

124. Victoria Toensing, "CIA's 'Cone of Silence' Guards Glass Ceiling," *Seattle Times*, 4 May 1995; Peter Carlson, "Looking to Sue the CIA? First Find Janine Brookner," *Washington Post*, 10 March 2004. Brookner's trouble began when "she reported her male deputy [in Jamaica] for his repeated and admitted wife beating, at least once to the point of the wife's collapse." See Toensing, "CIA's 'Cone of Silence.'"

125. Phillips, *The Night Watch*, 68.

126. Ibid., 67; see also Piero Gleijeses, *Shattered Hope: The Guatemalan Revolution and the United States, 1944–1954* (Princeton, NJ: Princeton University Press, 1991), 294–296.

127. Phillips, *The Night Watch*, 66.

128. Cullather, *Secret History*, xi, 76–77.

129. Phillips, *The Night Watch*, 352.

130. Ibid., 286; for Phillips's account of the task force, see ibid., 282–287.

131. Peter Kornbluh, *The Pinochet File: A Declassified Dossier on Atrocity and Accountability* (New York: New Press, 2003), 14.

132. Ibid., 17.

133. Ibid., 34–35.

134. Ibid., 29.

135. Phillips, *The Night Watch*, 352.

136. Ibid., 286–287.

137. Ibid., 352.

138. Cord Meyer, *Facing Reality: From World Federalism to the CIA* (New York: Harper & Row, 1980), 187.

139. Ibid., 189.

140. Kornbluh, *The Pinochet File*, 114.

141. Ibid., 90.

142. Phillips, *The Night Watch*, 327.

143. Kornbluh, *The Pinochet File*, 90.

144. Ibid., 111; Kornbluh demonstrates that the CIA concocted a propaganda scheme "designed to convince the Chilean generals that Allende was secretly plotting with Castro to undermine the army high command." The objective, of course, was to set the stage for a coup. Ibid., 94.

145. Ibid., 114.

146. Seymour Hersh, "Huge C.I.A. Operation Reported in U.S. against Antiwar Forces, Other Dissidents in Nixon Years," *New York Times,* 22 December 1974.

147. Meyer, *Facing Reality,* 209.

148. Ibid., 216.

149. Ibid., 215; Angus Mackenzie discovered in his investigation that Meyer received a thorough briefing on Operation MHCHAOS in 1972. Richard Ober, the project manager, outlined "the tremendous scope of MHCHAOS." See Mackenzie, *Secrets,* 55.

150. *Final Reports,* Select Comm. to Study Governmental Operations with Respect to Intelligence Activities [Church Committee], *Supplementary Detailed Staff Reports on Intelligence Activities and the Rights of Americans,* Book 3, S. Rep. No. 94-755 (1976), 697.

151. Phillips, *The Night Watch,* 350.

152. "[Rockefeller] Commission on CIA Activities Within the United States," *Report to the President by the Commission on CIA Activities Within the United States* (Washington, DC: Government Printing Office, 1975), 130.

153. Colby and Forbath, *Honorable Men,* 412.

154. "C.I.A. Aide Quitting to Defend Agency," 39.

155. Journal Office of Legislative Counsel, 14 January 1976, 2, CREST System, National Archives at College Park, College Park, MD.

156. Stafford T. Thomas to Herbert Hetu, 29 August 1979, 1, CREST System, National Archives at College Park, College Park, MD.

157. Jay Vogel, "Faculty Accused of Affiliation: 14 Linked with CIA Alleges Kelly," newspaper clipping, 2 February 1979, *Georgetown University Hoya,* part 1: container 26, folder 18, Papers of Ray Cline, Library of Congress Manuscript Division.

158. Ray Cline to M. Jon Vondracek, 31 January 1979, part 1: container 26, folder 18, Papers of Ray Cline, Library of Congress Manuscript Division.

159. Ray Cline to Admiral Stansfield Turner, 14 March 1977, part 1: container 26, folder 14, Papers of Ray Cline, Library of Congress Manuscript Division.

160. Ray Cline to Admiral Stansfield Turner, 18 July 1977, part 1: container 26, folder 14, Papers of Ray Cline, Library of Congress Manuscript Division.

161. Cline eventually turned against the Carter administration and joined Ronald Reagan's campaign in 1980. In a letter to Daniel Schorr in September 1979, Cline referred to Turner as "poor old Stan." See Cline to Schorr, 24 September 1979, 2, part 1: container 26, folder 18, Papers of Ray Cline, Library of Congress Manuscript Division.

162. Trevor McCrisken, "The Housewife, the Vigilante and the Cigarette-Smoking Man: The CIA and Television, 1975–2001," *History* 100 (April 2015): 295.

163. Cullather, *Secret History,* 122.

164. Ibid.

165. As with any organization, it is important to emphasize that differences

of opinion sometimes surfaced within ARIO. There was an early dispute over Phillips's decision to grant membership to Sam Adams, the former CIA analyst who had tangled with the Pentagon during the Vietnam War. At least one person resigned from ARIO in protest. See David A. Phillips to Board Members, 30 July 1976, 2, part 1: container 7, folder 4, Papers of Ray Cline, Library of Congress Manuscript Division; in addition, when the organization created the George Bush Award to honor contributions to the intelligence community, several members complained that the prize should have been named after someone with a more distinguished record than Bush, such as William Donovan. For the press release announcing the George Bush Award and the resulting controversy, see correspondence in part 1: container 7, folder 3, Papers of Ray Cline, Library of Congress Manuscript Division.

166. Schwarz quoted in Frank J. Smist Jr., *Congress Oversees the United States Intelligence Community, 1947–1994*, 2nd ed. (Knoxville: University of Tennessee Press, 1994), 64; for the most thorough overview of the public relations surrounding Welch's assassination, see Olmsted, *Challenging the Secret Government*, 151–155; see also Scott M. Cutlip, "Public Relations in the Government," *Public Relations Review* 2 (Summer 1976): 14–15.

167. "Slain C.I.A. Man Honored," *New York Times*, 31 December 1975; Eugene L. Meyer, "Slain CIA Agent Receives Unusual Honor," *Washington Post*, 31 December 1975; Olmsted, *Challenging the Secret Government*, 152; see also Loch K. Johnson, *A Season of Inquiry: The Senate Intelligence Investigation* (Lexington: University Press of Kentucky, 1985), 161–162.

168. "Colleagues Pay Tribute to Welch," *Washington Post*, 1 January 1976.

169. Laurence Stern, "CIA Agent Welch Buried," *Washington Post*, 7 January 1976; James M. Naughton, "Ford at Funeral for C.I.A. Officer," *New York Times*, 7 January 1976; Olmsted, *Challenging the Secret Government*, 152–153.

170. Stern, "CIA Agent Welch Buried."

171. Church quoted in Smist, *Congress Oversees*, 64.

172. Dan Morgan, "Slain Agent Feared for CIA Lives," *Washington Post*, 26 December 1975.

173. Ibid.

174. Phillips, *The Night Watch*, 271.

175. Olmsted, *Challenging the Secret Government*, 151; Morton H. Halperin, "CIA News Management," *Washington Post*, 23 January 1977.

176. Prados, *Lost Crusader*, 329.

177. Mackenzie, *Secrets*, 89. Mackenzie notes that two other publications had identified Welch: Julius Mader's *Who's Who in the CIA* in 1968 and a Peruvian journal in 1974. Ibid., 89; see also Philip Agee, *On the Run* (Secaucus, NJ: Lyle Stuart, 1987), 133.

178. Anthony Lewis, "Death and Secrecy," *New York Times*, 8 January 1976.

179. Ibid.

180. Nashel, *Edward Lansdale's Cold War*, 98.

181. Phillips, *The Night Watch*, 378; Phillips subsequently wrote a guide on how to start a career in the intelligence field. "If we decide that covert action is wrong because it constitutes meddling in other peoples' affairs," he said in

the chapter on the CIA, "we should re-examine not only our intelligence activities but our entire foreign policy, our foreign aid program, and our tariff policies (to mention only a few examples) because each of these can have a profound effect on the internal affairs of any number of countries and very often is designed to have just such an effect." See Phillips, *Careers in Secret Operations: How to Be a Federal Intelligence Officer* (Frederick, MD: University Publications of America, 1984), 38.

Chapter 2. Admiral Stansfield Turner, Herbert Hetu, and the Legend of CIA Openness, 1977–1980

1. Kathryn S. Olmsted, *Challenging the Secret Government: The Post-Watergate Investigations of the CIA and FBI* (Chapel Hill: University of North Carolina Press, 1996), 169.
2. E. H. Knoche to Admiral Turner, "Tour of Agency Headquarters-Congressional Sponsors," 19 April 1977, Suggestions for CIA Outreach to the Public, CREST System, National Archives at College Park, College Park, MD. Most sections of the document were declassified in 2002.
3. Ibid.
4. Ibid.
5. E. H. Knoche to Admiral Turner, "Meetings with Directors of University Area Study Centers," 19 April 1977, Suggestions for CIA Outreach to the Public, CREST System, National Archives at College Park, College Park, MD.
6. Ibid.
7. E. H. Knoche to Admiral Turner, "A Series of Agency Forums with Directors of Private Think Tanks," 19 April 1977, Suggestions for CIA Outreach to the Public, CREST System, National Archives at College Park, College Park, MD.
8. E. H. Knoche to Admiral Turner, "Public Affairs Suggestion" [High School and College Career Programs], 19 April 1977, Suggestions for CIA Outreach to the Public, CREST System, National Archives at College Park, College Park, MD.
9. E. H. Knoche to Admiral Turner, "Public Affairs Suggestion" [Expanded Public Speaking Program], 19 April 1977, Suggestions for CIA Outreach to the Public, CREST System, National Archives at College Park, College Park, MD.
10. E. H. Knoche to Admiral Turner, "Public Visitation Day," 19 April 1977, p. 1, Suggestions for CIA Outreach to the Public, CREST System, National Archives at College Park, College Park, MD.
11. Ibid., 2.
12. Stansfield Turner, *Secrecy and Democracy: The CIA in Transition* (Boston: Houghton Mifflin, 1985), 104.
13. Jeanne Edmunds, "They Didn't Laugh When I Invited CBS to Film the CIA," *Washington Post*, 15 July 1984; for background on Hetu, see Ronald Kessler, *Inside the CIA: Revealing the Secrets of the World's Most Powerful Spy Agency* (New York: Pocket Books, 1992), 215–220; for an overview of Hetu's career in the

navy, see Herbert Hetu, interview by Paul Stillwell, *The Reminiscences of Captain Herbert E. Hetu U.S. Navy (Retired)*, (Annapolis: Naval Institute Press, 2003); see also Christopher Moran, *Company Confessions: Secrets, Memoirs, and the CIA* (New York: St. Martin's, 2015), 163–173.

14. Hetu, interview by Stillwell, *The Reminiscences of Captain Herbert E. Hetu*, 42–44; according to Hetu, "I wrote all the first communiqués, and for the first 12–18 hours, everything in the press worldwide was coming out of the [USS] *Salem*, and I was writing it." Ibid., 43.

15. As Hetu explained the term, "those were the first people after World War II who, when the Navy decided to make public information a specialty, a separate designator, 1650, 1655, these were the first 40 people. People now are not sure there were exactly 40, but I'm working on that in my other hat as the [head of] public affairs [in the] alumni association." Ibid., 50. "Pickett Lumpkin was one of the greatest guys we've ever had in this business. He was a sweet, smart, nice man and taught me an enormous amount about public affairs," said Hetu. Ibid., 67.

16. Ibid., 72.

17. Ibid.,153. Interestingly, Hetu described the Watergate scandal as "a terrible PR blunder" and even suggested that President Nixon might have survived the crisis. "You know, if Nixon would have hung a couple of those guys on the White House lawn, they would be making gold statues of him. He would have been a hero." Ibid., 154.

18. Seth Jacobs, *America's Miracle Man in Vietnam* (Durham: Duke University Press, 2004), 154; see also Jonathan Nashel, *Edward Lansdale's Cold War* (Amherst: University of Massachusetts Press, 2005), 62–63. James T. Fisher says that the Office of Naval Intelligence compiled a dossier on Dooley that was seven hundred pages. This dossier included graphic descriptions of Dooley's sexual encounters with informants. See Fisher, *Dr. America: The Lives of Thomas A. Dooley, 1927–1961* (Amherst: University of Massachusetts Press, 1997), 84–89.

19. Hetu, interview by Stillwell, *The Reminiscences of Captain Herbert E. Hetu*, 60; Fisher, *Dr. America*, 86.

20. Jacobs, *America's Miracle Man*, 111. Jacobs points out that "*The Ugly American* became one of the most popular books in U.S. history, remaining on the best-seller list for seventy-eight weeks and ultimately selling over five million copies." Ibid. See also Nashel, *Edward Lansdale's Cold War*, 173–178.

21. Hetu, interview by Stillwell, *The Reminiscences of Captain Herbert E. Hetu*, 69.

22. Ibid., 75–79. Hetu explained that the navy would "bring the ships around and put them off the beach for a day or two, so they could shoot these scenes with the ships in the background." Ibid., 77.

23. Ibid., 97.

24. Ibid., 98; later Hetu was a consultant on Otto Preminger's film *In Harm's Way* (1965). Ibid., 132–137.

25. Ibid., 236.

26. Ibid., 237.

27. Herbert E. Hetu, "Public Relations During Peacetime Naval Disaster" (master's thesis, Boston University, 1965), 108; he also observed: "It becomes

obvious that the actions taken before disaster occurs are often the most important. When disaster strikes, the organizations which have planned to meet the
informational requirements are the ones which most effectively survive public
scrutiny. Perhaps the two most important words to remember in a disaster situation are—*Planning* and *Candor*." Ibid., 50.

28. Ibid., 80.

29. Hetu, interview by Stillwell, *The Reminiscences of Captain Herbert E. Hetu,*
229; in April 1969, when North Korea attacked an EC-121 spy plane, Hetu
managed the public relations response for the navy. Ibid., 209–214.

30. "If the P.I.O. [public information officer] can establish himself as an
ally of the stricken society rather than a potential enemy, he will most probably
serve that community, his organization, and the media in a positive and constructive manner," Hetu observed. Hetu, "Public Relations During Peacetime
Naval Disaster," 18.

31. Hetu quoted in Edmunds, "They Didn't Laugh When I Invited CBS to
Film the CIA"; see also Turner, *Secrecy and Democracy*, 105. "We are trying a new
openness policy," said Hetu. "We want advice on how better to serve the media."
Robert Green, "New CIA Image," 27 October 1977, *Manila Bulletin*, CREST
System, National Archives at College Park, College Park, MD.

32. Edmunds, "They Didn't Laugh When I Invited CBS to Film the CIA."

33. Hugh Sidey and John L. Steele to Admiral Turner, 9 August 1977, CREST
System, National Archives at College Park, College Park, MD; Herbert E. Hetu
to Acting Deputy Director of Central Intelligence, "Briefing of *Time*-Sponsored
Tour of Western European Industrialists," 25 August 1977, CREST System, National Archives at College Park, College Park, MD.

34. Leonard Levitt, "CIA Visits Glen Cove," 19 November 1977, *Newsday*,
CREST System, National Archives at College Park, College Park, MD.

35. Herbert E. Hetu to Acting Deputy Director for Administration, Public Briefings, 29 November 1977, CREST System, National Archives at College
Park, College Park, MD.

36. Paul V. Walsh to Herbert E. Hetu, "CBS—'Who's Who,'" 14 April 1977,
CREST System, National Archives at College Park, College Park, MD.

37. Robert W. Gambino to Deputy Director for Administration, "CBS—
'Who's Who,'" 13 April 1977, CREST System, National Archives at College
Park, College Park, MD.

38. Herbert E. Hetu to Admiral Turner, "CBS—'Who's Who,'" 18 April
1977, p. 2, CREST System, National Archives at College Park, College Park,
MD.

39. Ibid., 1.

40. Herbert E. Hetu, Second Meeting with ABC *Good Morning America* Rep-
resentatives, memorandum, 4 August 1977, Document No. CK3100202459,
Declassified Documents Reference System (DDRS). This database is now titled
U.S. Declassified Documents Online.

41. Herbert E. Hetu to Admiral Turner, "ABC—*Good Morning America*," 10
August 1977, p. 1, Document No. CK3100202460/CK3100202461, DDRS.

42. Herbert E. Hetu to Acting Deputy Director of Central Intelligence,

"ABC *Good Morning America*," 24 August 1977, Document No. CK3100202462, DDRS.

43. Herbert E. Hetu to Admiral Turner, "*Good Morning America* Program," 16 September 1977, Document No. CK3100202463/CK3100202464, DDRS; Hetu provided Turner with a briefing book to help prepare for the show, and they conducted a walk-through of 2430 E Street the day before the interview. Hetu also offered advice on how to dress: "I suggest you wear a light-weight, dark colored summer suit and a loose-fitting, comfortable shirt. You might consider bringing an additional shirt of the same color on a hanger to change during one of the lengthy film segments." Ibid., 2. For related documents on the *Good Morning America* interview, see Sonya Selby-Wright to Herbert E. Hetu, 28 June 1977, Document No. CK3100202458, DDRS; Sonya Selby-Wright to Herbert E. Hetu, 29 September 1977, Document No. CK3100202552, DDRS; and David Hartman to Herbert E. Hetu, 3 October 1977, Document No. CK3100202553, DDRS. See also Simon Willmetts, "The CIA and the Invention of Tradition," *Journal of Intelligence History* 14, no. 2 (2015): 124.

44. Nomination for Congressional Award for Exemplary Service to the Public, 14 October 1980, p. 2–3, CREST System, National Archives at College Park, College Park, MD.

45. Frank Carlucci to Incentive Awards Branch, 14 October 1980, Office of Personnel Management, CREST System, National Archives at College Park, College Park, MD.

46. Nomination for Congressional Award, 14 October 1980, 1–2.

47. Ibid., 2.

48. Ibid.

49. "Briefing Book Prepared by Public Affairs Office for Admiral Turner," 19 September 1977, Document No. CK3100202484-CK3100202532, Tab E, 2, DDRS.

50. Charles A. Briggs to Deputy Director for Administration, "Inspection Report of the Office of Public Affairs," July 1981, chap. 5, p. 2, the Publications Review Board (PRB), CREST System, National Archives at College Park, College Park, MD.

51. Ibid., 5. Between 1977 and June 4, 1981, there were 420 submissions to the PRB, of which 360 were described as "non-fiction," while the remaining 60 were categorized as "fiction." Ibid.

52. U.S. House of Representatives, Subcommittee on Oversight, Permanent Select Committee on Intelligence, *Prepublication Review and Secrecy Agreements*, 96th Cong., 2d sess. (16 and 24 April and 1 May 1980), 4.

53. Angus Mackenzie, *Secrets: The CIA's War at Home* (Berkeley: University of California Press, 1997), 71; for background on the PRB, see Moran, *Company Confessions*, 179–182.

54. Aspin quoted in George Lardner Jr., "CIA Defends Its Selective Censorship of Ex-Agents' Writings," *Washington Post*, 6 April 1980.

55. "Inspection Report of the Office of Public Affairs," July 1981, chap. 5, p. 4; of the 198 submissions to the board during the first three years of its existence, Hetu testified in March 1980 that they completely rejected three

while four were withdrawn from consideration. Lardner Jr., "CIA Defends Its Selective Censorship."

56. "Inspection Report of the Office of Public Affairs," July 1981, chap. 5, p. 5–6.

57. Kermit Roosevelt, *Countercoup: The Struggle for the Control of Iran* (New York: McGraw-Hill, 1979), 198.

58. Ibid., 199.

59. Richard and Gladys Harkness, "The Mysterious Doings of CIA," *Saturday Evening Post*, 6 November 1954; see also Hugh Wilford, "'Essentially a Work of Fiction': Kermit 'Kim' Roosevelt, Imperial Romance, and the Iran Coup of 1953," *Diplomatic History* 40, no. 5 (November 2016): 940–941.

60. "Iran 1953: The Strange Odyssey of Kermit Roosevelt's *Countercoup*," 12 May 2014, Document 11, ed. Malcolm Byrne, *National Security Archive Briefing Book No. 468*, accessed 22 Jun 2017, http://nsarchive.gwu.edu/NSAEBB/NSAEBB468/.

61. Ibid.

62. "Iran 1953: The Strange Odyssey," 12 May 2014, Document 17, accessed 22 June 2017, http://nsarchive.gwu.edu/NSAEBB/NSAEBB468/; see also Wilford, "'Essentially a Work of Fiction,'" 944.

63. For a detailed account of Snepp's odyssey, see Moran, *Company Confessions*, chap. 5.

64. Snepp quoted in Seymour M. Hersh, "Ex-C.I.A. Man Assails Saigon Evacuation," *New York Times*, 18 November 1977; see also Seymour M. Hersh, "C.I.A. Says Agent Violated Oath by Publishing Book About Saigon," *New York Times*, 19 November 1977; and Seymour M. Hersh, "Ex-Analyst Says C.I.A. in Saigon Gave False Reports to Newsmen," *New York Times*, 21 November 1977.

65. "U.S. Sues Ex-CIA Agent for Book Profits," *Washington Post*, 16 February 1978; for a description of the complex legal battle, see Frank Snepp, *Irreparable Harm: A Firsthand Account of How One Agent Took On the CIA in an Epic Battle Over Secrecy and Free Speech* (New York: Random House, 1999), esp. parts 3 and 4; see also Mackenzie, *Secrets*, 73–77.

66. Fred Barbash, "Snepp Breached Contract, Judge Says," *Washington Post*, 22 June 1978.

67. Fred Barbash, "Appeals Court Says CIA Agent Was Punished Improperly for Violating Secrecy Agreement," *Washington Post*, 21 March 1979.

68. Fred Barbash, "High Court Backs Secrecy Restraint on U.S. Workers," *Washington Post*, 20 February 1980. According to the three dissenters (John P. Stevens, William Brennan, and Thurgood Marshall), "The court seems unaware of the fact that its drastic new remedy has been fashioned to enforce a species of prior restraint on a citizen's right to criticize his government." Ibid.

69. Jim Mann, "Snepp and the CIA: A Few Troubling Questions Remain," *Los Angeles Times*, 2 March 1980.

70. "Third Ex-C.I.A. Agent Sued by U.S. for Profits," *New York Times*, 4 March 1980.

71. Laurence Stern, "Ex-CIA Chief Bares More in French," *Washington Post*, 19 November 1978. Colby revealed details about the *Glomar Explorer* and iden-

tified a station chief by name. Ibid.; John Prados, *Lost Crusader: The Secret Wars of CIA Director William Colby* (New York: Oxford University Press, 2003), 338; Snepp, *Irreparable Harm*, 114–115, 156–158, 308–309.

72. "Inspection Report of the Office of Public Affairs," July 1981, chap. 5, p. 11.

73. Ibid., 11–12.

74. George Lardner Jr., "CIA Defends Its Selective Censorship."

75. George Lardner Jr., "CIA Delays Printing of Ex-Aide's Book," *Washington Post*, 3 April 1980.

76. Ibid.; Wilbur C. Eveland, *Ropes of Sand: America's Failure in the Middle East* (New York: W. W. Norton, 1980), 13–14; Mackenzie, *Secrets*, 129–133. The CIA later released the secrecy contract. As Mackenzie explains, however, Eveland had not signed the document. "Even more important," says Mackenzie, "the employment contract contained no explicit assertion of a prepublication review agreement." After the CIA threatened litigation, Eveland reluctantly agreed to sign a secrecy pledge in December 1982. Mackenzie, *Secrets*, 131. See also Moran, *Company Confessions*, 207–212.

77. Snepp quoted in George Lardner Jr., "CIA to Snepp: Delete Name of (Known) Agent in Novel," *Washington Post*, 14 July 1980.

78. Ibid.

79. "Bob" quoted in Ralph W. McGehee, *Deadly Deceits: My 25 Years in the CIA* (1983; repr., Melbourne: Ocean Press, 1999), 197.

80. Ibid.

81. Ibid., 198.

82. Ibid.

83. Ibid., 199.

84. Ibid.

85. Ibid., 202.

86. Ibid., 203.

87. Bill Moyers, "In the Kingdom of the Half-Blind," 9 December 2005, The National Security Archive, accessed 28 July 2006, http://www.gwu.edu/~ns archiv/anniversary/moyers.htm.

88. Permanent Select Committee on Intelligence, Central Intelligence Agency Information Act, H.R. Rep. No. 98-726, pt. 1, at 6 (1984).

89. U.S. House of Representatives, Subcommittee on Government Information and Individual Rights of the Committee on Government Operations, *The Freedom of Information Act: Central Intelligence Agency Exemptions. Hearings on H.R. 5129, H.R. 7055, and H.R. 7056 to Enhance the Foreign Intelligence and Law Enforcement Activities of the United States by Improving the Protection of Information Necessary to Their Effective Operation*, 96th Cong., 2d sess. (20 February and 29 May 1980), 71.

90. U.S. House of Representatives, Subcommittee on Legislation of the Permanent Select Committee on Intelligence, "Statement of Mark H. Lynch on Behalf of the American Civil Liberties Union," *Legislation to Modify the Application of the Freedom of Information Act to the Central Intelligence Agency*, 98th Cong., 2d sess. (8 February 1984), 40.

91. John F. Blake to deputy DCI, "IPS Report on Impact of the FOIA and Privacy Act," 6 December 1978, p. 7, 10, 11, CREST System, National Archives at College Park, College Park, MD. CIA officials blamed the extensive backlog of FOIA cases on the agency's records management system. David Wise has vividly shown the limitations of these firewalls in his study of Aldrich Ames, the CIA turncoat arrested in 1994. "On June 13, 1985, in his fourth-floor office, Ames wrapped up between five and seven pounds of cable traffic and other secret documents in plastic bags, took the elevator down, and pushed his laminated ID card into the turnstiles that block the exits from headquarters. . . . No guard asked to look inside the plastic bags." Wise, *Nightmover: How Aldrich Ames Sold the CIA to the KGB for $4.6 Million* (New York: HarperCollins, 1995), 118.

92. John F. Blake to deputy DCI, "IPS Report on Impact of the FOIA and Privacy Act," 6 December 1978, p. 15. "While we take no issue with the concept that the American public has a right to know what its Government is doing," the report claimed, "we do submit that in the case of foreign intelligence records the public benefits deriving from the Act have not been commensurate with the costs." Ibid.

93. Ibid.

94. Ibid., 15–16.

95. Ibid., 16.

96. Ibid., 17.

97. John Stockwell, *In Search of Enemies: A CIA Story* (London: Andre Deutsch, 1978), 169; Athan G. Theoharis, "Researching the Intelligence Agencies: The Problem of Covert Activities," *Public Historian* 6 (Spring 1984): 69.

98. Stockwell, *In Search of Enemies,* 228n.

99. Theoharis, "Researching the Intelligence Agencies," 68.

100. *The Freedom of Information Act: Central Intelligence Agency Exemptions,* 23. There were other bills in both the House and the Senate at the time that would have provided the CIA with exemptions to FOIA. See, for instance, H.R. 6316, H.R. 7055, H.R. 7056, S. 2216, and S. 2284; Mackenzie, *Secrets,* 79–80.

101. *The Freedom of Information Act: Central Intelligence Agency Exemptions,* 29–31.

102. Ibid., 28, 67.

103. Ibid., 31.

104. "IPS Report on Impact of the FOIA and Privacy Act," 7.

105. *The Freedom of Information Act: Central Intelligence Agency Exemptions,* 26; historian Lloyd Gardner questioned Carlucci's accusation that foreign governments had expressed concern about FOIA, noting that the State Department had encouraged countries to complain during the controversy over the Pentagon Papers. The objective, of course, was to manufacture protest that would help justify the government's position in its case against Daniel Ellsberg. He implied that the CIA might have used similar tactics to build support for restricting FOIA. Interestingly, the revelations about the State Department resulted from a FOIA request filed by a student of Walter LaFeber. Ibid., 181.

106. Ibid., 25.

107. Ibid., 25, 28.

108. Ibid., 24.

109. Ibid., 53.

110. Ibid., 58.

111. Ibid., 70.

112. Ibid.

113. Ibid., 51, 62.

114. Ibid., 66.

115. Ibid., 94.

116. Ibid., 95.

117. Ibid., 171.

118. Ibid.

119. Ibid., 186.

120. Ibid., 184

121. John D. Marks, *The Search for the "Manchurian Candidate": The CIA and Mind Control* (1979; repr., New York: W. W. Norton, 1991), xix.

122. Ibid.

123. Jennifer McBride, "The CIA on Campus: 1969–1971," *Flat Hat*, 18 April 1980.

124. Ibid. For more information on Project Resistance, see David S. McCarthy, "'The Sun Never Sets on the Activities of the CIA': Project Resistance at William & Mary," *Intelligence and National Security* 28, no. 5 (October 2013): 611–633.

Chapter 3. The Culture of Secrecy Unleashed, 1981–1987

1. George Lardner Jr., "CIA Is Lowering the Blinds, Closing More Shutters," *Washington Post*, 30 June 1981; "Intelligence Agency Will Abolish Office Providing Press Data," *New York Times*, 1 July 1981.

2. Lardner, "CIA Is Lowering the Blinds"; Joseph E. Persico, *Casey: From the OSS to the CIA* (New York: Penguin Books, 1990), 270; Bob Woodward, *Veil: The Secret Wars of the CIA, 1981–1987* (New York: Simon & Schuster, 1987), 139.

3. According to Ronald Kessler, Hetu had previously sent Casey a memo in which he urged his new boss to reconsider the decision to end press briefings. Casey responded poorly: "I didn't ask you to debate it. I asked you to stop it. Now I'm ordering you to stop it. Stop it today. If you have any scheduled today, cancel them." Kessler, *Inside the CIA: Revealing the Secrets of the World's Most Powerful Spy Agency* (New York: Pocket Books, 1992), 220.

4. "Intelligence Agency Will Abolish Office Providing Press Data."

5. Robert M. Gates, *From the Shadows: The Ultimate Insider's Story of Five Presidents and How They Won the Cold War* (New York: Simon & Schuster, 1996), 211.

6. Ibid., 210.

7. Ibid., 211.

8. Cord Meyer, "Casey Picks Amateur for Most Sensitive CIA Job," *Washington Star*, 15 May 1981, Papers of Cord Meyer, container 5, folder 6, Library of

Congress Manuscript Division; Persico, *Casey*, 245; "C.I.A. Acknowledges Ex–Campaign Official Is Placed in Key Post," *New York Times*, 16 May 1981.

9. "The Company Mr. Casey Keeps," *New York Times*, 22 May 1981; Persico, *Casey*, 246; Woodward, *Veil*, 133.

10. Woodward, *Veil*, 131.

11. Bob Woodward and Patrick E. Tyler, "Hugel Denies Leaking Inside Business Information," *Washington Post*, 14 July 1981.

12. Ibid.

13. Ibid.

14. "Letters in Hugel Resignation," *New York Times*, 15 July 1981; for a good overview of the entire Hugel affair, see Persico, *Casey*, 243–252; see also Woodward, *Veil*, 140–147.

15. Hugel quoted in Persico, *Casey*, 250.

16. Persico, *Casey*, 268.

17. For an assessment of the controversy surrounding Casey's finances, see ibid., 254–261, 267–269; Woodward, *Veil*, 148–152; Paul L. Montgomery, "Judge Asserts Casey, C.I.A. Chief, Misled Stock Buyers in '68," *New York Times*, 15 July 1981; Judith Miller, "Senate Panel to Review Charges on Chief of C.I.A.," *New York Times*, 18 July 1981; Terence Smith, "Moynihan Assails White House on Casey Files," *New York Times*, 22 July 1981; Judith Miller, "Some Call for Resignation," *New York Times*, 25 July 1981; "Financial Filings at Issue," *New York Times*, 25 July 1981; Judith Miller, "Director of C.I.A. Asking [for] a Hearing to Answer Critics," *New York Times*, 27 July 1981; Judith Miller, "Casey Summoned to Testify Today," *New York Times*, 29 July 1981; and Arnold H. Lubasch, "Judge Withdraws Decision against Casey in Suit," *New York Times*, 11 November 1981.

18. Persico, *Casey*, 261; Judith Miller, "Senate Committee Finds Casey Fit for C.I.A. Job but Pursues Inquiry," *New York Times*, 30 July 1981.

19. Persico, *Casey*, 300.

20. Woodward, *Veil*, 265–266. Casey named Clair George the Congressional liaison. Persico, *Casey*, 301; Kessler, *Inside the CIA*, 220–222.

21. Lauder quoted in Persico, *Casey*, 455; George V. Lauder to Mike Wallace, 7 July 1986. Released by the CIA to the author on 19 September 2006 in response to a FOIA request; Senator Barry Goldwater often referred to Casey as "flappy" and "flapper lips." Woodward, *Veil*, 148.

22. For the most part, the eight letters are routine: George V. Lauder to William Casey, 23 April 1985; George V. Lauder to William Casey, 24 April 1985; George V. Lauder to William Casey, 9 October 1985; George V. Lauder to William Casey, 3 January 1986; George V. Lauder to William Casey, 9 May 1986; George V. Lauder to William Casey, 15 May 1986; George V. Lauder to William Casey, 16 May 1986; George V. Lauder to William Casey, 30 May 1986, CREST System, National Archives at College Park, College Park, MD.

23. George V. Lauder to Emil Slaboda, 17 September 1985. Released by the CIA to the author on 19 September 2006 in response to a FOIA request; Lauder's letter was published in the *Trentonian*. "CIA Response," *Trentonian*, 25 September 1985. Copy released by the CIA to the author on 19 September 2006 in response to a FOIA request.

24. George V. Lauder to Max Frankel, 15 October 1984. Released by the CIA to the author on 19 September 2006 in response to a FOIA request.

25. Ibid.

26. See, for example, Greg Grandin, *Empire's Workshop: Latin America, the United States, and the Rise of the New Imperialism* (New York: Henry Holt, 2006), chap. 3, esp. 95; see also Michael McClintock, *The American Connection: State Terror and Popular Resistance in El Salvador* (London: Zed Books, 1985).

27. George V. Lauder to Earl W. Foell, 21 October 1986. Released by the CIA to the author on 19 September 2006 in response to a FOIA request.

28. George V. Lauder to Leslie Gelb, 3 June 1986. Released by the CIA to the author on 19 September 2006 in response to a FOIA request; Lauder had previously issued a denial to the *Wall Street Journal*: "The CIA has made no information public concerning Mr. Yurchenko. Moreover, it is forbidden by Presidential Executive Order 12333 from propagandizing or attempting to influence the American public." George V. Lauder to Robert Bartley, 5 November 1985. Released by the CIA to the author on 19 September 2006 in response to a FOIA request.

29. Lauder to Bartley, 5 November 1985.

30. George V. Lauder to Bob Woodward, 20 February 1986, p. 2. Released by the CIA to the author on 19 September 2006 in response to a FOIA request.

31. George V. Lauder to Daniel S. Wheeler, 29 October 1986, p. 2. Released by the CIA to the author on 19 September 2006 in response to a FOIA request.

32. George V. Lauder to John Seigenthaler, 21 April 1986, p. 2. Released by the CIA to the author on 19 September 2006 in response to a FOIA request.

33. George V. Lauder to Arnaud de Borchgrave, 22 October 1985. Released by the CIA to the author on 19 September 2006 in response to a FOIA request.

34. George V. Lauder to Arnaud de Borchgrave, 12 December 1985. Released by the CIA to the author on 19 September 2006 in response to a FOIA request.

35. George V. Lauder to Arnaud de Borchgrave, 27 December 1985, p. 2. Released by the CIA to the author on 19 September 2006 in response to a FOIA request.

36. Ibid., 1.

37. Ibid., 2.

38. George V. Lauder to Jack N. Anderson, 26 December 1984. Released by the CIA to the author on 19 September 2006 in response to a FOIA request; Jack Anderson, "Ex-Agent Cites CIA Drug Scheme," *Washington Post*, 26 December 1984.

39. Lauder to Anderson, 26 December 1984.

40. David Crook, "CIA Sought His News Sources, Anderson Says," *Los Angeles Times*, 11 January 1985.

41. Ibid.

42. Ibid.

43. Kenneth B. Noble, "Firm Citing C.I.A. Link Is Charged," *New York Times*, 25 August 1984.

44. "According to reports by bankruptcy trustees, Rewald spent $250,000 on a fleet of cars, including three Cadillacs, two Mercedes-Benzes, a Rolls-Royce and a Jaguar; $66,000 on boats; $82,000 on jewelry and art; $154,000 on travel; $102,000 on relatives; $225,000 on household help, including tutors; and $541,000 on horses and other polo club expenses." See Howard Kurtz, "Investors Say Bankrupt Firm Had CIA Tie," *Washington Post*, 16 April 1984.

45. For good overviews of the Rewald affair, see Jonathan Kwitny, "Suits Focus on Extent of CIA Involvement in an Alleged Fraud," *Wall Street Journal*, 18 April 1984; Jonathan Kwitny, "House Panel Seeks Justice, SEC Records as Probe of Rewald-CIA Case Is Launched," *Wall Street Journal*, 22 May 1984; John Kelly, "Cover to Cover: Rewald's CIA Story," *Counterspy* 8, no. 4 (June–August 1984): 8–17, 48–57; Marita Hernandez, "Hawaii Investment Adviser Held in Fraud," *Los Angeles Times*, 1 September 1984; and David Crook, "Adventures in Paradise: How ABC Enraged the CIA—and Why the CIA Fought Back," *Los Angeles Times*, 5 May 1985.

46. Kurtz, "Investors Say Bankrupt Firm Had CIA Tie."

47. Ibid.

48. Jonathan Kwitny, "Suits Focus on Extent of CIA Involvement."

49. Ibid.

50. Kurtz, "Investors Say Bankrupt Firm Had CIA Tie"; David Crook, "Adventures in Paradise"; Jack Anderson said that "at least 17" CIA officers used BBRDW for cover. Anderson, "Ex-Agent Cites CIA Drug Scheme"; see also Jack Anderson, "CIA Role Was More Than Low-Level," *Washington Post*, 2 November 1984.

51. Jonathan Kwitny, "Suits Focus on Extent of CIA Involvement."

52. David Crook, "Adventures in Paradise."

53. John Kelly, the editor of *Counterspy*, actually helped to ensure that the story received wider coverage. See David Crook, "Adventures in Paradise."

54. Ibid.

55. Ibid.

56. "C.I.A. Denies a Murder Effort," *New York Times*, 28 September 1984.

57. "Complaint by C.I.A. Over Report on TV," *New York Times*, 22 November 1984; Ward Sinclair, "In FCC Complaint, CIA Says ABC Distorted News," *Washington Post*, 22 November 1984; David Crook, "CIA Asks FCC to Probe ABC Report for Fairness," *Los Angeles Times*, 27 November 1984; "CIA and ABC," *Washington Post*, 27 November 1984; David Crook, "ABC Retraction of CIA Murder Plot Detailed," *Los Angeles Times*, 13 December 1984.

58. "Complaint by C.I.A. Over Report on TV."

59. For the FCC's response to the complaint, see George Lardner Jr., "FCC Rejects CIA Complaint of 'News Distortion' by ABC," *Washington Post*, 11 January 1985; and David Crook, "FCC Staff Rejects CIA Complaint against ABC," *Los Angeles Times*, 11 January 1985. For an overview of the CIA's appeal, see David Crook, "CIA Renews Its Charges against ABC," *Los Angeles Times*, 9 February 1985; David Crook, "CIA Comes Out Firing against ABC," *Los Angeles Times*, 11 February 1985; and Penny Pagano, "FCC Dismisses CIA Charges against ABC," *Los Angeles Times*, 13 July 1985.

60. David Crook, "'Chilling Effect' Cited in FCC Decision," *Los Angeles Times,* 16 July 1985.

61. Robert Parry and Peter Kornbluh, "Iran-Contra's Untold Story," *Foreign Policy* 72 (Fall 1988): 5.

62. Raymond graduated from the College of William & Mary in 1950. Phillips had attended the college before World War II, but in the aftermath of a wild road trip, he missed his exams. According to Phillips's account: "I had attended a weekend prom at a now defunct girls' school in Washington and accepted, perhaps in an alcoholic haze, an invitation from a convivial fellow to ride with him back to school. I slept well in his car, but unfortunately his school turned out to be Yale." He then enrolled at Texas Christian University. See Phillips, *The Night Watch* (New York: Ballantine, 1977), 3.

63. Robert Parry, *Lost History: Contras, Cocaine, the Press & 'Project Truth'* (Arlington: Media Consortium, 1999), 49.

64. *Report of the Congressional Committee Investigating the Iran-Contra Affair,* H.R. Rep. No. 100-433, S. Rep. No. 100-216, appendix B: vol. 22, at 155 (1988) (deposition of Walter Raymond Jr.).

65. National Security Decision Directive No. 77, 14 January 1983, "Management of Public Diplomacy Relative to National Security," accessed 29 March 2008, http://www.fas.org/irp/offdocs/nsdd/nsdd-077.htm. Parry and Kornbluh, "Iran-Contra's Untold Story," 9; Parry, *Lost History,* 49–50; Grandin, *Empire's Workshop,* chap. 4, esp. 123–124; Malcolm Byrne, *Iran-Contra: Reagan's Scandal and the Unchecked Abuse of Presidential Power* (Lawrence: University Press of Kansas, 2014), 21–22.

66. Parry and Kornbluh, "Iran-Contra's Untold Story," 9; Parry, *Lost History,* 50.

67. Parry and Kornbluh, "Iran-Contra's Untold Story," 9; *Report of the Congressional Committee Investigating the Iran-Contra Affair,* appendix B: vol. 22, at 166.

68. "Letters," *Foreign Policy* 73 (Winter 1988–1989): 173.

69. Ibid., 177; *Report of the Congressional Committee Investigating the Iran-Contra Affair,* appendix B: vol. 22, at 70–71.

70. *Report of the Congressional Committee Investigating the Iran-Contra Affair,* appendix B: vol. 22, at 71.

71. Walter Raymond Jr. to John M. Poindexter, "Central American Outreach," 29 August 1983, repr. as OLN-220 in *Iran-Contra Investigation* in S. Select Committee on Secret Military Assistance to Iran and the Nicaraguan Opposition and H.R. Select Committee to Investigate Covert Arms Transactions with Iran, Cong. Rep. 100-7, part 3: appendix A, at 874 (Washington, DC: Government Printing Office, 1988); Parry and Kornbluh, "Iran-Contra's Untold Story," 11.

72. Parry and Kornbluh, "Iran-Contra's Untold Story," 27; "They were trying to manipulate [US] public opinion . . . using the tools of Walt Raymond's trade craft which he learned from his career in the CIA covert operation shop," explained an anonymous insider from the National Security Council. Ibid., 4–5; *Iran-Contra Investigation,* 843.

73. Raymond to Poindexter, *Iran-Contra Investigation*, part 3: appendix A, at 843.

74. Parry and Kornbluh, "Iran-Contra's Untold Story," 11; *Report of the Congressional Committee Investigating the Iran-Contra Affair*, appendix B: vol. 22, at 49.

75. Parry and Kornbluh, "Iran-Contra's Untold Story," 20. They observed that "in its first year alone, [the Office of Public Diplomacy's] activities included booking more than 1,500 speaking engagements, including radio, television, and editorial board interviews; publishing three booklets on Nicaragua; and distributing materials to 1,600 college libraries, 520 political science faculties, 122 editorial writers, and 107 religious organizations." Ibid., 17.

76. *Report of the Congressional Committee Investigating the Iran-Contra Affair*, appendix B: vol. 22, at 88.

77. Raymond to Poindexter, *Iran-Contra Investigation*, part 3: appendix A, at 859; Raymond said that he was not involved in this effort. *Report of the Congressional Committee Investigating the Iran-Contra Affair*, appendix B: vol. 22, at 124; "North's calendars show some 70 public diplomacy strategy sessions with Raymond between 1984 and 1986—though Raymond has asserted that North was 'not a regular attendee' at the meetings." Parry and Kornbluh, "Iran-Contra's Untold Story," 12.

78. Parry and Kornbluh, "Iran-Contra's Untold Story," 28.

79. Ibid., 10; Raymond to Poindexter, *Iran-Contra Investigation*, part 3: appendix A, at 875; Parry, *Lost History*, 62.

80. Parry and Kornbluh, "Iran-Contra's Untold Story," 5–6.

81. Persico, *Casey*, 532–533; Woodward, *Veil*, 486–487; for background on the tense relationship between Casey and Leahy, see Gates, *From the Shadows*, 370–371.

82. Rowland Evans and Robert Novak, "Congress Is Crippling the CIA," *Reader's Digest*, November 1986, 99.

83. George Lardner Jr., "CIA Is Sued Over Its Censorship of Article on Fabricating Data," *Washington Post*, 28 March 1981.

84. George Lardner Jr., "CIA Veteran Decries Effort to 'Reclassify' Material in His Book," *Washington Post*, 1 April 1982; Ralph W. McGehee, *Deadly Deceits: My 25 Years in the CIA* (1983; repr., Melbourne: Ocean Press, 1999), 200–203.

85. McGehee, *Deadly Deceits*, 200.

86. Stansfield Turner, *Secrecy and Democracy: The CIA in Transition* (Boston: Houghton Mifflin, 1985), x.

87. Ibid., xii.

88. Snepp quoted in Seymour Hersh, "Ex–Intelligence Director Disputes Censorship of His Book on C.I.A.," *New York Times*, 18 May 1983. "I think Turner deserves everything the censors visit on him because he failed to recognize just how dangerous censorship was in the first place," Snepp remarked. Ibid.

89. "Students Punished for Protest," *New York Times*, 9 December 1984; Cory Dean, "Student Activism Alive at Brown U[niversity]," *New York Times*, 14 February 1985; there was also controversy involving the CIA at Harvard University. This scandal began in the fall of 1985 when the *Harvard Crimson* revealed that the director of the school's Center for Middle Eastern Studies, Nadav

Safran, had taken around $46,000 from the CIA to finance a conference. It also emerged that the CIA had paid over $100,000 to assist Safran with the researching and writing of *Saudi Arabia: The Ceaseless Quest for Security*. See Stuart Lavietes, "Nadav Safran, 77, a Professor and an Expert in Mideast Politics," *New York Times*, 27 July 2003; "C.I.A. Aid for Meeting Protested," *New York Times*, 14 October 1985; Charles R. Babcock, "Author Defends CIA Aid for Book About Saudis," *Washington Post*, 15 October 1985; Colin Campbell, "Harvard Widens Inquiry in C.I.A. Aid to Professor," *New York Times*, 20 October 1985; Colin Campbell, "C.I.A. Grant Raises Questions on Research Rules at Harvard," *New York Times*, 5 November 1985; Fox Butterfield, "Scholar to Quit Post at Harvard Over C.I.A. Tie," *New York Times*, 2 January 1986.

90. According to the CIA's website, "Harvard, Princeton, Georgetown, University of South Carolina, University of Oregon, University of Kentucky, Texas A&M, Marquette University, Ohio State University and the military academies" are a few of the universities that have participated in the project. "Officer in Residence Program," Center for the Study of Intelligence, accessed 16 July 2007, https://www.cia.gov/library/center-for-the-study-of-intelligence/academic -relations/officer-in-residence-program.html. "CIA hopes to demonstrate the quality and competence of its people, and the Agency benefits when its officers can work in an academic environment. The officers, and the Agency, benefit from the substantive outreach to students, faculty, and administrators on US campuses." Ibid.

91. John Hollister Hedley, "Twenty Years of Officers in Residence," *Studies in Intelligence* 49, no. 4 (2005), accessed 21 July 2006, https://www.cia.gov/csi /studies/vo149no4/Officers_in_Residence_3.htm.

92. Persico, *Casey*, 456.

93. Casey quoted in Ibid.

94. Ibid.

95. Ibid., 231. According to Persico, "to Casey, the Freedom of Information Act was democracy turned on its head." Ibid., 290.

96. William J. Casey, "The American Intelligence Community," *Presidential Studies Quarterly* 12, no. 2 (Spring 1982): 151.

97. "Pious Deceptions," *New York Times*, 12 September 1982.

98. Ibid.

99. Ibid.

100. William J. Casey, "Freedom of Information Harmful to the C.I.A.," *New York Times*, 1 October 1982.

101. Judge Gerhardt Gesell quoted in ibid. The irony, of course, is that the CIA Information Act of 1984 continued to allow first-person FOIA requests. Since Agee was asking for information pertaining to him, the exemptions did not apply. See Philip Agee, *On the Run* (Secaucus, NJ: Lyle Stuart, 1987), 42–44, 90–91, 331, 340. Frank Carlucci had used the same tactic in 1980. See George Lardner Jr., "CIA Uses Agee Case in War on Freedom of Information Act," *Washington Post*, 15 March 1980. Melvin Wulf, an attorney who represented Agee, claimed that the CIA was "working the Agee angle in order to destroy the Freedom of Information Act." Ibid.

102. Angus Mackenzie, *Secrets: The CIA's War at Home* (Berkeley: University of California Press, 1997), 105; Mackenzie described the relationship between Lynch and Mayerfeld in the following way:

> For eight years, while fighting against Mayerfeld in court over the FOIA, Lynch had grown to respect his opponent, despite the fact that the men seemed in every respect such opposites—Mayerfeld, a shrewd, tough fireplug of a man; Lynch, tall and fragile-looking with an unfortunately naive demeanor. Lynch's idealism compelled him to follow his vision of what ought to be, while Mayerfeld was a crafter of opportunity, carefully exploiting each opening. Mayerfeld was expert at creating the impression that he might accommodate his opponent's desires—without ever doing so. (Ibid., 113.)

103. Ibid., 106–107.

104. Robert Pear, "C.I.A. Is Nearer [to] Pact on Release of Certain Files," *New York Times*, 30 May 1983; Paul Taylor, "Limited Exemption for CIA Under FOIA Now Acceptable," *Washington Post*, 31 May 1983.

105. "The Plot Thickens," *Nation*, 18 June 1983, 1; Mackenzie, *Secrets*, 114–115.

106. "Clarification," *Nation*, 2 July 1983, 2; Mackenzie, *Secrets*, 115.

107. Angus Mackenzie, "A C.I.A.-A.C.L.U. Deal? The Operational Files Exemption," *Nation*, 24 September 1983, 234; Mackenzie, *Secrets*, 115–116.

108. Morton H. Halperin and Allan Adler, "There Is No Deal," *Nation*, 24 September 1983, 234.

109. Mackenzie, *Secrets*, 116.

110. Persico, *Casey*, 290.

111. Ibid.

112. Victor S. Navasky, "Why Sue the C.I.A.?" *New York Times*, 26 October 1982; the Supreme Court accepted a case involving a FOIA lawsuit against the CIA a few years later, ruling in favor of the agency in 1985 (CIA v. Sims). The FOIA requester was seeking "the names of the institutions and individuals that had performed MKULTRA research." James X. Dempsey, "The CIA and Secrecy," in *A Culture of Secrecy: The Government Versus the People's Right to Know*, ed. Athan G. Theoharis (Lawrence: University Press of Kansas, 1998), 42. "As a result of the *Sims* case," says Dempsey, "the phrase 'sources and methods' [the B-3 exemption] has attained talismanic significance as grounds for withholding from the public information about the CIA. Protecting sources and methods trumps other values." Ibid., 44.

113. Navasky, "Why Sue the C.I.A.?"

114. McMahon quoted in "C.I.A. Seeks Protection against Opening Files," *New York Times*, 22 June 1983; McMahon made the same claim to a House subcommittee in February 1984. See "C.I.A. Aide Complains of Deterrent to Agents," *New York Times*, 9 February 1984.

115. Nelson quoted in Robert Pear, "C.I.A. Data Access Runs into Snags," *New York Times*, 4 September 1983.

116. Ibid.

117. Congressman Mazzoli introduced H.R. 3460, and Congressman Whitehurst introduced H.R. 4431. In March 1984, Mazzoli, Whitehurst, and

two other congressmen introduced H.R. 5164, which was a compromise between the earlier versions.

118. *Legislation to Modify the Application of the Freedom of Information Act to the Central Intelligence Agency,* Subcommittee on Legislation of the Permanent Select Committee on Intelligence, at 5, 14 (1984).

119. Ibid., 15.

120. Ibid., 14.

121. Ibid., 39.

122. U.S. House of Representatives, Subcommittee on Government Information, Justice, and Agriculture of the Committee on Government Operations, *CIA Information Act: Hearing on H.R. 5164 to Amend the National Security Act of 1947 to Regulate Public Disclosure of Information Held by the Central Intelligence Agency, and for Other Purposes,* 98th Cong., 2d sess., 10 May 1984 [hereafter cited as *CIA Information Act*], 41; Stephen Engelberg, "C.I.A. and A.C.L.U. Support Curb on Information," *New York Times,* 11 May 1984.

123. *CIA Information Act,* 84.

124. Ibid.

125. Ibid., 87–88. There were eleven other pending cases listed by the CIA. Ibid., 85.

126. Ibid., 88. After it became clear that Congressman Mazzoli would not allow the CIA to use the legislation to block pending litigation, Mackenzie received the Operation MHCHAOS documents on May 15, 1984. See Mackenzie, *Secrets,* 117.

127. *CIA Information Act,* 89.

128. "Policy Adopted by Executive Committee of the ACLU of Southern California on June 5, 1984," repr. in ibid., 203. See also R. Samuel Paz and Ramona Ripston to Congressman Glenn English, 7 June 1984, repr. in ibid., 201–202.

129. Mae Churchill quoted in David Burnham, "The Increasing Dissent Within the A.C.L.U.," *New York Times,* 14 August 1984.

130. David Burnham, "A.C.L.U. Reviews Support of Information Bill," *New York Times,* 9 September 1984.

131. Mackenzie, *Secrets,* 117–118; George Lardner Jr., "Measure Protecting CIA Files Blocked in House," *Washington Post,* 18 September 1984; "Shielding CIA Files," *Washington Post,* 20 September 1984; "House Approves a Bill Restricting C.I.A. Files," *New York Times,* 20 September 1984. The final vote was 369–36.

132. Woodward, *Veil,* 383–384.

133. "Statement on Signing the Central Intelligence Agency Information Act, 15 October 1984, *Public Papers of the Presidents of the United States: Ronald Reagan, 1984, Book 2: June 30 to December 31, 1984* (Washington, DC: Government Printing Office, 1987), 1541.

134. Jeffrey T. Richelson, "Holding Back: How Agencies Thwart the Freedom of Information Act," *Bulletin of the Atomic Scientists* 59 (November/December 2003): 29–30.

135. William J. Casey to Cong. Edward P. Boland, 27 April 1984, repr. in

Central Intelligence Agency Information Act, Permanent Select Committee on Intelligence, H.R. Rep. No. 98-726, part 1, at 12–13 (1984).

136. Ibid., 13.

137. Dempsey, "The CIA and Secrecy," 48.

138. Ibid., 49; Steven Aftergood, "CIA Expands Operational File Secrecy," *Secrecy News,* 19 April 2006.

139. "Long, Secret History of C.I.A. Sheds Light on Battles Over Authority," *New York Times,* 28 November 1989.

Chapter 4. The Rise and Fall of the New Era of Openness at the CIA, 1988–2001

Epigraphs

*Warren F. Kimball, "Openness and the CIA," *Studies in Intelligence,* no. 10 (Winter–Spring 2001): 65.

†US House of Representatives, Subcommittee on Government Information, Justice, and Agriculture of the Committee on Government Operations, *CIA Information Act: Hearing on H.R. 5164 to Amend the National Security Act of 1947 to Regulate Public Disclosure of Information Held by the Central Intelligence Agency, and for Other Purposes,* 98th Cong., 2d sess., 10 May 1984 [hereafter cited as *CIA Information Act*], "Statement of Charles S. Rowe," 63.

‡Aftergood quoted in Elaine Sciolino, "Cameras Are Being Turned on a Once-Shy Spy Agency," *New York Times,* 6 May 2001.

1. Arthur S. Hulnick, "Openness: Being Public About Secret Intelligence," *International Journal of Intelligence and Counterintelligence* 12, no. 4 (Winter 1999): 469–470; Ronald Kessler, *Inside the CIA: Revealing the Secrets of the World's Most Powerful Spy Agency* (New York: Pocket Books, 1992), 222–227, 232–235. "When Baker took over the CIA's public affairs in June 1987," says Kessler, "he found that much of the good work Herb Hetu had accomplished under Turner had been torpedoed by Casey." Ibid., 224.

2. Members of the Task Force on Greater CIA Openness to Gates, "Task Force Report on Greater CIA Openness," 20 December 1991, p. 6, accessed 24 March 2006, http://www.cia-on-campus.org/foia/pao1.html.

3. In June 2017, nearly three deades later, the State Department released an update. See "Iran 1953: State Department Finally Releases Updated Official History of Mosaddeq Coup" [Electronic Record]; Malcolm Byrne, ed., *National Security Archive Briefing Book No. 598,* retrieved from http://nsarchive.gwu.edu /NSAEBB/NSAEBB598-State-Department-releases-documents-on-US-backed -1953-coup-in-Iran/, 15 June 2017.

4. Warren I. Cohen, "At the State Dept., Historygate," *New York Times,* 8 May 1990; "History Bleached at State," *New York Times,* 16 May 1990; for a superb overview of the background to Cohen's resignation and its complicated aftermath, see Page Putnam Miller, "We Can't Yet Read Our Own Mail: Access to the Records of the Department of State," in *A Culture of Secrecy: The Government Versus the People's Right to Know,* ed. Athan G. Theoharis (Lawrence: University

Press of Kansas, 1998), 186–210. See also Matthew Jones and Paul McGarr, "'Real Substance, Not Just Symbolism'? The CIA and the Representation of Covert Operations in the *Foreign Relations of the United States* Series," in *Intelligence Studies in Britain and the US: Historiography Since 1945*, ed. Christopher R. Moran and Christopher J. Murphy (Edinburgh, UK: Edinburgh University Press, 2013), 65–89.

5. Miller, "We Can't Yet Read Our Own Mail, 195; Kimball, "Openness and the CIA," 66–67.

6. Helms quoted in Miller, "We Can't Yet Read Our Own Mail," 199.

7. Kimball, "Openness and the CIA," 66–67.

8. *Nomination of Robert M. Gates, to Be Director of Central Intelligence*, S. Select Committee on Intelligence, 102d Cong., 3 vols., vol. 2, at 143 (Washington, DC: Government Printing Office, 1992).

9. Ibid., 193.

10. Ibid., 261; see also Angus Mackenzie, *Secrets: The CIA's War at Home* (Berkeley: University of California Press, 1997), 183.

11. *Nomination of Robert M. Gates*, vol. 1, at 444; for Gates's assessment of the confirmation process in 1991, see Robert M. Gates, *From the Shadows: The Ultimate Insider's Story of Five Presidents and How They Won the Cold War* (New York: Simon & Schuster, 1996), 545–552.

12. Gates, *From the Shadows*, 551.

13. *Nomination of Robert M. Gates*, vol. 1, at 444; for background on the hearings, see Richard L. Berke, "Bradley Goes One-on-One with Gates," *New York Times*, 18 September 1991; Elaine Sciolino, "Gates Almost a Side Issue in Hearings," *New York Times*, 1 October 1991; and "Excerpts from Senate Hearing on Nomination of C.I.A. Chief," *New York Times*, 2 October 1991.

14. Robert M. Gates to Joseph R. DeTrani, "Greater CIA Openness," 18 November 1991. Released by the CIA to the author on 29 November 2005 in response to a FOIA request. See also Mackenzie, *Secrets*, 184.

15. Joseph R. DeTrani to Robert M. Gates, "Task Forces on Greater CIA Openness and Internal Agency Communication," 22 November 1991, p. 1. Released by the CIA to the author on 29 November 2005 in response to a FOIA request. With the exception of DeTrani, all of the names of task force participants are redacted from the document. Ibid., 1. A task force on internal agency communication was established at the same time, but the group had different members. John Hedley became its chairperson. Ibid., 2.

16. Joseph R. DeTrani to Robert M. Gates, "Report of First Meeting of Task Force on Greater CIA Openness," 26 November 1991. Released by the CIA to the author on 29 November 2005 in response to a FOIA request.

17. Ibid.

18. Joseph R. DeTrani to Robert M. Gates, "Task Force on Greater CIA Openness—Week Two," 6 December 1991, p. 1. Released by the CIA to the author on 29 November 2005 in response to a FOIA request.

19. Ibid., 2; Mackenzie contends that "'openness' [for Gates] meant adopting a well-crafted public relations scheme aimed at the most important opinion-makers in the nation." Mackenzie, *Secrets*, 187.

20. DeTrani to Gates, "Task Force on Greater CIA Openness—Week Two," 1.

21. Ibid. DeTrani outlined additional recommendations from Tenet in his memo: "Whatever path we pursue on openness, be consistent. . . . If we aren't consistent, our efforts could be seen as manipulation or politicization"; "admit when we are wrong and work to find ways to cover dissent in our product"; "recognize the dilemma in the intelligence success/policy failure sequence and how to deal with that as an executive branch agency"; and "be excellent in what we do in public." Ibid.

22. Joseph R. DeTrani to Robert M. Gates, "Task Force on Greater CIA Openness—Week Three," 13 December 1991. Released by the CIA to the author on 29 November 2005 in response to a FOIA request.

23. Members of Task Force on Greater CIA Openness to Robert M. Gates, "Task Force Report on Greater CIA Openness," 20 December 1991, p. 2.

24. Ibid., 3.

25. Ibid.

26. Ibid.

27. Ibid., 7.

28. Ibid., 8.

29. Robert M. Gates, "Task Force Report on Greater CIA Openness," 6 January 1992, p. 2. Released by the CIA to the author on 29 November 2005 in response to a FOIA request. Gates prohibited his subordinates from offering "groups of reporters unclassified background briefings when there is a major international event" unless he gave approval. Ibid., 3; Mackenzie, *Secrets*, 186–187.

30. Gates, "Task Force Report on Greater CIA Openness," 2. Gates also supported the attempt to publish an anthology of selected articles from the CIA's in-house journal, *Studies in Intelligence*. Ibid.

31. Members of Task Force on Greater CIA Openness to Gates, 12; Mackenzie, *Secrets*, 187.

32. Gates, "Task Force Report on Greater CIA Openness," 4.

33. Ibid., 1; Mackenzie, *Secrets*, 184.

34. Members of Task Force on Greater CIA Openness to Gates, 11.

35. Elaine Sciolino, "Panel from C.I.A. Urges Curtailing of Agency Secrecy," *New York Times*, 12 January 1992; Michael Isikoff, "CIA Task Force Urges Speedier Declassifications," *Washington Post*, 13 January 1992.

36. Joseph R. DeTrani to Robert M. Gates, "Re: Stories on Openness Task Force," 13 January 1992. Released by the CIA to the author on 29 November 2005 in response to a FOIA request.

37. Robert M. Gates, "CIA and Openness," Oklahoma Press Association, 21 February 1992, p. 2. Released by the CIA to the author on 29 November 2005 in response to a FOIA request.

38. Ibid., 11.

39. Ibid., 25; for coverage of the speech in the press, see "CIA May Lift Its Veil," *Houston Chronicle*, 22 February 1992; George Lardner Jr., "Gates Acts to Promote CIA Openness," *Washington Post*, 22 February 1992.

40. DeTrani told Mackenzie on January 14 that the report had to remain classified since Gates had not finished reviewing it. In reality, as Mackenzie ob-

serves, Gates had completed this review eight days earlier. See Mackenzie, *Secrets*, 186.

41. George Lardner Jr., "CIA Report on Openness Classified Secret," *Washington Post*, 23 April 1992.

42. Handwritten note from Robert M. Gates to Cong. Lee H. Hamilton, 13 April 1992. Released by the CIA to the author on 29 November 2005 in response to a FOIA request.

43. Foster quoted in Lardner, "CIA Report on Openness Classified Secret"; Mackenzie, *Secrets*, 186.

44. Leslie Harris quoted in Lardner, "CIA Report on Openness Classified Secret."

45. *Secrecy & Government Bulletin*, no. 7 (February 1992). Aftergood also remarked that "the major change is that Director Gates is on TV a lot more, and has testified at several open Congressional hearings." He cited one source as describing the openness policy as "media puffery." Ibid.

46. Members of Task Force on Greater CIA Openness to Gates, 6; see also Lardner, "CIA Report on Openness Classified Secret."

47. Members of Task Force on Greater CIA Openness to Gates, 6; Mackenzie, *Secrets*, 185.

48. Members of Task Force on Greater CIA Openness to Gates, 8.

49. Joseph R. DeTrani to Robert M. Gates, "Progress Report on Actions/ Recommendations Relating to the DCI Task Force Report on Greater CIA Openness," 18 February 1992.

50. Ibid.

51. Mary V. Dearborn, *Mailer: A Biography* (New York: Houghton Mifflin, 1999), 409.

52. Ibid., 410.

53. Ibid.

54. Ibid., 414; Elaine Sciolino, "Mailer Visits C.I.A. and Finds He's in Friendly Territory. Really," *New York Times*, 3 February 1992.

55. Sciolino, "Mailer Visits C.I.A. and Finds He's in Friendly Territory. Really."

56. Members of Task Force on Greater CIA Openness to Gates, 3–4.

57. Robert M. Gates, "CIA and Openness," 20.

58. Ibid. For background on the law, see "Archive Calls on CIA and Congress to Address Loophole Shielding CIA Records from the Freedom of Information Act," 15 October 2004, *National Security Archive Electronic Briefing Book No. 138*, accessed 25 May 2006, http://www.gwu.edu/~nsarchiv/NSAEBB /NSAEBB138/.

59. James X. Dempsey, "The CIA and Secrecy," in *A Culture of Secrecy*, ed. Athan G. Theoharis (Lawrence: University Press of Kansas, 1998), 53; Nick Cullather, *Secret History: The CIA's Classified Account of Its Operations in Guatemala, 1952–1954* (Stanford: Stanford University Press, 1999), xii; Karl E. Meyer, "Inside the C.I.A.: A Bit of Sunlight on the Missile Crisis," *New York Times*, 24 October 1992; Zachary Karabell, "CIA Clings to Secrecy," *Christian Science Monitor*, 23 February 1993, 18.

60. Dempsey, "The CIA and Secrecy," 54.

61. Cullather, *Secret History*, xii.

62. Charles Fenyvesi, "Washington Whispers," *U.S. News & World Report*, 22 August 1994, 22; for background on Woolsey, see Michael R. Gordon, "Campus Activist to Insider: Journey of the C.I.A. Nominee," *New York Times*, 11 January 1993; for the details of Woolsey's troubled relationship with the Clinton White House, see Tim Weiner, "Tension with White House Leaves C.I.A. Chief Out in the Cold," *New York Times*, 25 December 1993.

63. Douglas Jehl, "C.I.A. Releases Files on Korea and Cold War," *New York Times*, 1 October 1993; Weiner, "C.I.A. Opening Files on Cold War Role," *New York Times*, 29 August 1993.

64. *Increasing Accessibility to CIA Documents*, H.R. Permanent Select Committee on Intelligence, 103d Cong., at 4 (Washington, DC: Government Printing Office, 1994).

65. John Kelly, "CBS as CIA," *Counterspy* 5, no. 1 (November 1980–January 1981): 3–4; "Hollywood Plots a CIA TV Series," *Washington Post Magazine*, 17 August 1980, 2.

66. "Hollywood Plots a CIA TV Series," 2.

67. Dennis R. Boxx to Executive Director [of CIA], "CIA Television Series," memorandum, 16 April 1996, p. 1. Released by the CIA to the author on 21 December 2005 in response to a FOIA request.

68. Ibid., 1.

69. Ibid., 2.

70. In addition to Boxx's April 1996 memo, another memo was released to the author on 21 December 2005 in response to a FOIA request. [Redacted] to Dennis Boxx, Vin Swasey, [Redacted], "CIA Television Series Project," 3 October 1995.

71. From the perspective of Jack Myers, a cofounder of TPP: "I have no doubt that if DCI Woolsey had still been at the helm of the CIA [in 1996], our program would've made it onto the air, especially since we already had a signed contract with Twentieth Century Fox and Steve Tisch had agreed to produce it." See Tricia Jenkins, *The CIA in Hollywood: How the Agency Shapes Film and Television* (Austin: University of Texas Press, 2012), 45.

72. Chase Brandon, telephone interview by the author, 8 September 2005.

73. Paul Barry took over as the entertainment industry liaison in June 2007 and served until 2008. See Amy Argetsinger and Roxanne Roberts, "The CIA Has a New Man on a Special Mission—to Hollywood," *Washington Post*, 5 June 2007; "CIA Names New Entertainment Liaison," *CIA Press Releases & Statements*, 4 June 2007, accessed 3 August 2007, https://www.cia.gov/news-information/press-releases-statements/cia-names-new-entertainment-liaison.html. Brandon later published a spy novel. See Chase Brandon, *The Cryptos Conundrum* (New York: Forge, 2012).

74. Jenkins, *The CIA in Hollywood*, 3. "According to [Paul] Barry," says Jenkins, "Chase Brandon took his contacts and files in order to build his own Hollywood consulting business in the private sector." Ibid., 139n3.

75. Chase Brandon, e-mail to the author, 24 May 2005.

76. Robert Dreyfuss, "Left Out in the Cold," *Mother Jones*, January/February 1998, accessed 20 July 2006, http://www.motherjones.com/news/feature /1998/01/dreyfuss.html. For a thorough discussion of Chase Brandon, see Jenkins, *The CIA in Hollywood*, chap. 4.

77. Chase Brandon, telephone interview by the author.

78. Ibid.

79. Ibid.

80. David L. Robb, *Operation Hollywood: How the Pentagon Shapes and Censors the Movies* (Amherst, NY: Prometheus, 2004), 150.

81. Dan Neil, "Spy vs. Lie," *Los Angeles Times, West Magazine*, 28 May 2006, 45.

82. Ibid.

83. Josh Young, "Spook Shows," *Entertainment Weekly*, 23 March 2005, accessed 20 July 2006, http://www.ew.com/ew/report/0,6115,254697_7%7C29 166%7C%7C0_o_,00.html.

84. Robb, *Operation Hollywood*, 149.

85. Mackenzie, *Secrets*, 186.

86. Chase Brandon, telephone interview by the author.

87. "Patrick Stewart Visits CIA Headquarters," *What's News at CIA*, no. 483 (24 December 1997). Released by the CIA to the author on 21 December 2005 in response to a FOIA request.

88. Ibid.

89. Ibid.

90. "Dan Ackroyd [*sic*] Developing Television Series on CIA," *What's News at CIA*, no. 358 (24 October 1996); "Mr. Smith Goes to CIA," *What's News at CIA*, no. 488 (21 January 1998); "Superman Visits Headquarters," *What's News at CIA*, no. 799 (10 October 2000). The CIA released all three articles to the author on 21 December 2005 in response to a FOIA request.

91. *Sum of All Fears*, Production Notes, accessed 20 July 2006, http://www .contactmusic.com/new/home.nsf/webpages/fearsproductionx25x07x02. See also Jenkins, *The CIA in Hollywood*, 85.

92. Matheson quoted in "DCI Meets Director of 'The Agency' [from *In the Company of Spies*]," *What's News at CIA*, no. 519 [publication date redacted]. Released by the CIA to the author on 21 December 2005 in response to a FOIA request.

93. Silver quoted in "The Agency's Lead Characters Visit Headquarters," *What's News at CIA*, no. 528 [publication date redacted]; Alice Krige also journeyed to the CIA. See "Actress Alice Krige Visits Headquarters," *What's News at CIA*, no. 532 [publication date redacted]. The CIA released both articles on 21 December 2005 in response to a FOIA request.

94. Chase Brandon, "Lights . . . Camera . . . Action!" *What's News at CIA*, no. 538 [publication date redacted]. Released by the CIA to the author on 21 December 2005 in response to a FOIA request.

95. The original title was *The Agency*.

96. Vernon Loeb, "The CIA's Operation Hollywood," *Washington Post*, 14 October 1999; Charles Strum, "The C.I.A. As (Surprise!) the Good Guys,"

New York Times, 24 October 1999; "Agency Hosts Movie Premiere and Sneak Preview," *What's News at CIA*, no. 683 [publication date redacted]; released by the CIA to the author on 21 December 2005 in response to a FOIA request; "Central Intelligence Agency Hosts Premiere Screening of Showtime and Paramount Network Television Spy Thriller, *In the Company of Spies*," *CIA Press Releases & Statements*, 14 October 1999; released by the CIA to the author on 21 December 2005 in response to a FOIA request; "Showtime Movie a Hit," *What's News at CIA*, no. 685 [publication date redacted]; released by the CIA to the author on 21 December 2005 in response to a FOIA request.

97. Tenet quoted in Loeb, "The CIA's Operation Hollywood."

98. Sciolino, "Cameras Are Being Turned on a Once-Shy Spy Agency."

99. Loeb, "The CIA's Operation Hollywood."

100. Ibid; Sciolino, "Cameras Are Being Turned on a Once-Shy Spy Agency."

101. Aftergood quoted in Loeb, "The CIA's Operation Hollywood." For an overview of the movie, see Jenkins, *The CIA in Hollywood*, 58–61.

102. Herb Adelman quoted in "'The Agency' Gets the Green Light," *What's News at CIA*, no. 882 (17 May 2001); released by the CIA to the author on 21 December 2005 in response to a FOIA request. Sciolino, "Cameras Are Being Turned on a Once-Shy Spy Agency,"; Duncan Campbell, "Hollywood Helps CIA Come In from the Cold," *Guardian*, 6 September 2001; John Patterson, "The Caring, Sharing CIA: Central Intelligence Gets a Makeover," *Guardian*, 5 October 2001; for the most detailed assessment of the television show, see Jenkins, *The CIA in Hollywood*, 61–70.

103. Chase Brandon, telephone interview by the author; Mark Rahner, "Eyes on Spies," *Seattle Times*, 12 October 2003.

104. Untitled video, http://www.cia.gov/employment/garner/index.html (accessed 4 September 2004). "Innovative Additions to the CIA Career Website Include Jennifer Garner Recruitment Video," *What's News at CIA*, no. 1281 (10 March 2004); released by the CIA to the author on 21 December 2005 in response to a FOIA request.

105. *The Recruit*, directed by Roger Donaldson (Burbank, CA: Touchstone Home Entertainment, 2003), DVD.

106. Ibid.

107. Ibid.

108. A. O. Scott, "Hard Lessons in a Devilishly Devious C.I.A.," *New York Times*, 31 January 2003.

109. Stephen Hunter, "*The Recruit*: Haven't We Met Somewhere Before?" *Washington Post*, 31 January 2003.

110. Chase Brandon, telephone interview by the author.

111. Ibid.

112. Robb, *Operation Hollywood*, 152. See also Jenkins, *The CIA in Hollywood*, 77–85.

113. Chase Brandon, telephone interview by the author.

114. *Nomination of George J. Tenet to Be Director of Central Intelligence*, S. Select Committee on Intelligence, 105th Cong., at 55 (Washington, DC: Government Printing Office, 1998); for a discussion of Tenet's testimony, see Jonathan

Nashel, "The Rise of the CIA and American Popular Culture," in *Architects of the American Century: Individuals and Institutions in Twentieth-Century U.S. Foreign Policymaking*, ed. David F. Schmitz and T. Christopher Jespersen (Chicago: Imprint Publications, 1999), 77; see also Cullather, *Secret History*, xv.

115. Tim Weiner, "C.I.A.'s Openness Derided As a 'Snow Job,'" *New York Times*, 20 May 1997.

116. George C. Herring, "My Years with the CIA," newsletter, Organization of American Historians, May 1997, accessed 20 May 2006, http://www.fas.org /sgp/eprint/herring.html.

117. Ibid.

118. Ibid.

119. Cullather, *Secret History*, xiv.

120. Tim Weiner, "C.I.A. Destroyed Files on 1953 Iran Coup," *New York Times*, 29 May 1997; "CIA Says It Is Trying to Determine Extent of Document Destruction," *St. Louis Post Dispatch*, 30 May 1997.

121. James Risen, "How a Plot Convulsed Iran in '53 (and in '79)," *New York Times*, 16 April 2000.

122. Ibid.

123. *Bay of Pigs Declassified: The Secret CIA Report on the Invasion of Cuba*, ed. Peter Kornbluh (New York: New Press, 1998), 5, 10.

124. Ibid., 15.

125. Tim Weiner, "C.I.A., Breaking Promises, Puts Off Release of Cold War Files," *New York Times*, 15 July 1998; George Lardner Jr., "CIA Won't Declassify Files, Blames Budget," *Washington Post*, 16 July 1998.

126. Cullather, *Secret History*, xv.

127. Jonathan Riskind, "Bill Ok'd to Open U.S. Files on Nazis," *Columbus Dispatch*, 7 August 1998; Mark Fritz, "CIA Opens Its Files on Third Reich Figures," *Boston Globe*, 27 April 2001. Fritz wrote a nine-part series in the *Boston Globe* based on records declassified in 2001. See "The Secret History of WWII," 11 March 2001, 15 April 2001, 31 May 2001, 1 July 2001, 2 July 2001, 26 August 2001, 19 November 2001, 3 December 2001, and 26 December 2001; the first volume of documents was published in 2004. See Richard Breitman, Norman J. W. Goda, Timothy Naftali, and Robert Wolfe, *U.S. Intelligence and the Nazis* (New York: Cambridge University Press, 2005).

128. Scott Shane, "C.I.A. Knew Where Eichmann Was Hiding," *New York Times*, 7 June 2006; Christopher Lee, "CIA Ties With Ex-Nazis Shown," *Washington Post*, 7 June 2006.

129. Shane, "C.I.A. Knew Where Eichmann Was Hiding."

130. Peter Kornbluh, *The Pinochet File: A Declassified Dossier on Atrocity and Accountability* (New York: New Press, 2003), 472.

131. Kornbluh quoted in Vernon Loeb, "Top CIA Officials Won't Declassify Some Chile Files," *Washington Post*, 11 August 2000; for more on the conflict between the White House and Langley, see Kornbluh, *The Pinochet File*, 472–476.

132. Miller, "We Can't Yet Read Our Own Mail," 206.

133. Ibid., 203; Dempsey, "The CIA and Secrecy," 55; Karla Haworth, "His-

torians' Panel Faults CIA for Delays in Declassification," *Chronicle of Higher Education*, 5 September 1997.

134. George Lardner Jr., "History of U.S.-Greek Ties Blocked," *Washington Post*, 17 August 2001.

135. For more information on the Indonesia volume, see "CIA Stalling State Department Histories: Archive Posts One of Two Disputed Volumes on Web," The National Security Archive, 27 July 2001, accessed 7 July 2006, http://www.gwu.edu/~nsarchiv/NSAEBB/NSAEBB52/ 7 July 2006.

136. James E. Miller quoted in Lardner, "History of U.S.-Greek Ties Blocked."

137. Dempsey, "The CIA and Secrecy," 50–51.

138. Ibid., 51.

139. "CIA Releases Five Million Pages of Historical Records," *CIA Press Releases and Statements*, 20 November 2003, accessed 9 July 2006, http://www.cia.gov/cia/public_affairs/press_release/2003/pr11202003.htm.

140. "CREST: 25-Year Program Archive," Central Intelligence Agency, accessed 21 June 2017, https://www.cia.gov/library/readingroom/collection/crest-25-year-program-archive.

141. "About MuckRock," MuckRock, accessed 21 June 2017, https://www.muckrock.com/about/; Michael Morisy, "How We Sued the CIA and (Mostly) Won: Agency Agrees to Post Declassified Documents Online," MuckRock, 14 December 2016, accessed 21 June 2017, https://www.muckrock.com/news/archives/2016/dec/14/lawsuit-cia-crest/.

142. Michael Best, "Publishing CIA's Declassified Vault," Kickstarter, accessed 21 June 2017, https://www.kickstarter.com/projects/285662323/publishing-cias-declassified-vault.

143. Thomas Powers, *The Man Who Kept the Secrets: Richard Helms and the CIA* (New York: Alfred A. Knopf, 1979), 344.

Chapter 5. *"We Either Get Out and Sell, or We Get Hammered"*

1. Don van Natta Jr. and Souad Mekhennet, "German's Claim of Kidnapping Brings Investigation of U.S. Link," *New York Times*, 9 January 2005.

2. Ibid.

3. Khaled el-Masri, "America Kidnapped Me," *Los Angeles Times*, 18 December 2005. El-Masri also told his story to CBS. El-Masri, interview by Scott Pelley, "Rendition," *60 Minutes*, CBS, season 38, episode 13, aired 18 December 2005.

4. *Committee Study of the Central Intelligence Agency's Detention and Interrogation Program* [hereafter cited as *Committee Study of Detention and Interrogation Program*], Executive Summary, at 128 (2014).

5. The inspector general of the CIA determined in July 2007 that el-Masri was wrongfully detained. According to the report, "[the] Agency's prolonged detention of al-Masri[sic] was unjustified." Ibid., 129.

6. Jane Mayer published a detailed account of the CIA's rendition program in February 2005. This secret program began in the 1990s, but it was expanded after the 9/11 attacks. See Mayer, "Outsourcing Torture: The Secret History of America's 'Extraordinary Rendition' Program," *New Yorker*, 14 Febru-

ary 2005, accessed 4 December 2017, https://www.newyorker.com/magazine
/2005/02/14/outsourcing-torture. For a detailed history of the CIA's use of
detention and interrogation, see John Prados, *The Family Jewels: The CIA, Secrecy,
and Presidential Power* (Austin: University of Texas Press, 2013), chap. 5.

7. *Committee Study of Detention and Interrogation Program*, Executive Summary,
441.

8. Ibid.

9. Ibid., 442.

10. Ibid., 403.

11. Ibid. For example, the CIA cooperated with *Dateline* on NBC. Ibid., 196,
404.

12. Ibid., 8.

13. Ibid., 123n727.

14. Ibid.

15. Ibid., 442.

16. Dana Priest, "CIA Holds Terror Suspects in Secret Prisons," *Washington
Post*, 2 November 2005.

17. Ibid.

18. *Committee Study of Detention and Interrogation Program*, Executive Summary, 151–152; "While she [Priest] had some facts wrong," notes José A. Rodriguez, "she had others uncomfortably right." See José A. Rodriguez Jr. with Bill
Harlow, *Hard Measures: How Aggressive CIA Actions After 9/11 Saved American Lives*
(New York: Simon & Schuster, 2012), 118. Rodriguez argues that a top official
inside the Office of the Inspector General leaked the information to Priest. See
ibid., 172–173.

19. *Committee Study of Detention and Interrogation Program*, Executive Summary,
153. For a detailed account of the CIA's prison in Romania, see Adam Goldman and Matt Apuzzo, "Inside Romania's Secret CIA Prison," *Associated Press*, 8
December 2011, accessed 5 June 2006, http://www.cbsnews.com/news/inside
-romanias-secret-cia-prison/.

20. *Committee Study of Detention and Interrogation Program*, Executive Summary, 5.

21. He was fired in 1997. Rodriguez Jr., *Hard Measures*, 157–164.

22. Michael Isikoff and David Corn, *Hubris: The Inside Story of Spin, Scandal,
and the Selling of the Iraq War* (New York: Three Rivers, 2006), 270. Harlow currently operates a crisis public relations firm. A modified version of this quote
appears on his website. See "Bill Harlow," *15-Seconds*, accessed 31 May 2016,
http://www.15-seconds.com/bill-harlow/.

23. George Tenet with Bill Harlow, *At the Center of the Storm: My Years at the
CIA* (New York: HarperCollins, 2007). According to Rodriguez,

> I always marveled at the ease and speed with which Bill took my words and
> turned them into clear and readable prose. When I first approached Bill
> about helping me with this book I did not realize what a partnership it
> would become and how much trust and confidence in each other it would
> require. We have become very close as a result and I am grateful for his con-
> tribution and for his friendship. (Rodriguez Jr., *Hard Measures*, 266)

24. Rodriguez Jr., *Hard Measures*, 62.

25. Ibid., 115.

26. *Committee Study of Detention and Interrogation Program*, Executive Summary, 10.

27. Ibid., 12. According to the Senate Select Committee on Intelligence, "this is a conservative calculation and includes only CIA detainees whom the CIA itself determined did not meet the standard for detention." Ibid., 16.

28. Ibid., 51.

29. Ibid., 110.

30. Ibid., 4. Rodriguez says, "Agency officers visited the U.S. Bureau of Prisons to learn about how to create the most effective holding facility." Rodriguez Jr., *Hard Measures*, 115. He neglects to mention that representatives from the bureau were shocked by the CIA prison system: "They have never been in a facility where individuals are so sensory deprived, i.e., constant white noise, no talking, everyone in the dark, with the guards wearing a light on their head when they collected and escorted a detainee to an interrogation cell, detainees constantly . . . shackled to the wall or floor, and the starkness of each cell (concrete and bars)." See *Committee Study of Detention and Interrogation Program*, Executive Summary, 60.

31. *Committee Study of Detention and Interrogation Program*, Executive Summary, 4.

32. Ibid., 50n240.

33. Ibid., 11; according to the executive summary, "the CIA did not conduct its first training course until November 2002, by which time at least nine detainees had already been subjected to the techniques." Ibid., 104. The problems extended far beyond the Salt Pit. For example, the CIA officer in charge of the secret prison in Romania expressed frustration at

> what appears to be a lack of resolve at Headquarters to deploy to the field the brightest and most qualified officers for service at [the detention site]. Over the course of the last year the quality of personnel . . . has declined significantly. With regard to debriefers, most are mediocre, a handful are exceptional and more than a few are basically incompetent. . . . The result, quite naturally, is the production of mediocre or, I dare say, useless intelligence. . . . If this program truly does represent one of the agency's most secret activities then it defies logic why inexperienced, marginal, underperforming and/or officers with potentially significant [counterintelligence] problems are permitted to deploy to this site. (Ibid., 144)

34. Ibid., 59.

35. Ibid., 50.

36. Ibid.

37. Ibid., 54.

38. Ibid., 63n314.

39. Ibid., 56n278.

40. Ibid., 54.

41. Ibid., 55. For more information on Rahman, see "Death Investigation— Gul Rahman," CIA FOIA Electronic Reading Room, "Documents Related to

the Former Detention and Interrogation Program," accessed 4 July 2016, https://www.cia.gov/library/readingroom/docs/0006555318.pdf. See also Central Intelligence Agency Inspector General, Report of Investigation, "Death of a Detainee in [Redacted]," 27 April 2005, CIA FOIA Electronic Reading Room, "Documents Related to the Former Detention and Interrogation Program," accessed 4 July 2016, https://www.cia.gov/library/readingroom/docs/0006541713.pdf. Both of these documents were released to the ACLU in response to a FOIA request.

42. Rodriguez briefly mentions "the deaths of two detainees who were not part of the interrogation program run by CTC." Rodriguez Jr., *Hard Measures*, 250. He is apparently referring to Abdul Wali and Manadel al-Jamadi. Both prisoners died in 2003, Wali in June and al-Jamadi in November. David A. Passaro, a CIA contractor, was convicted for his involvement in Wali's death. James Dao, "A Man of Violence, or Just '110 Percent' Gung-Ho," *New York Times*, 19 June 2004; Clyde Haberman, "A Singular Conviction Amid the Debate on Torture and Terrorism," *New York Times*, 19 April 2015; see also Jane Mayer, *The Dark Side: The Inside Story of How the War on Terror Turned into a War on American Ideals* (New York: Doubleday, 2008), chap. 10.

43. *Committee Study of Detention and Interrogation Program*, Executive Summary, 57.

44. Rodriguez Jr., *Hard Measures*, 244.

45. John Rizzo, *Company Man: Thirty Years of Controversy and Crisis in the CIA* (New York: Scribner, 2014), 209–210.

46. *Committee Study of Detention and Interrogation Program*, Executive Summary, 71.

47. Ibid.

48. Ibid., 44.

49. Ibid., 45, 473–474. According to the executive summary, internal CIA investigations of the Salt Pit found

> the use of the CIA's enhanced interrogation techniques—and other coercive interrogation techniques—was more widespread than was reported in contemporaneous CIA cables. Specifically, the interrogation techniques that went unreported in CIA cables included standing sleep deprivation in which a detainee's arms were shackled above his head, nudity, dietary manipulation, exposure to cold temperatures, cold showers, "rough takedowns," and, in at least two instances, the use of mock executions. (Ibid., 56)

50. Ibid., 43.

51. "Throughout my career," says Rodriguez, "controversy followed me around like a hungry dog." Rodriguez Jr., *Hard Measures*, 11.

52. *Committee Study of Detention and Interrogation Program*, Executive Summary, 123. To be clear, Rodriguez was not the only CIA official manipulating the historical record. General Michael Hayden, director of the CIA between 2006 and 2009, allegedly told a subordinate "to keep the detainee number at 98—pick whatever date . . . needed to make that happen but the number is 98." Ibid., 15.

53. Rodriguez Jr., *Hard Measures*, 230–231.

54. It is important to emphasize that the full committees were *not* briefed on the program. Ibid., xiii.

55. U.S. Department of Justice Office of Legal Counsel to John Rizzo, "The Torture Archive," memorandum, 1 August 2002, p. 2, The National Security Archive, accessed 28 April 2015, http://nsarchive.gwu.edu/torture_archive /topten.html. For more information on the legal memos underpinning the detention and interrogation program, see Rizzo, *Company Man*, chap. 11.

56. Dept. of Justice Office of Legal Counsel to Rizzo, "The Torture Archive," 3–4.

57. Ibid., 4.

58. Rodriguez Jr., *Hard Measures*, 69–70.

59. Ibid., 70.

60. *Committee Study of Detention and Interrogation Program*, Executive Summary, 43–44.

61. Ibid., 86.

62. Ibid.

63. Ibid., 35.

64. Ibid., 491.

65. Ibid., 35.

66. Rodriguez Jr., *Hard Measures*, 239.

67. Ibid., 65.

68. *Committee Study of Detention and Interrogation Program*, Executive Summary, 77.

69. Ibid., 101. For the names of the seventeen detainees, see ibid., 102.

70. Ibid., 51n245.

71. Ibid., 105.

72. Ibid., 106.

73. Ibid., 107.

74. Ibid.

75. Rodriguez Jr., *Hard Measures*, 96.

76. *Committee Study of Detention and Interrogation Program*, Executive Summary, 82.

77. For background on the CIA prison in Poland, see Adam Goldman, "The Hidden History of the CIA's Prison in Poland," *Washington Post,* 23 January 2014.

78. *Committee Study of Detention and Interrogation Program*, Executive Summary, 84–85.

79. Ibid., 85.

80. Ibid., 88.

81. Ibid., 90.

82. Ibid., 92.

83. Ibid., 83.

84. Ibid., 92.

85. Ibid.

86. Jane Mayer, "The Unidentified Queen of Torture," *New Yorker,* 18 De-

cember 2014, accessed 4 December 2017, https://www.newyorker.com/news
/news-desk/unidentified-queen-torture.

87. *Committee Study of Detention and Interrogation Program*, Executive Summary, 95.

88. Ibid., 94.

89. Ibid., 95.

90. Ibid.

91. Massimo Calabresi, "Ex–CIA Counterterror Chief: 'Enhanced Interrogation' Led U.S. to bin Laden," *Time*, 4 May 2011, accessed 4 December 2017, http://swampland.time.com/2011/05/04/did-torture-get-the-us-osama-bin-laden/.

92. Michael B. Mukasey, "The Waterboarding Trail to bin Laden," *Wall Street Journal*, 6 May 2011.

93. *Committee Study of Detention and Interrogation Program*, Executive Summary, 378n2137.

94. Rodriguez Jr., *Hard Measures*, 111–112.

95. The coordinated public relations strategy would be used again after the Senate released the *Committee Study of Detention and Interrogation Program* in December 2014. The campaign featured a website (http://ciasavedlives.com/) and ultimately led to the publication of an anthology that strongly defended the CIA's program. Bill Harlow, the former director of the Office of Public Affairs at the agency, edited the book, and George Tenet wrote the introduction. Porter J. Goss, General Michael Hayden, John McLaughlin, Michael Morell, Philip Mudd, John Rizzo, and José A. Rodriguez Jr. contributed the essays. See Bill Harlow, ed., *Rebuttal: The CIA Responds to the Senate Intelligence Committee's Study of Its Detention and Interrogation Program* (Annapolis: Naval Institute Press, 2015). See also Mark Mazzetti, "Ex-Chief of C.I.A. Shapes Response to Detention Report," *New York Times*, 25 July 2014.

96. Panetta attempts to downplay the significance of the public relations effort in Leon Panetta with Jim Newton, *Worthy Fights: A Memoir of Leadership in War and Peace* (New York: Penguin, 2014), 315:

> I knew that if we went ahead with this [operation], it would be a matter of intense international interest, and the press would clamor for details—a complicated situation because we would want to be responsive but also to zealously protect against the release of information that might compromise any prosecutions (if we captured bin Laden) or future operations. I had great confidence in our lead communications person, George Little, so I brought him into the circle as well.

97. *Committee Study of Detention and Interrogation Program*, Executive Summary, 379n2137.

98. Mark Mazzetti, Helene Cooper, and Peter Baker, "Behind the Hunt for Bin Laden," *New York Times*, 2 May 2011.

99. Ibid.

100. Central Intelligence Agency, Office of Inspector General Investigations Staff, "Potential Ethics Violations Involving Film Producers," 16 September

2013, p. 4, accessed 27 June 2016, https://www.scribd.com/doc/279621337/CIA-ZDT-wm#fullscreen. This report was released to Vice News in response to a FOIA request.

101. Ibid., 67.

102. "Marie Harf June 7 Oscars Email," Judicial Watch, accessed 27 June 2016, http://www.judicialwatch.org/document-archive/marie-harf-june-7-oscars-email/.

103. "Potential Ethics Violations Involving Film Producers," 67.

104. Central Intelligence Agency, Office of Inspector General, Report of Investigation, "Alleged Disclosure of Classified Information by Former D/CIA [Leon Panetta]," 12 March 2014, p. 99, accessed 27 June 2016, https://www.scribd.com/doc/279621337/CIA-ZDT-wm#fullscreen. This report was released to Vice News in response to a FOIA request.

105. Ibid.

106. The other guests sitting at the table were Christiane Amanpour, Senator Evan Bayh (D-IN), Ian Cameron, Jonathan Karl, Maria Karl, Martha Raddatz, and Jamie Rubin. Ibid., 118. Although Panetta does not mention the internal investigation in his memoir, he does briefly describe the incident in a footnote. "I was under the impression that everyone in the audience enjoyed a security clearance, but learned later that one of the producers [Boal] of *Zero Dark Thirty* was allowed to attend. Some critics pounced on that; all I can say is that my shout-out to the SEAL team member that day was meant to congratulate him, not to expose him, and was made only because I had been assured that everyone in the audience was cleared." Panetta, *Worthy Fights*, 331.

107. "Alleged Disclosure of Classified Information," 98.

108. Harf explained in a memo that "Kathryn is not interested in doing the deep dives that Mark did; she simply wants to meet the people that Mark has been talking to." See "Marie Harf July 14 internal memo," Judicial Watch, accessed 27 June 2016, http://www.judicialwatch.org/document-archive/marie-harf-july-14-internal-memo/. When *Zero Dark Thirty* was released, Morell was acting director of the CIA. Ironically, he issued a statement to agency employees that was sharply critical of the movie:

> The film creates the strong impression that the enhanced interrogation techniques that were part of our former detention and interrogation program were the key to finding Bin Ladin. That impression is false. As we have said before, the truth is that multiple streams of intelligence led CIA analysts to conclude that Bin Ladin was hiding in Abbottabad. Some came from detainees subjected to enhanced techniques, but there were many other sources as well. And, importantly, whether enhanced interrogation techniques were the only timely and effective way to obtain information from those detainees, as the film suggests, is a matter of debate that cannot and never will be definitively resolved.

It is important to note that the statement directly contradicts the public relations strategy that the CIA unleashed in May 2011. See "Message from the Acting Director: *Zero Dark Thirty*," 21 December 2012, accessed 5 July 2016, https://

NOTES TO PAGES 113–116 | 181

www.cia.gov/news-information/press-releases-statements/2012-press-releasese
-statements/message-from-adcia-zero-dark-thirty.html.

109. "Marie Harf July 17 Email," Judicial Watch, accessed 27 June 2016,
http://www.judicialwatch.org/document-archive/marie-harf-july-17-email/.

110. Ibid.

111. "Potential Ethics Violations Involving Film Producers," 5.

112. "Leven Marie Harf July 13–14 Email," Judicial Watch, accessed 27 June
2016, http://www.judicialwatch.org/document-archive/leven-marie-harf-july
-13–14-email/.

113. "Mario Bryant Boal Email July 20," Judicial Watch, accessed 28 June
2016, http://www.judicialwatch.org/document-archive/mario-bryant-boal
-email-july-20/.

114. Ibid.

115. These conversations took place on October 26, November 1, November 18, and December 5. See "Potential Ethics Violations Involving Film Producers," 68.

116. "Boal CIA Memo," 2, accessed 28 June 2016, https://www.document
cloud.org/documents/696468-boal-cia-memo.html#document/p1. This document was released to *Gawker* in response to a FOIA request. Adrian Chen,
"Newly Declassified Memo Shows CIA Shaped *Zero Dark Thirty's* Narrative,"
Gawker, 6 May 2013.

117. "Boal CIA Memo," 2.

118. Randall B. Woods, *Shadow Warrior: William Egan Colby and the CIA* (New
York: Basic Books, 2013), 191.

119. "Boal CIA Memo," 1.

120. Maureen Dowd, "Downgrade Blues," *New York Times,* 6 August 2011.

121. "Marie Harf Mark Mazzetti August 5 Email," Judicial Watch, accessed
27 June 2016, http://www.judicialwatch.org/document-archive/marie-harf
-mark-mazzetti-august-5-email/.

122. *Zero Dark Thirty,* scene 1, directed by Kathryn Bigelow (Hollywood, CA:
Columbia Pictures, 2013), DVD.

123. Ibid.

124. Ibid.

125. Ibid.

126. *Zero Dark Thirty,* scene 6, DVD.

127. *Zero Dark Thirty,* scene 8, DVD.

128. Frank Bruni, "Bin Laden, Torture and Hollywood," *New York Times,* 8
December 2012.

129. Ibid.

130. David Edelstein, "Epic Pileup," *New York Magazine,* 10 December 2012,
4 December 2017, http://nymag.com/movies/reviews/zero-dark-thirty-hobbit
-2012-12/.

131. Ibid.

132. Manohla Dargis, "By Any Means Necessary," *New York Times,* 17 December 2012.

133. *Charlie Rose,* PBS, 6 December 2012.

134. *Zero Dark Thirty,* production notes, 3, accessed 28 June 2016, http://gregorymancuso.com/wp-content/uploads/2013/07/Zero-Dark-Thirty-movie-production-notes-pdf-download.pdf.

135. Senators Dianne Feinstein, Carl Levin, and John McCain to Michael Lynton, 19 December 2012, p. 1, accessed 1 May 2015, http://www.feinstein.senate.gov/public/index.cfm/press-releases?ID=b5946751-2054-404a-89b7-b81e1271efc9.

136. Ibid.

137. Ibid., 2.

138. Ibid., 2–3.

139. Kathryn Bigelow, "Kathryn Bigelow Addresses *Zero Dark Thirty* Torture Criticism," *Los Angeles Times,* 15 January 2013.

140. Ibid.

141. Ibid.

142. Ibid.

143. Matt Taibbi, "'Zero Dark Thirty' Is Osama Bin Laden's Last Victory Over America," *Rolling Stone,* 16 January 2013. "Here's my question: if it would have been dishonest to leave torture out of the film entirely, how is it not dishonest to leave out how generally ineffective it was, how morally corrupting, how totally it enraged the entire Arab world, how often we used it on people we knew little to nothing about, how often it resulted in deaths, or a hundred other facts?" Ibid.

144. Ibid.

145. Ibid.

146. Peter Maass, "Don't Trust *Zero Dark Thirty,*" *Atlantic,* 13 December 2012, 4 December 2017, https://www.theatlantic.com/entertainment/archive/2012/12/dont-trust-zero-dark-thirty/266253/.

147. Ibid.

148. Ibid.

149. Ibid.

150. Ibid.

151. Steve Coll, "'Disturbing' and 'Misleading,'" *New York Review of Books,* 7 February 2013.

152. Ibid.

153. Ibid.

154. Ibid.

155. José A. Rodriguez Jr., "A CIA Veteran on What *Zero Dark Thirty* Gets Wrong About the Bin Laden Manhunt," *Washington Post,* 3 January 2013. "Indeed, as I watched the story unfold on the screen, I found myself alternating between repulsion and delight." Ibid.

156. Ibid.

157. Ibid. According to Rodriguez, "the successes and the failures in this mission were the work of many, not a few." Ibid.

158. Ibid.

159. Roger Ebert, "*Zero Dark Thirty,*" 2 January 2013, accessed 4 July 2016, http://www.rogerebert.com/reviews/zero-dark-thirty-2013.

160. Coll, "'Disturbing' and 'Misleading.'"

161. Taibbi, "*Zero Dark Thirty* Is Osama Bin Laden's Last Victory Over America."

162. The *Washington Post* revealed her name in January 2014. See Greg Miller and Adam Goldman, "A Hard-Edged Defender of Spy Agencies," *Washington Post*, 12 January 2014.

163. *Committee Study of the Central Intelligence Agency's Detention and Interrogation Program*, Executive Summary, 3 December 2014, 91.

164. Matthew Cole, "Bin Laden Expert Accused of Shaping CIA Deception on 'Torture' Program," NBC News, 16 December 2014, 4 December 2017, https://www.nbcnews.com/news/investigations/bin-laden-expert-accused-shaping-cia-deception-torture-program-n269551; for more information on Bikowsky, see Greg Miller, "In *Zero Dark Thirty*, She's the Hero; In Real Life, CIA Agent's Career Is More Complicated," *Washington Post*, 10 December 2012.

165. *Committee Study of the Central Intelligence Agency's Detention and Interrogation Program*, Executive Summary, 3 December 2014, 192; see also Cole, "Bin Laden Expert Accused of Shaping CIA Deception on 'Torture' Program."

166. *Committee Study of the Central Intelligence Agency's Detention and Interrogation Program*, Executive Summary, 3 December 2014, 192.

167. "Potential Ethics Violations Involving Film Producers," 32.

168. Ibid., 37.

169. Ibid., 38.

170. Ibid., 36. During an internal investigation, the CIA had the earrings appraised in 2012. "The jeweler estimated the value to be no more than $200 and stated if he was to sell them, he would ask between $60 and $70." Ibid., 41.

171. Ibid., 35.

172. Jason Leopold and Ky Henderson, "Tequila, Painted Pearls, and Prada—How the CIA Helped Produce *Zero Dark Thirty*," Vice News, 9 September 2015, accessed 4 July 2016, https://news.vice.com/article/tequila-painted-pearls-and-prada-how-the-cia-helped-produce-zero-dark-thirty.

173. C. Michael Hiam, *Who the Hell Are We Fighting? The Story of Sam Adams and the Vietnam Intelligence Wars* (Hanover, NH: Steerforth, 2006), 124.

Conclusion

1. Joseph R. DeTrani to Robert M. Gates, "Task Force on Greater CIA Openness—Week Two," memorandum, 6 December 1991, p. 1. Released by the CIA to the author on 29 November 2005 in response to a FOIA request.

2. "CIA Adds Eight Stars to Memorial Wall for Fallen Officers," NBC News, accessed 29 June 2017, http://www.nbcnews.com/card/cia-adds-eight-stars-memorial-wall-fallen-officers-n764336. See also Ted Gup, *The Book of Honor: The Secret Lives and Deaths of CIA Operatives* (New York: Doubleday, 2000).

3. Nicholas Dujmovic, "Two CIA Prisoners in China, 1952–73," *Studies in Intelligence* 50, no. 4 (2006), accessed 13 July 2016, https://www.cia.gov

/library/center-for-the-study-of-intelligence/csi-publications/csi-studies/studies/vo150no4/two-cia-prisoners-in-china-1952201373.html.

4. Ibid.

5. The film was released to the public in 2011. Center for the Study of Intelligence, *Extraordinary Fidelity*, video, YouTube, accessed 11 July 2016, https://www.youtube.com/watch?v=ZoMh7EiXRJI.

6. Dujmovic, "Two CIA Prisoners in China, 1952–73."

7. Ibid.

8. "No record of an inquiry into the decision to send Downey and Fecteau on the flight appears to exist. It is clear that no one was ever disciplined for it, probably because it was a wartime decision in the field." Ibid. For an excellent introduction to how the CIA tells its history, see Simon Willmetts, "The CIA and the Invention of Tradition," *Journal of Intelligence History* 14, no. 2 (2015): 112–128.

9. Tricia Jenkins, *The CIA in Hollywood: How the Agency Shapes Film and Television* (Austin: University of Texas Press, 2012), 82.

10. Ibid.

11. Church quoted in Loch K. Johnson, *A Season of Inquiry: The Senate Intelligence Investigation* (Lexington: University Press of Kentucky, 1985), 57.

12. For example, see Christopher Moran, *Company Confessions: Secrets, Memoirs, and the CIA* (New York: St. Martin's, 2015), 171.

13. Helms quoted in David S. McCarthy, "'The Sun Never Sets on the Activities of the CIA': Project Resistance at William and Mary," *Intelligence and National Security* 28 (October 2013), 612.

14. Ibid.

15. "General Hayden's Remarks at SHAFR Conference," 21 June 2007, Central Intelligence Agency News and Information, accessed 26 March 2008, https://www.cia.gov/news-information/speeches-testimony/2007/general-hayden-remarks-at-shafr-conference.html.

16. Ibid.

17. Ibid. Hayden pledged that the CIA would continue to release material for the State Department's *FRUS* series; that officials would review classified CIA documents housed in the libraries of former presidents; and that more National Intelligence Estimates and Cold War reports would be declassified. The audience also received complimentary copies of a volume that contained "147 documents amounting to more than 11,000 pages of analysis done between 1953 and 1973" on the Soviet Union, China, and their often tense relationship with each other. Hayden's gifts, however, were overshadowed by an announcement he made at the beginning of the speech: the "Family Jewels," an infamous collection of memos and other documents assembled in the early 1970s that detailed illegal CIA activities, would soon be turned over to the public. In the media frenzy surrounding the release of the "Family Jewels," most reporters failed to explain that a FOIA request had been filed for the collection as early as 1992. Hayden had the audacity to characterize the CIA's processing of FOIA requests as "very successful." Ibid. For media coverage of the "Family Jewels," see Scott Shane, "C.I.A. to Release Documents on Decades-Old Misdeeds," *New York Times*, 22 June 2007; Karen DeYoung and Walter Pincus, "CIA to Air

Decades of Its Dirty Laundry," *Washington Post,* 22 June 2007; Mark Mazzetti, "C.I.A. Chief Tries Preaching a Culture of More Openness," *New York Times,* 23 June 2007; Karen DeYoung and Walter Pincus, "CIA Releases Files on Past Misdeeds," *Washington Post,* 27 June 2007; and Mark Mazzetti and Tim Weiner, "Files on Illegal Spying Show C.I.A. Skeletons from Cold War," *New York Times,* 27 June 2007.

18. In March of 2003, President Bush signed Executive Order 13292. This order amended Executive Order 12958, making it easier for the government to keep material classified. It also gave the vice president increased power to classify (and declassify) government records.

19. Scott Shane, "U.S. Reclassifies Many Documents in Secret Review," *New York Times,* 21 February 2006; Jeffrey R. Young, "How the National Archives Struck a Deal with the CIA," *Chronicle of Higher Education,* 5 May 2006, 43; Matthew M. Aid, "Declassification in Reverse: the U.S. Intelligence Community's Secret Historical Document Reclassification Program," The National Security Archive, 21 February 2006, accessed 25 May 2006, http://www.gwu.edu/~ns archiv/NSAEBB/NSAEBB179/; Matthew M. Aid, "The Secret Reclassification Program," *OAH Newsletter* 34 (May 2006), 1, 10, 18–19; Bruce Craig, "Historians Expose Government Reclassification Effort," *Perspectives* 44 (April 2006), 29–30.

20. "Memorandum of Understanding between the National Archives and Records Administration and the Central Intelligence Agency," October 2001, p. 2, accessed 25 May 2006, https://nsarchive2.gwu.edu/news/20060419 /mou-nara-cia.pdf.

21. Aid, *OAH Newsletter,* 19n9.

22. Ibid., 18; Craig, "Historians Expose Government Reclassification Effort," 30.

23. Edmund Cohen, "The CIA and the Historical Declassification of History Programs," *International Journal of Intelligence and Counterintelligence,* 12 (Fall 1999): 341; the agency's decision to unveil the documents from the Korean War had received coverage in the *New York Times.* See Douglas Jehl, "C.I.A. Releases Files on Korea and Cold War," *New York Times,* 1 October 1993.

24. Priest's article was published on November 2. The videotapes were shredded on November 9. Rodriguez later provided the following description of the shredder that was used: "The device's five spinning and two stationary steel blades are designed to chop up DVDs, CDs, cell phones, credit cards, X-rays, and other optical media and produce tiny, unrecognizable bits that are vacuumed out into giant, heavy-duty, plastic trash bags. Our problem had been reduced to confetti—or so we thought." Rodriguez Jr., *Hard Measures,* 193–194.

25. Rodriguez Jr., *Hard Measures,* 193. For Haspel's appointment, see Greg Miller, "CIA Officer with Ties to 'Black Sites' Named Deputy Director," *Washington Post,* 2 February 2017; Dexter Filkins, "The New C.I.A. Deputy Chief's Black-Site Past," *New Yorker,* 3 February 2017; and Matthew Rosenberg, "New C.I.A. Deputy Director, Gina Haspel, Had Leading Role in Torture," *New York Times,* 2 February 2017.

26. John Rizzo, a veteran CIA lawyer, called the incident an "act of gross insubordination." John Rizzo, *Company Man: Thirty Years of Controversy and Crisis*

in the CIA (New York: Scribner, 2014), 20. In his assessment, "He [Rodriguez] had chosen to ignore and defy the White House, the director of national intelligence, and the director of the CIA." Ibid., 19.

27. Scott Shane and Mark Mazzetti, "Tapes by C.I.A. Lived and Died to Save Image," *New York Times,* 30 December 2007. For the initial story on the tapes, see Mark Mazzetti, "C.I.A. Destroyed 2 Tapes Showing Interrogations," *New York Times,* 7 December 2007.

28. Peter Finn and Julie Tate, "2005 Destruction of Interrogation Tapes Caused Concern at CIA, E-Mails Show," *Washington Post,* 16 April 2010.

29. "Sen. Feinstein Accuses CIA of Searching Congressional Computers," video, 11 March 2014, C-SPAN, accessed 11 July 2016, http://www.c-span.org/video/?c4486712/sen-feinstein-accuses-cia-searching-congressional-computers.

30. Ibid.

31. Halimah Abdullah, "Feinstein Says CIA Spied on Senate Computers," CNN, 12 March 2014, accessed 13 July 2016, http://www.cnn.com/2014/03/11/politics/senate-cia/.

32. Central Intelligence Agency, Inspector General, "Summary of Report," 31 July 2014, p. 327, accessed 13 July 2016, https://www.scribd.com/document/274285608/Senate-Docs-Syp-Wm#fullscreen&from_embed.

33. Ibid. For a detailed exposé of the scandal, see Jason Leopold, "The Google Search That Made the CIA Spy on the US Senate," Vice News, 12 August 2015, accessed 7 July 2016, https://news.vice.com/article/the-google-search-that-made-the-cia-spy-on-the-us-senate.

34. Mark Mazzetti and Carl Hulse, "Inquiry by C.I.A. Affirms It Spied on Senate Panel," *New York Times,* 31 July 2014.

35. "Most View the CDC Favorably; VA's Image Slips," Pew Research Center, accessed 13 July 2016, http://www.people-press.org/2015/01/22/most-view-the-cdc-favorably-vas-image-slips/.

36. Cynthia M. Nolan, "Seymour Hersh's Impact on the CIA," *International Journal of Intelligence and Counterintelligence* 12, no. 1 (1999): 21.

37. Christopher Endy, "The Empire Sneaks Back," review of *Remaking France: Americanization, Public Diplomacy, and the Marshall Plan,* by Brian A. McKenzie, *Diplomatic History* 31, no. 4 (September 2007): 763.

38. Jonathan Nashel, "The Rise of the CIA and American Popular Culture," in *Architects of the American Century: Individuals and Institutions in Twentieth-Century U.S. Foreign Policymaking,* ed. David F. Schmitz and T. Christopher Jespersen (Chicago: Imprint Publications, 1999), 77.

39. Kimball quoted in Aid, *OAH Newsletter,* 10.

40. *Alleged Assassination Plots Involving Foreign Leaders,* Select Committee to Study Governmental Operations with Respect to Intelligence Activities [Church Committee], S. Rep. No. 94-465, at 285 (1975).

41. Edward R. Murrow, "Speech to the Radio-Television News Directors Association and Foundation, Chicago, Illinois," 15 October 1958, Radio Television Digital News Association, accessed 18 June 2017, https://www.rtdna.org/content/edward_r_murrow_s_1958_wires_lights_in_a_box_speech.

Bibliography

Library of Congress, Manuscript Division

Cord Meyer Papers
David A. Phillips Papers
Ray Cline Papers

Government Records

CIA Records Search Tool (CREST). College Park, MD: National Archives II.
Commission on CIA Activities Within the United States [Rockefeller Commission]. *Report to the President by the Commission on CIA Activities Within the United States*. Washington, DC: Government Printing Office, 1975.
Declassified Documents Reference System (DDRS). Farmington Hills, MI: Gale Group, 2008.
The 9/11 Commission Report: Final Report of the National Commission on Terrorist Attacks upon the United States. New York: W. W. Norton, 2004.
U.S. Congress. *Report of the Congressional Committees Investigating the Iran-Contra Affair*. 100th Cong., 1st sess., H.R. Rep. 100-433, S. Rept. 100-216. Appendix B: vol. 22. Washington, DC: Government Printing Office, 1987.
U.S. Congress. Senate Select Committee on Secret Military Assistance to Iran and the Nicaraguan Opposition. House Select Committee to Investigate Covert Arms Transactions with Iran. *Iran-Contra Investigation*. 100th Cong., 1st sess., 100-7. Part III: Appendix A. Washington, DC: Government Printing Office, 1988.
U.S. House of Representatives. Committee on Government Operations, Subcommittee on Government Information and Individual Rights. *The Freedom of Information Act: Central Intelligence Agency Exemptions. Hearings on H.R. 5129, H.R. 7055, and H.R. 7056 to Enhance the Foreign Intelligence and Law Enforcement Activities of the United States by Improving the Protection of Information Necessary to Their Effective Operation*. 96th Cong., 2d sess. Washington, DC: Government Printing Office, 1981.
U.S. House of Representatives. Committee on Government Operations, Subcommittee on Government Information, Justice, and Agriculture. *CIA Information Act: Hearing on H.R. 5164 to Amend the National Security Act of 1947 to Regulate Public Disclosure of Information Held by the Central Intelligence Agency, and for Other Purposes*. 98th Cong., 2d sess. Washington, DC: Government Printing Office, 1984.

U.S. House of Representatives. Permanent Select Committee on Intelligence. *Central Intelligence Agency Information Act.* 98th Cong., 2d sess., 1984. H.R. Rep. 98-726.

U.S. House of Representatives. Permanent Select Committee on Intelligence. *Increasing Accessibility to CIA Documents.* 103d Cong., 1st sess. Washington, DC: Government Printing Office, 1994.

U.S. House of Representatives. Permanent Select Committee on Intelligence, Subcommittee on Legislation. *Legislation to Modify the Application of the Freedom of Information Act to the Central Intelligence Agency.* 98th Cong., 2d sess. Washington, DC: Government Printing Office, 1984.

U.S. House of Representatives. Permanent Select Committee on Intelligence, Subcommittee on Oversight. *Prepublication Review and Secrecy Agreements.* 96th Cong., 2d sess., 1980.

U.S. Senate. Select Committee on Intelligence. Committee on Human Resources, Subcommittee on Health and Scientific Research. *Project MKULTRA, the CIA's Program of Research in Behavioral Modification.* 95th Cong., 1st sess. Washington, DC: Government Printing Office, 1977.

U.S. Senate. Select Committee on Intelligence. *Nomination of George J. Tenet to be Director of Central Intelligence.* 105th Cong., 1st sess. Washington, DC: Government Printing Office, 1998.

U.S. Senate. Select Committee on Intelligence. *Nomination of Robert M. Gates to Be Director of Central Intelligence.* 3 vols. 102d Cong., 1st sess. Washington, DC: Government Printing Office, 1992.

U.S. Senate. Select Committee to Study Governmental Operations with Respect to Intelligence Activities [Church Committee]. *Final Reports.* 94th Cong., 2d sess., 1976. *Supplementary Detailed Staff Reports on Intelligence Activities and the Rights of Americans* (Book III). S. Rep. No. 94-755.

Newspapers

Boston Globe
Chicago Sun-Times
Christian Science Monitor
Dallas Times Herald
Los Angeles Times
Manila Bulletin
Newsday
New York Times
Seattle Times
Village Voice
Wall Street Journal
Washington Post
Washington Star

Periodicals

Commentary
Counter-Spy
Harper's
Jump Cut
Look
Mother Jones
Nation
Newsweek
New Yorker
New York Times Magazine
Ramparts
Reader's Digest
Saturday Evening Post
Time
U.S. News & World Report
Washington Monthly

Articles

Adams, Sam. "Vietnam Cover-Up: Playing War with Numbers." *Harper's* (May 1975): 41–44, 62–73.
Casey, Steven. "Selling NSC-68: The Truman Administration, Public Opinion, and the Politics of Mobilization, 1950–51." *Diplomatic History* 29, no. 4 (September 2005): 655–690.
Casey, William J. "The American Intelligence Community." *Presidential Studies Quarterly* 12, no. 2 (Spring 1982): 150–153.
Cohen, Edmund. "The CIA and the Historical Declassification of History Programs." *International Journal of Intelligence and Counterintelligence* 12 (Fall 1999): 338–345.
Cutlip, Scott M. "Public Relations in the Government." *Public Relations Review* 2 (Summer 1976): 5–28.
Davis, Earle. "Howard Hunt and the Peter Ward–CIA Spy Novels." *Kansas Quarterly* 10, no. 4 (Fall 1978): 85–95.
Dempsey, James X. "The CIA and Secrecy." In *A Culture of Secrecy: The Government Versus the People's Right to Know,* edited by Athan G. Theoharis, 37–59. Lawrence: University Press of Kansas, 1998.
Der Derian, James. "The CIA, Hollywood, and Sovereign Conspiracies." *Queen's Quarterly* 100, no. 2 (Summer 1993): 329–347.
Deutsch, James I. "'I Was a Hollywood Agent': Cinematic Representations of the Office of Strategic Services in 1946." *Intelligence and National Security* 13 (Summer 1998): 85–99.

De Vries, Tity. "The 1967 Central Intelligence Agency Scandal: Catalyst in a Transforming Relationship between State and People." *Journal of American History* 98, no. 4 (March 2012): 1075–1092.

Eldridge, David N. "'Dear Owen': The CIA, Luigi Luraschi and Hollywood, 1953." *Historical Journal of Film, Radio and Television* 20, no. 2 (2000): 149–196.

Evans, Rowland, and Robert Novak. "Congress Is Crippling the CIA." *Reader's Digest* (November 1986): 99–103.

Ferris, John. "Coming in from the Cold War: The Historiography of American Intelligence, 1945–1990." *Diplomatic History* 19, no. 1 (Winter 1995): 87–115.

Fletcher, Katy. "Evolution of the Modern American Spy Novel." *Journal of Contemporary History* 22, no. 2 (April 1987): 319–331.

Hadley, David P. "A Constructive Quality: The Press, the CIA, and Covert Intervention in the 1950s." *Intelligence and National Security* 31, no. 2 (2016): 246–265.

Hedley, John Hollister. "Twenty Years of Officers in Residence." *Studies in Intelligence* 49, no. 4 (2005): 31–39.

Hixson, Walter L. "'Red Storm Rising': Tom Clancy Novels and the Cult of National Security." *Diplomatic History* 17, no. 4 (Fall 1993): 599–613.

Hulnick, Arthur S. "Openness: Being Public About Secret Intelligence." *International Journal of Intelligence and Counterintelligence* 12, no. 4 (Winter 1999): 463–483.

Jenkins, Tricia. "How the Central Intelligence Agency Works with Hollywood: An Interview with Paul Barry, the CIA's New Entertainment Industry Liaison." *Media, Culture & Society* 31, no. 3 (2009): 489–495.

Johnson, Loch K. "Accountability and America's Secret Foreign Policy: Keeping a Legislative Eye on the Central Intelligence Agency." *Foreign Policy Analysis* 1 (2005): 99–120.

———. "The Church Committee Investigation of 1975 and the Evolution of Modern Intelligence Accountability." *Intelligence and National Security* 23 (April 2008): 198–225.

———. "The CIA and the Media." *Intelligence and National Security* 1 (May 1986): 143–169.

———. "Congress and the American Experiment in Holding Intelligence Agencies Accountable." *Journal of Policy History* 28, no. 3 (2016): 494–514.

———. "A Conversation with Former DCI William E. Colby, Spymaster During the 'Year of the Intelligence Wars.'" In *Strategic Intelligence: Intelligence and Accountability, Safeguards against the Abuse of Secret Power,* vol. 5, edited by Loch K. Johnson, 47–66. Westport, CT: Praeger Security International, 2007.

———. "Supervising America's Secret Foreign Policy: A Shock Theory of Congressional Oversight for Intelligence." In *American Foreign Policy in a Globalized World,* edited by David P. Forsythe, Patrice C. McMahon, and Andrew Wedeman, 173–192. New York: Routledge, 2006.

Kimball, Warren F. "Openness and the CIA." *Studies in Intelligence,* no. 10 (Winter–Spring 2001): 63–67.

Kinsman, N. Richard. "Openness and the Future of the Clandestine Service." *Studies in Intelligence,* no. 10 (Winter–Spring 2001): 55–61.

Marchetti, Victor. "Propaganda and Disinformation: How the CIA Manufactures History." *Journal of Historical Review* 9 (Fall 1989): 305–320.

Marks, John. "How to Spot a Spook." *Washington Monthly* 6 (November 1974): 5–11.

McCarthy, David S. "'The Sun Never Sets on the Activities of the CIA': Project Resistance at William and Mary." *Intelligence and National Security* 28 (October 2013): 611–633.

McCrisken, Trevor. "The Housewife, the Vigilante and the Cigarette-Smoking Man: The CIA and Television, 1975–2001." *History* 100 (April 2015): 293–310.

Millar, James R., et al. "Survey Article: An Evaluation of the CIA's Analysis of Soviet Economic Performance, 1970–90." *Comparative Economic Studies* 35, no. 2 (1993): 33–57.

Miller, Page Putnam. "We Can't Yet Read Our Own Mail: Access to the Records of the Department of State." In *A Culture of Secrecy: The Government Versus the People's Right to Know,* edited by Athan G. Theoharis, 186–210. Lawrence: University Press of Kansas, 1998.

Moran, Christopher. "The Last Assignment: David Atlee Phillips and the Birth of CIA Public Relations." *International History Review* 35, no. 2 (2013): 337–355.

Nashel, Jonathan. "The Rise of the CIA and American Popular Culture." In *Architects of the American Century: Individuals and Institutions in Twentieth-Century U.S. Foreign Policymaking,* edited by David F. Schmitz and T. Christopher Jespersen, 65–80. Chicago: Imprint Publications, 1999.

Nolan, Cynthia M. "Seymour Hersh's Impact on the CIA." *International Journal of Intelligence and Counterintelligence* 12 (March 1999): 18–34.

Parry, Robert, and Peter Kornbluh. "Iran-Contra's Untold Story." *Foreign Policy* (Fall 1988): 3–30.

Rausch, G. Jay, and Diane K. Rausch. "Developments in Espionage Fiction." *Kansas Quarterly* 10, no. 4 (Fall 1978): 71–82.

Richelson, Jeffrey T. "Holding Back: How Agencies Thwart the Freedom of Information Act." *Bulletin of the Atomic Scientists* 59, no. 6 (November–December 2003): 26–32.

Sarchett, Barry W. "Unreading the Spy Thriller: The Example of William F. Buckley Jr." *Journal of Popular Culture* 26, no. 2 (Fall 1992): 127–139.

Schwarz, Frederick A. O., Jr. "The Church Committee and a New Era of Intelligence Oversight." *Intelligence and National Security* 22 (April 2007): 270–297.

Theoharis, Athan G. "Researching the Intelligence Agencies: The Problem of Covert Activities." *Public Historian* 6, no. 2 (Spring 1984): 67–76.

Thomas, Evan. "A Singular Opportunity: Gaining Access to CIA's Records." *Studies in Intelligence* 39, no. 5 (1996): 19–23.

Waters, Robert, and Gordon Daniels. "The World's Longest General Strike: The AFL-CIO, the CIA, and British Guiana." *Diplomatic History* 29, no. 2 (April 2005): 279–307.

Wilford, Hugh. "'Essentially a Work of Fiction': Kermit 'Kim' Roosevelt, Imperial Romance, and the Iran Coup of 1953." *Diplomatic History* 40, no. 5 (November 2016): 922–947.

———. "Still Missing: The Historiography of U.S. Intelligence." *Passport* 47, no. 2 (September 2016): 20–25.

Willmetts, Simon. "The Burgeoning Fissures of Dissent: Allen Dulles and the Selling of the CIA in the Aftermath of the Bay of Pigs." *History* 100 (April 2015): 167–188.

———. "The CIA and the Invention of Tradition." *Journal of Intelligence History* 14, no. 2 (2015): 112–128.

Memoirs, Books, and Unpublished Theses and Dissertations

Adams, Sam. *War of Numbers: An Intelligence Memoir.* South Royalton, VT: Steerforth, 1994.

Agee, Philip. *Inside the Company: CIA Diary.* London: Allen Lane, 1975.

———. *On the Run.* Secaucus, NJ: Lyle Stuart, 1987.

Allen, George W. *None So Blind: A Personal Account of the Intelligence Failure in Vietnam.* Chicago: Ivan R. Dee, 2001.

Ambrose, Stephen E., and Richard H. Immerman. *Ike's Spies: Eisenhower and the Espionage Establishment.* New York: Doubleday, 1981.

Andrew, Christopher. *For the President's Eyes Only: Secret Intelligence and the American Presidency from Washington to Bush.* New York: HarperCollins, 1995.

Baer, Robert. *See No Evil: The True Story of a Ground Soldier in the CIA's War on Terrorism.* New York: Three Rivers, 2002.

Bamford, James. *The Puzzle Palace: A Report on America's Most Secret Agency.* Boston: Houghton Mifflin, 1982.

Barnouw, Erik. *Tube of Plenty: The Evolution of American Television.* New York: Oxford University Press, 1982.

Barrett, David M. *The CIA & Congress: The Untold Story from Truman to Kennedy.* Lawrence: University Press of Kansas, 2005.

Bergen, Peter L. *Manhunt: The Ten-Year Search for Bin Laden from 9/11 to Abbottabad.* New York: Crown, 2012.

Berman, William C. *William Fulbright and the Vietnam War: The Dissent of a Political Realist.* Kent, OH: Kent State University Press, 1988.

Bill, James A. *The Eagle and the Lion: The Tragedy of American-Iranian Relations.* New Haven, CT: Yale University Press, 1988.

Bird, Kai. *The Good Spy: The Life and Death of Robert Ames.* New York: Broadway, 2014.

Blum, William. *The CIA: A Forgotten History.* Atlantic Highlands, NJ: Zed Books, 1986.

Breckinridge, Scott D. *The CIA and the U.S. Intelligence System.* Boulder: Westview, 1986.

Breitman, Richard, Norman J. W. Goda, Timothy Naftali, and Robert Wolfe. *U.S. Intelligence and the Nazis.* New York: Cambridge University Press, 2005.

Brewin, Bob, and Sydney Shaw. *Vietnam on Trial: Westmoreland vs. CBS.* New York: Atheneum, 1987.

Buford, Kate. *Burt Lancaster: An American Life.* New York: Alfred A. Knopf, 2000.

Byrne, Malcolm. *Iran-Contra: Reagan's Scandal and the Unchecked Abuse of Presidential Power.* Lawrence: University Press of Kansas, 2014.

Cahn, Anne H. *Killing Détente: The Right Attacks the CIA.* University Park: Pennsylvania State University Press, 1998.

Callahan, David. *Dangerous Capabilities: Paul Nitze and the Cold War.* New York: HarperCollins, 1990.

Cannon, Lou. *President Reagan: The Role of a Lifetime.* New York: Public Affairs, 2000.

Cawelti, John G., and Bruce A. Rosenberg. *The Spy Story.* Chicago: University of Chicago Press, 1987.

Cecil, Matthew. *Branding Hoover's FBI: How the Boss's PR Men Sold the Bureau to America.* Lawrence: University Press of Kansas, 2016.

———. *Hoover's FBI and the Fourth Estate: The Campaign to Control the Press and the Bureau's Image.* Lawrence: University Press of Kansas, 2014.

Clarridge, Duane. *A Spy for All Seasons: My Life in the CIA.* New York: Scribner, 2002.

Cline, Ray. *Secrets, Spies, and Scholars: Blueprint of the Essential CIA.* Washington, DC: Acropolis, 1976.

Cockburn, Leslie. *Out of Control: The Story of the Reagan Administration's Secret War in Nicaragua, the Illegal Arms Pipeline, and the Contra Drug Connection.* New York: Atlantic Monthly Press, 1987.

Colby, William, and Peter Forbath. *Honorable Men: My Life in the CIA.* New York: Simon & Schuster, 1978.

Coll, Steve. *Ghost Wars.* New York: Penguin Books, 2004.

Corn, David. *Blond Ghost: Ted Shackley and the CIA's Crusades.* New York: Simon & Schuster, 1994.

Cullather, Nick. *Secret History: The CIA's Classified Account of Its Operations in Guatemala, 1952–1954.* Stanford, CA: Stanford University Press, 1999.

Dinges, John. *The Condor Years: How Pinochet and His Allies Brought Terrorism to Three Continents.* New York: New Press, 2004.

Draper, Theodore. *A Very Thin Line: The Iran-Contra Affairs.* New York: Hill and Wang. 1991.

Dulles, Allen. *The Craft of Intelligence.* New York: Harper & Row, 1963.

Emery, Fred. *Watergate: The Corruption of American Politics and the Fall of Richard Nixon.* New York: Random House, 1994.

Eveland, Wilbur Crane. *Ropes of Sand: America's Failure in the Middle East.* New York: W. W. Norton, 1980.

Ewen, Stuart. *PR! A Social History of Spin.* New York: Basic Books, 1996.

Fisher, James T. *Dr. America: The Lives of Thomas A. Dooley, 1927–1961.* Amherst: University of Massachusetts Press, 1997.

Fishgall, Gary. *Against Type: The Biography of Burt Lancaster.* New York: Scribner, 1995.

Foerstel, Herbert N. *Freedom of Information and the Right to Know: The Origins and Applications of the Freedom of Information Act.* Westport, CT: Greenwood, 1999.

Freedman, Lawrence. *US Intelligence and the Soviet Strategic Threat.* Boulder: Westview, 1977.

Fulbright, J. W. *The Pentagon Propaganda Machine.* New York: Liveright, 1970.

Gaddis, John Lewis. *The United States and the End of the Cold War: Implications, Reconsiderations, Provocations.* New York: Oxford University Press, 1992.

Garthoff, Douglas F. *Directors of Central Intelligence as Leaders of the U.S. Intelligence Community, 1946–2005.* Washington, DC: Potomac, 2007.

Gates, Robert M. *From the Shadows: The Ultimate Insider's Story of Five Presidents and How They Won the Cold War.* New York: Simon & Schuster, 1996.

Gilbey, Ryan. *It Don't Worry Me: The Revolutionary American Films of the Seventies.* New York: Faber & Faber, 2003.

Gleijeses, Piero. *Shattered Hope: The Guatemalan Revolution and the United States, 1944–1954.* Princeton, NJ: Princeton University Press, 1991.

Goldberg, Robert Alan. *Enemies Within: The Culture of Conspiracy in Modern America.* New Haven, CT: Yale University Press, 2001.

Grandin, Greg. *Empire's Workshop: Latin America, the United States, and the Rise of the New Imperialism.* New York: Henry Holt, 2006.

Gregg, Robert W. *International Relations on Film.* Boulder: Lynne Rienner, 1998.

Grose, Peter. *Gentleman Spy: The Life of Allen Dulles.* Boston: Houghton Mifflin, 1994.

Gup, Ted. *The Book of Honor: The Secret Lives and Deaths of CIA Operatives.* New York: Doubleday, 2000.

Guthrie, Lindsay Mara. "Public Exposure vs. Public Disclosure: How the Central Intelligence Agency's Public Image Deteriorated from 'Gentlemen Spies' to 'Rogue Elephants' in American Society, from 1947 to 1975." Senior thesis, College of William & Mary, 2003.

Harding, Bill. *The Films of Michael Winner.* London: Frederick Muller, 1978.

Helms, Richard. *A Look Over My Shoulder.* New York: Random House, 2003.

Hepburn, Allan. *Intrigue: Espionage and Culture.* New Haven, CT: Yale University Press, 2005.

Hersh, Burton. *The Old Boys: The American Elite and the Origins of the CIA.* New York: Charles Scribner's Sons, 1992.

Hetu, Herbert E. "Public Relations During Peacetime Naval Disaster." Master's thesis, Boston University, 1965.

Hiam, C. Michael. *Who the Hell Are We Fighting? The Story of Sam Adams and the Vietnam Intelligence Wars.* Hanover, NH: Steerforth, 2006.

Higgins, Trumbull. *The Perfect Failure: Kennedy, Eisenhower, and the CIA at the Bay of Pigs.* New York: W. W. Norton, 1987.

Hitz, Frederick P. *The Great Game: The Myth and Reality of Espionage.* New York: Alfred A. Knopf, 2004.

Holm, Richard L. *The American Agent: My Life in the CIA.* London: St. Ermins, 2003.

Hunt, E. Howard. *Undercover: Memoirs of an American Secret Agent.* New York: Berkley Publishing, 1974.

Jacobs, Seth. *America's Miracle Man in Vietnam*. Durham: Duke University Press, 2004.

Jeffreys-Jones, Rhodri. *The CIA and American Democracy*. 3rd ed. New Haven, CT: Yale University Press, 2003.

———. *Cloak and Dollar: A History of American Secret Intelligence*. New Haven, CT: Yale University Press, 2002.

Jeffreys-Jones, Rhodri, and Christopher Andrew. *Eternal Vigilance? 50 Years of the CIA*. Portland, OR: Frank Cass, 1997.

Jenkins, Tricia. *The CIA in Hollywood: How the Agency Shapes Film and Television*. Austin: University of Texas Press, 2012.

Johnson, Loch K. *America's Secret Power: The CIA at Home and Abroad*. New York: Oxford University Press, 1989.

———. *Bombs, Bugs, Drugs, and Thugs: Intelligence and America's Quest for Security*. New York: New York University Press, 2000.

———. *A Season of Inquiry: The Senate Intelligence Investigation*. Lexington: University Press of Kentucky, 1985.

———. *Secret Agencies: U.S. Intelligence in a Hostile World*. New Haven, CT: Yale University Press, 1996.

Karalekas, Anne. *History of the Central Intelligence Agency*. Laguna Hills, CA: Aegean Park, 1977.

Karlow, S. Peter. *Targeted by the CIA*. Paducah, KY: Turner Publishing, 2001.

Kent, Sherman. *Strategic Intelligence for American World Policy*. Princeton, NJ: Princeton University Press, 1966.

Kessler, Ronald. *Inside the CIA: Revealing the Secrets of the World's Most Powerful Spy Agency*. New York: Pocket Books, 1992.

Kirkpatrick, Lyman. *The Real CIA*. New York: MacMillan, 1968.

Knott, Stephen F. *Secret and Sanctioned: Covert Operations and the American Presidency*. New York: Oxford University Press, 1996.

Kornbluh, Peter, ed. *Bay of Pigs Declassified: The Secret CIA Report on the Invasion of Cuba*. New York: New Press, 1998.

———. *The Pinochet File: A Declassified Dossier on Atrocity and Accountability*. New York: New Press, 2003.

LaFeber, Walter. *America, Russia, and the Cold War, 1945–2000*. 9th ed. New York: McGraw-Hill, 2002.

Leab, Daniel J. *Orwell Subverted: The CIA and the Filming of Animal Farm*. University Park: Pennsylvania State University Press, 2007.

Leary, William M. *Perilous Missions: Civil Air Transport and CIA Covert Operations in Asia*. Tuscaloosa: University of Alabama Press, 1984.

Lee, Martin, and Bruce Shlain. *Acid Dreams: The CIA, LSD and the Sixties Rebellion*. New York: Grove, 1985.

Lefever, Ernest W., and Roy Godson. *The CIA and the American Ethic: An Unfinished Debate*. Washington, DC: Ethics and Policy Center, Georgetown University, 1979.

Lev, Peter. *American Films of the 70s: Conflicting Visions*. Austin: University of Texas Press, 2000.

Longaker, Richard P. *The Presidency and Individual Liberties*. Ithaca, NY: Cornell University Press, 1961.

Mackenzie, Angus. *Secrets: The CIA's War at Home.* Berkeley: University of California Press, 1997.

Maltby, Richard. *Harmless Entertainment: Hollywood and the Ideology of Consensus.* Metuchen, NJ: Scarecrow, 1983.

Mangold, Tom. *Cold Warrior: James Jesus Angleton.* New York: Simon & Schuster, 1991.

Mann, James. *Rise of the Vulcans: The History of Bush's War Cabinet.* New York: Viking, 2004.

Marchand, Roland. *Creating the Corporate Soul: The Rise of Public Relations and Corporate Imagery in American Big Business.* Berkeley: University of California Press, 1998.

Marchetti, Victor. *The Rope-Dancer.* New York: Dell, 1971.

Marchetti, Victor, and John D. Marks. *The CIA and the Cult of Intelligence.* New York: Alfred A. Knopf, 1974.

Marks, John D. *The Search for the "Manchurian Candidate": The CIA and Mind Control.* Reprint, New York: W. W. Norton, 1991.

Martin, David C. *Wilderness of Mirrors.* New York: Harper & Row, 1980.

Mayer, Jane. *The Dark Side: The Inside Story of How the War on Terror Turned into a War on American Ideals.* New York: Doubleday, 2008.

Mazzetti, Mark. *The Way of the Knife: The CIA, a Secret Army, and a War at the Ends of the Earth.* New York: Penguin Books, 2013.

McClintock, Michael. *The American Connection: State Terror and Popular Resistance in El Salvador.* London: Zed Books, 1985.

McCoy, Alfred W. *A Question of Torture: CIA Interrogation, from the Cold War to the War on Terror.* New York: Metropolitan, 2006.

McGarvey, Patrick J. *The CIA: The Myth and the Madness.* New York: Saturday Review, 1972.

McGehee, Ralph W. *Deadly Deceits: My 25 Years in the CIA.* New York: Sheridan Square, 1983.

Melanson, Philip H. *Secrecy Wars: National Security, Privacy, and the Public's Right to Know.* Washington, DC: Brassey's, 2001.

Meyer, Cord. *Facing Reality: From World Federalism to the CIA.* New York: Harper & Row, 1980.

Meyer, Janet L. *Sydney Pollack: A Critical Filmography.* Jefferson, NC: McFarland, 1998.

Miller, Karen S. *The Voice of Business: Hill & Knowlton and Postwar Public Relations.* Chapel Hill: University of North Carolina Press, 1999.

Mills, Ami Chen. *CIA Off Campus: Building the Movement against Agency Recruitment and Research.* Boston: South End, 1991.

Montague, Ludwell Lee. *General Walter Bedell Smith as Director of Central Intelligence October 1950–February 1953.* University Park: Pennsylvania State University Press, 1992.

Moran, Christopher R. *Company Confessions: Secrets, Memoirs, and the CIA.* New York: St. Martin's, 2015.

Moran, Christopher R., and Christopher J. Murphy, eds. *Intelligence Studies in Britain and the US: Historiography Since 1945.* Edinburgh, UK: Edinburgh University Press, 2013.

Moran, Lindsay. *Blowing My Cover: My Life as a CIA Spy.* New York: Putnam, 2005.

Morgan, Ted. *A Covert Life: Jay Lovestone.* New York: Random House, 1999.

Moynihan, Daniel Patrick. *Secrecy: The American Experience.* New Haven, CT: Yale University Press, 1998.

Nashel, Jonathan. *Edward Lansdale's Cold War.* Amherst: University of Massachusetts Press, 2005.

Nitze, Paul H. *From Hiroshima to Glasnost: At the Center of Decision.* With Ann M. Smith and Steven L. Rearden. New York: Grove Weidenfeld, 1989.

Olmsted, Kathryn S. *Challenging the Secret Government: The Post-Watergate Investigations of the CIA and FBI.* Chapel Hill: University of North Carolina Press, 1996.

———. *Real Enemies: Conspiracy Theories and American Democracy, World War I to 9/11.* New York: Oxford University Press, 2009.

Panetta, Leon. *Worthy Fights: A Memoir of Leadership in War and Peace.* With Jim Newton. New York: Penguin, 2014.

Parmet, Herbert S. *George Bush: The Life of a Lone Star Yankee.* New York: Scribner, 1997.

Parry, Robert. *Lost History: Contras, Cocaine, the Press & "Project Truth."* Arlington: Media Consortium, 1999.

Paseman, Floyd. *A Spy's Journey: A CIA Memoir.* St. Paul, MN: Zenith, 2004.

Persico, Joseph E. *Casey: From the OSS to the CIA.* New York: Penguin Books, 1990.

Petrusenko, Vitalii V. *A Dangerous Game: CIA and the Mass Media.* Translated by Nicolai Kozelsky and Vladimir Leonov. Prague: Interpress, 1979.

Phillips, David A. *Careers in Secret Operations: How to Be a Federal Intelligence Officer.* Frederick, MD: University Publications of America, 1984.

———. *The Night Watch.* New York: Ballantine, 1977.

Potter, Claire. *War on Crime: Bandits, G-Men, and the Politics of Mass Culture.* New Brunswick, NJ: Rutgers University Press, 1998.

Powers, Richard Gid. *G-Men: Hoover's FBI in American Popular Culture.* Carbondale: Southern Illinois University Press, 1983.

Powers, Thomas. *Intelligence Wars: American Secret History from Hitler to al-Qaeda.* New York: New York Review of Books, 2004.

———. *The Man Who Kept the Secrets: Richard Helms and the CIA.* New York: Alfred A. Knopf, 1979.

Prados, John. *The Family Jewels: The CIA, Secrecy, and Presidential Power.* Austin: University of Texas Press, 2013.

———. *The Ghosts of Langley: Into the CIA's Heart of Darkness.* New York: New Press, 2017.

———. *Lost Crusader: The Secret Wars of CIA Director William Colby.* New York: Oxford University Press, 2003.

———. *Safe for Democracy: The Secret Wars of the CIA.* Chicago: Ivan R. Dee, 2006.

———. *The Soviet Estimate.* New York: Dial Press, 1982.

Pratt, Ray. *Projecting Paranoia: Conspiratorial Visions in American Film.* Lawrence: University Press of Kansas, 2001.

Prouty, L. Fletcher. *The Secret Team: The CIA and Its Allies in Control of the United States and the World.* Englewood Cliffs, NJ: Prentice-Hall, 1973.

198 | BIBLIOGRAPHY

Radosh, Ronald. *American Labor and United States Foreign Policy.* New York: Vintage, 1969.

Ranelagh, John. *The Agency: The Rise and Decline of the CIA.* New York: Simon & Schuster, 1986.

Rich, Frank. *The Greatest Story Ever Sold: The Decline and Fall of Truth from 9/11 to Katrina.* New York: Penguin, 2006.

Richardson, Peter. *A Bomb in Every Issue: How the Short, Unruly Life of "Ramparts" Magazine Changed America.* New York: New Press, 2009.

Richelson, Jeffrey T. *The Wizards of Langley: Inside the CIA's Directorate of Science and Technology.* Boulder: Westview, 2001.

Risen, James. *State of War: The Secret History of the CIA and the Bush Administration.* New York: Free Press, 2006.

Rizzo, John. *Company Man: Thirty Years of Controversy and Crisis in the CIA.* New York: Scribner, 2014.

Robb, David L. *Operation Hollywood: How the Pentagon Shapes and Censors the Movies.* Amherst, NY: Prometheus, 2004.

Roberts, Alasdair. *Blacked Out: Government Secrecy in the Information Age.* New York: Cambridge University Press, 2006.

Rodriguez, José A., Jr. *Hard Measures: How Aggressive CIA Actions After 9/11 Saved American Lives.* With Bill Harlow. New York: Simon & Schuster, 2012.

Roosevelt, Kermit. *Countercoup: The Struggle for the Control of Iran.* New York: McGraw-Hill, 1979.

Rudgers, David F. *Creating the Secret State: The Origins of the Central Intelligence Agency.* Lawrence: University Press of Kansas, 2000.

Saunders, Frances Stonor. *The Cultural Cold War: The CIA and the World of Arts and Letters.* New York: New Press, 1999.

Sayre, Nora. *Running Time: Films of the Cold War.* New York: Dial Press, 1982.

Schmitz, David F. *The United States and Right-Wing Dictatorships, 1965–1989.* New York: Cambridge University Press, 2006.

Schroen, Gary C. *First In: An Insider's Account of How the CIA Spearheaded the War on Terror in Afghanistan.* New York: Ballantine, 2005.

Schudson, Michael. *The Rise of the Right to Know: Politics and the Culture of Transparency, 1945–1975.* Cambridge, MA: Harvard University Press, 2015.

Schwarz, Frederick A. O., Jr. *Democracy in the Dark: The Seduction of Government Secrecy.* New York: New Press, 2015.

Schwarz, Frederick A. O., Jr., and Aziz Z. Huq. *Unchecked and Unbalanced: Presidential Power in a Time of Terror.* New York: New Press, 2007.

Shackley, Ted. *Spymaster: My Life in the CIA.* With Richard A. Finney. Dulles, VA: Potomac, 2005.

Shils, Edward A. *The Torment of Secrecy: The Background and Consequences of American Security Policies.* Glencoe, IL: Free Press, 1956.

Sklar, Robert. *Movie-Made America: A Social History of American Movies.* New York: Random House, 1975.

Smist, Frank J., Jr. *Congress Oversees the United States Intelligence Community, 1947–1994.* 2nd ed. Knoxville: University of Tennessee Press, 1994.

Smith, Joseph B. *Portrait of a Cold Warrior.* New York: Ballantine, 1976.

Snepp, Frank. *Irreparable Harm: A Firsthand Account of How One Agent Took on the CIA in an Epic Battle Over Secrecy and Free Speech.* New York: Random House, 1999.

Srodes, James. *Allen Dulles: Master of Spies.* Washington, DC: Regnery, 1999.

Stillwell, Paul, ed. *The Reminiscences of Captain Herbert E. Hetu U.S. Navy (Retired).* Annapolis: Naval Institute Press, 2003.

Stockton, Bayard. *Flawed Patriot: The Rise and Fall of CIA Legend Bill Harvey.* Washington, DC: Potomac, 2006.

Stockwell, John. *In Search of Enemies: A CIA Story.* London: Andre Deutsch, 1978.

Streeby, Shelley. *American Sensations: Class, Empire, and the Production of Popular Culture.* Berkeley: University of California Press, 2002.

Swartz, James E. "The Professionalization of Pentagon Public Affairs: The Evolution of a Role in the United States Federal Government, 1947–1967." PhD diss., University of Iowa, 1985.

Szulc, Tad. *Compulsive Spy: The Strange Career of E. Howard Hunt.* New York: Viking, 1974.

Taylor, William R. *Sydney Pollack.* Boston: Twayne Publishers, 1981.

Tenet, George. *At the Center of the Storm: My Years at the CIA.* With Bill Harlow. New York: HarperCollins, 2007.

Theoharis, Athan G., ed. *A Culture of Secrecy: The Government Versus the People's Right to Know.* Lawrence: University Press of Kansas, 1998.

Thomas, Evan. *The Very Best Men: Four Who Dared.* New York: Simon & Schuster, 1995.

Toplin, Robert Brent, ed. *Hollywood as Mirror: Changing Views of "Outsiders" and "Enemies" in American Movies.* Westport, CT: Greenwood, 1993.

Turner, Stansfield. *Secrecy and Democracy: The CIA in Transition.* Boston: Houghton Mifflin, 1985.

Tye, Larry. *The Father of Spin: Edward L. Bernays & the Birth of Public Relations.* New York: Crown, 1998.

Valentine, Douglas. *The Phoenix Program.* New York: William Morrow, 1990.

Wark, Wesley K., ed. *Spy Fiction, Spy Films and Real Intelligence.* Portland, OR: Frank Cass, 1991.

Weber, Ralph E., ed. *Spymasters: Ten CIA Officers in Their Own Words.* Wilmington, DE: Scholarly Resources, 1999.

Weiner, Tim. *Legacy of Ashes: The History of the CIA.* New York: Doubleday, 2007.

Westerfield, H. Bradford, ed. *Inside CIA's Private World: Declassified Articles from the Agency's Internal Journal, 1955–1992.* New Haven, CT: Yale University Press, 1995.

Whitfield, Stephen. *The Culture of the Cold War.* Baltimore: Johns Hopkins University Press, 1991.

Wilford, Hugh. *The Mighty Wurlitzer: How the CIA Played America.* Cambridge, MA: Harvard University Press, 2008.

Willmetts, Simon. *In Secrecy's Shadow: The OSS and CIA in Hollywood Cinema, 1941–1979.* Edinburgh: Edinburgh University Press, 2016.

Wilson, James Q. *Bureaucracy: What Government Agencies Do and Why They Do It.* New York: Basic Books, 1989.

Winks, Robin W. *Cloak & Gown: Scholars in the Secret War, 1939–1961.* New York: William Morrow, 1987.

Wise, David. *Nightmover: How Aldrich Ames Sold the CIA to the KGB for $4.6 Million.* New York: HarperCollins, 1995.

Wise, David, and Thomas B. Ross. *The Invisible Government.* New York: Random House, 1964.

Wood, Robin. *Hollywood from Vietnam to Reagan . . . and Beyond.* Revised, New York: Columbia University Press, 2003.

Woods, Randall B. *Shadow Warrior: William Egan Colby and the CIA.* New York: Basic Books, 2013.

Woodward, Bob. *Veil: The Secret Wars of the CIA, 1981–1987.* New York: Simon & Schuster, 1987.

Index